Rallies and Races

Rallies and Races

Motoring Adventures of Gatsonides

by William Leonard

CIP GEGEVENS KONINKLIJKE BIBLIOTHEEK, DEN HAAG

Leonard, Willem

Rallies and Races : Gatsonides' adventures / by Willem
Leonard ; [ill.: Jan Apetz ; transl. from the Dutch]. -
Amsterdam : The Greyhound Press - Ill.
Transl. of: Rallyes en Races : Gatsonides' avonturen. -
ISBN 90-75145-02-0
NUGI 466
Subject headings: Gatsonides, Gatso / racing drivers / car racing

Copyright English translation © 1995 by The Greyhound Press

Edited by Michael Allen

Translator: Willy Walter

Coverart and cartoons: Jan Apetz

All rights reserved. No part of this publication may be reproduced or transmitted in any form or by any means, electronic or mechanical, including photocopy, without permission in writing from The Greyhound Press. Reviewers may quote brief passages.

For information write to:

The Greyhound Press
Antwoordnummer 10709
1000 RA Amsterdam, The Netherlands

ISBN 90 75145 02 0

Contents

List of Illustrations		VII
Preface for the revised 1995 edition		XI
Original Preface		XIII
A Word with You before you Start		XV
Chapter 1	Monte Carlo Rally, 1936	1
Chapter 2	Monte Carlo Rally, 1937	7
Chapter 3	Liège-Rome-Liège, 1937	21
Chapter 4	Monte Carlo Rally, 1938	33
Chapter 5	Liège-Rome-Liège, 1938	45
Chapter 6	Monte Carlo Rally, 1939	55
Chapter 7	Sports Car Races at Zandvoort, 1939	65
Chapter 8	Liège-Rome-Liège, 1939	73
Chapter 9	Dumonceau Cup Trials	81
Chapter 10	The Dripping Cock Races	91
Chapter 11	French Alpine Rally, 1946	99
Chapter 12	Lisbon Rally, 1947	107
Chapter 13	French Alpine Rally, 1947	119
Chapter 14	First Post-War Sports Car Races	129
Chapter 15	Monte Carlo Rally, 1949	139
Chapter 16	Monte Carlo Rally, 1950	151
Chapter 17	Sports Car Races, Zandvoort, 1950	165
Chapter 18	The 1950 Les Mans 24 Hours Race	175
Chapter 19	French Alpine Rally, 1950	199
Chapter 20	Liège-Rome-Liège, 1950	213
The Culprits		223
'Gatso' on the 'Monte'		227
Postscript		233
International motorsport competitions		235

List of illustrations

Gatso: Maurice Gatsonides pictured at 40 years of age, already a legendary figure but still with his greatest achievements to come as the 1950s unfolded. XII

From left to right: William Leonard, Gatso, Louise and Jan Apetz, Ciska Gatsonides. XVII

Rally 1936 Monte Carlo route. XVIII

Strand in sight of the finish. Monte Carlo Rally 1936. 4

Plenty of snow on the route to the start at Umea. Monte Carlo Rally 1937. 8

The Gatsonides Hillman Minx stuck in deep snow on the way to the starting point at Umea. Monte Carlo Rally 1937. 9

The 'sledge' in position on the Minx, pictured on the boat toCopenhagen. Monte Carlo Rally 1937. 11

Bakker Schut's average-speedmeter, shown set for 50 kilometres travelled in one hour. 17

Berlescu's much-modified Ford V8, with three seats, and special snow-gear fitted at one side. 17

The Minx achieved an excellent result on the classifying test, Monte Carlo Rally 1937. 18

Tired, dirty, but very happy at the finish of the Liège-Rome-Liège, 1937. 30

In the ice between Nisj and Sofia, on the way to the start at Athens. On the roofrack are the snowsledge, shovels and spare wheels. 37

Van der Heijden's Studebaker and Bakker Schut's Ford V8 on a Greek 'Motorway'. 38

Still on the way to Athens, washing the Minx in a Greek river where the bridge had been washed away by heavy rains. 39

Winners of the 1938 Mont Carlo Rally. Left to right: Barendrecht, Bakker Schut, Ton. Behind: Dutch Sports Marshall Van Wickevoort Crommelin. 44

Finish Liège-Rome-Liège. Left to right: Gatso, Barendrecht (Holland), Wessely (Austria), Escalle (France) and Juszezynski (Poland) 51

A proud moment. King Leopold of Belgium congatulates Gatso and Barendrecht, Liège-Rome-Liège 1938. 52

Press reception for Gatso and Barendrecht at the Amsterdam Ford Factory. Liège-Rome-Liège 1938. 54

White loneliness on the way to the Athens start. Monte Carlo Rally 1939. 61

In a snowy ditch on the motorway still under construction from Belgrado to Sofia. Visible are young trees planted just before the winter set in. 62

Great tension in the last seconds before the 'off'. Hollands's first sports-car meeting, held on the temporary road circuit at Zandvoort in 1939. Car no. 38 is Gatso's 68

Liège-Rome-Liège route. 72

Peter Wssely's Steyer burning in a canal. Liège-Rome-Liège 1939. 76

Janus Van der Kamp's Opel after performing a half-somersault during the 1937 Dumonceau Cup Trial 84

A premature end in the Dumonceau Cup Trial for Eddy Holman's Hudson drophead coupé. 85

Dark glasses and a paint-spray mask help Gatso to combat hay fever on the dusty Dumonceau Cup Trial in 1938. The car is a Ford V8 borrowed from Henk Blijdenstein, who competed in Gatso's Riley Kastrel Sprite. .. 86

With Henk Richten navigating, Gatso's Ford V8 tackles the Kautenbach hill-climb near Luxembourg in the final staging of the Dumonceau Cup Trial. 89

Gatso and Theo van Ellinkhuizen at the San Sebastian control 1947. 111

The Gatso sports-car on the classification test at Estoril, Lisbon Rally 1947. 115

Kees Kruit and co-driver looking rather travel-stained on the Alpine Rally, 1947. 121

Jan Erens (left) and Lex van Strien with their notorious old Ford V8 'Blue Angel' having gained second place on the Alpine Rally, 1947. 126

International friendship in motorsport, 5 Frenchmen (one of which was a naturlised Austrian), 3 British, and 6 Dutch at the prizegiving. French Alpine Rally 1951. 127

The Gatso 1500 'Flatty' with Gatso himself at the wheel, establishing a Dutch one-hour endurance record dor 1.5-litre cars, at the Zandvoort circuit in November 1949. 'Flatty' covered 63.7 miles in the hour, with a fastest lap of speed of 65.4 m.p.h. 136

Techincal scrutineer Joop Van Wamelen, checking 'Flatty's' engine cylinder capacity after establishing the one-hour record at Zandvoort. 137

After being presented with the Silver Cup for 1st place in the 1.5-litre
class Gatso is interviewed by B.B.C. reprter, Peter Stevens. The presentation was made by Prince Rainier of Monaco, who can be seen seated at
the top left of the picture. At the top right is Faroux, who intervened the
following day. Incorrectly according to the FINA-rules. 148

An advertisement by the dutch Rootes car importers for the Hillman
Minx following the 1949 Monte Carlo Rally. 149

Dutch class-winners Han Van Der Heyden and Ies Langestraat with
their Panhard at the Monte Carlo start. These small Panhards won their
class in several events during 1950. 153

One of the many which dropped out between Nevers and Grasse. 157

The big Humber making good progress, going as fast as possible on the
frozen snow between Nevers and Grasse. 158

B.B.C. reporter Peter Stevens interviews Gatso after his toughest ever
Monte drive, in an 'unsuitable' car. 159

Left to right: Henri Secrèt and Marcel Becquart (winners), Klaas Barendrecht and Maurice Gatsonides ('moral winners'), and Pierre Lahaye (former winner) discussing who will win in 1950. 160

The 1950 win for Hotchkiss meant that for the second time this famous
French make of car had won the Monte three times in succession. Right:
Henri Secrèt, left: Marcel Bequart who became one of Gatso's best
friends and co-driver in many rallies and Le Mans races in the following
years until 1959. 162

Gatso's second-placed Humber Super Snipe was equipped with Dutch
Vredestein tyres. 163

Advertisement exclaiming that 'Specialists prefer Lodge', and showing
Gatso, in his 'inseparable' farmers hat, working on 'Flatty'. 164

'Flatty' leading Dries Van Der Lof's M.G. in the Tarzan Bend, Zandvoort
1950. 169

...... and suddenly the left rear wheel collapsed. 170

Van Dieten's Jaguar with Gatso's new 4000 Coupé right behind. Following them are Tielens (Delahaye) and Klaas Barendrecht in the other
Gatso 4-litre. 172

Map of Le Mans circuit 174

Whilst practising before the race Veuillet's Delahaye ended up in the protective sandbank at the side of the notorious Tertre Rouge corner. 181

1950 - Le Mans at night. On the left the pits, with spectators on the roof.
Grandstands on the right. 182

Smoky' leading Briggs Cunningham's 'Le Tank' between the Arnage corners (one left- and one right-hander). 188

IX

Four very happy Dutchmen after 24 hectic hours at Le Mans. Left to right: Geert Hoogeveen, Jan Apetz, Henk Hoogeveen and Maurice Gatsonides.	194
Talbot Lago advertisement. The 1950 Le Mans winning Talbot, driven by Louis Rosiér.	196
Shell lubricants kept the Aéro Minor going for 24 hours.	197
Gatso and Ciska tackle the Tre Groce mountain climb in their works Sunbeam Talbot. Alpine Rally 1950.	207
Absolutely unrecognisable after rolling some 200 feet down a ravine, the completely wrecked Allard of the two British boys Potter and Gill.	208
An action shot of Gatsonides crew's Sunbeam Talbot was chosen to illustrate a Ferodo advertisement.	210
Advertisement depicting the Dyna Panhard in the Alps, and listing the car's competition achievements in 1950. These small French cars were pwered by a 610cc two-cylinder aircooled engine.	211
In 'Parc Fermé' at Liège before the start in 1950.	214
Tyresoles newsletter page showing Gatso and Worledge sitting on the bonnet of the Zephyr	232
1994 gathering of veteran German rally drivers.	234
Gatso celebrated his 84th birthday by competing in his Replica Monte 1953 winning Ford Zephyr in the Monte Carlo Challenge 1995.	237

Preface for the revised 1995 edition

When William Leonard wrote this book over 40 years ago, the character whose motorsport adventures were being told, Maurice Gatsonides, was himself already more than 40 years old. In that time 'Gatso' had achieved considerable fame in motorsport. He already enjoyed legendary status and much adulation in his native Holland, and if he had decided then, in the early 1950s, to ease up and simply look back in satisfaction on his past successes, few would have been surprised.

However, that was not to be. Gatso was in fact to go on to even greater fame, boosting his already excellent reputation by winning the Monte Carlo Rally for Ford of Britain in 1953, driving a Zephyr Six. The story of that success is told in an Appendix to this reprint of the 1951 and 1952 editions of *Rallies & Races*. That victory in Monte Carlo was followed by many more international rallying awards in both British and Continental cars. Twice he won the GT Class at Monte Carlo, in 1955 in an Aston Martin, and again in 1961 when at 50 years of age he was successful in a French Facellia. It was not until 1970 that he finally retired from the international rally scene, to resume again in 1980 with oldtimers in historic rallies.

In addition to re-writing the English translation from the Dutch language of the original 20 chapters of *Rallies & Races* for this reprint, I have had the pleasure of working with the remarkable Gatso in recent years on a completely new book, *Gatso: The Never Ending Race*, published late in 1993. This begins with his childhood and continues to his 84th year, covering not only his motorsport activities, but his wartime adventures too, and also the fascinating story of the design and development of his 'Gatsometer' road traffic speed measuring equipment, which is making a significant contribution to road safety throughout the world today.

If you enjoy this reprint of *Rallies and Races*, you will surely also enjoy *Gatso: The Never Ending Race*.

Michael Allen, January 1995

Gatso: Maurice Gatsonides pictured at 40 years of age, already a legendary figure but still with his greatest acheivements to come as the 1950 unfolded.

Original Preface

Motoring sport, more than any other sport, breeds a camaraderie amongst its international devotees that can be only a force for good in this imperfect world. For that reason, as well as for my personal liking and regard for Maurice Gatsonides, it gives me great pleasure to write this preface to the English translation of William Leonard's book describing some of 'Gatso's' many adventures on road and race track. That the book will be read with interest and entertainment by British competitors in motoring sport I have no doubt, because many of them number themselves amongst Gatso's friends and have competed against him on several occasions, as I have done myself in Alpine Rallies.

Gatso is not only a fine driver, as those who read of his adventures in the following pages must inevitably conclude, but he is a fine sports man, remaining calm and unruffled either in victory or defeat. Bad luck is accepted with a shrug of the shoulders - 'it's all part of the game' - but if, on reflection, what appears to be 'bad luck' is finally judged by Gatso to be bad preparation of his car, then he is his own severest critic.

In action Gatso is intense, but still unruffled. He does not allow the fierce excitement of the race, and the Alpine Rally is a veritable race against the relentless clock, to mar his judgement or make him unregardful of his rivals. I well remember being passed many times by Gatso when he was driving a faster car than mine and starting behind me. He was never impatient to pass, he knew that I would give him room at the first opportunity, and when I drew in and he passed it was always with an acknowledging wave of the hand, and a cheery grin. And to see Gatso descend an Alpine pass is something to remember!

Good luck to you, Gatso; 'press on regardless!'

1950 - A.G. Douglas Clease, editor of *The Autocar*

A Word with You before You Start

When you consider that many ages ago our forefathers made crazy voyages in crazy ships, that Crusaders from all over Western Europe trekked trough far-away countries just for the pupose of teaching infidels the right religion the hard way, that later on both British and Dutch sailors sailed the seven seas, and when you realize that it was not only the search for new hunting grounds, the urge for conversation or the hope of undreamed riches that pushed the adventurous men on, but mainly the wish to kiss the wife and kids good-bye and enjoy a lively spot of adventure, you can easily understand why every year a couple of chaps feel the urge to get into a car, drive for thousands of miles with no more rest than a nap in the back seat can afford, to defy snow, rain and storm, be cold and dog-tired and at last arrive unwashed and unshaven, but supremely happy in Monte Carlo.

Then you can also understand why every year again these chaps think it worth while to risk their necks, their money and their conjugal happiness to participate in those hardest-of-them-all tests, the French Alpine Rally and Liège-Rome-Liège Rally. Then you'll see why all those hundreds of trials, those small national rallies, so popular all over the Continent, again and again draw hundreds of competitors who, immensely thrilled, appear at the start, eager to overcome the difficulties they voluntarily accept, to muddle through in dark and rainy nights over roads that hardly deserve that description.

It is the adventure that lures them. That rough-and-ready adventure in an time full of streamlined troubles like gloomy newspaper headlines, taxes and more taxes, and all the thousand and one problems that worry us.

That adventure can just easily be found in those small national events as in the big international rallies with all the cracks competing.

And I'm sure that you will not say: "I wish I were in bed" when you are digging like a slave to free a ditched car, when you are ploughing through the snow that awaits the Rally-driver in boundless quantities. Because these obstacles, once passed, give one the satisfaction of a task fullfilled, an effort well done and a goal reached the hard but pleasing way. A goal that in intself may be not so very important, but that receives its glamour because of the hard work done before it could be reached.

They are rather nice chaps, these Rally-drivers. And to give you an impression of them, I have been listening for many evenings to the tales of Maurice Gatsonides and have written them down for you. 'Gatso' himself rather prefers to be behind the wheel of a car than in front of a typewriter. He is one of the chaps whose performances are looked upon with some respect by that great international fraternity of drivers.

'Gatso' is not a Britisher, but still there is something to connect this very skilled driver, the best Holland has at the moment, with the British angle of the sport. His biggest successes have mainly been won with British cars. That he chose them is a sincere and well-earned compliment on the part of a man who, most of the time, was able to take his choise from many marques of many nationalities. He is going to stick to this choise because he appreciates the British cars he drove so succesfully for their dependability, their road-holding, their honesty and that extra-special quality that is so hard to define, but so important in a car that has to give just that little bit more than the others. In the Monte Carlo Rally he twice won the Barclays Bank Cup, the prize for the best placed British car. The last time he won it driving a Humber Super Snipe, a normal and rather stately car, in no way tuned-up, to second place in the 1950 Rally, when only five of the 365 cars got through unpenalized.

And then, Gatso is not one of the lucky chaps. Time after time the rottenest of luck snatched a certain victory from his hands. Time after time those little things that can go wrong, went wrong, through no fault of his. But then Gatsonides is always likely to learn from those unfortunate experiences and he regards them as being "all in the game."

In this book we've tried to make you a passenger in the many cars that Gatsonides drove in many Rallies and races. He will take you with him through the icy deserts of Scandinavia in winter, through the mud of the Balkans and the dust of the formidable passes of the Alps. He gives you an imaginary seat in his sports car, roaring through the hairpins of a spectator-packed circuit. In the beams of his headlights you'll see that renowned corner of Arnage on the Le Mans

Circuit approaching with a speed that will make you send up a little prayer or two.

I think we had better get on with the story, because Gatso is not fond of being presented as a sort of superman, one of those movie-heroes who keep their eyes fixed on a burning carburettor and have a handkerchief of the fair lady in the grandstand in their racing-helmet. He is quite an ordinary, likeable fellow, who likes rallies and races, who thinks it an excellent thing that people from all countries should meet in these events and become pals. That really is the reason why he likes rallies and races best. And that is why we humbly present this unpretentious narrative by a man who likes the British and their cars well.

William Leonard

From left to right: William Leonard, Gatso, Louise and Jan Apetz, Ciska Gatsonides

XVII

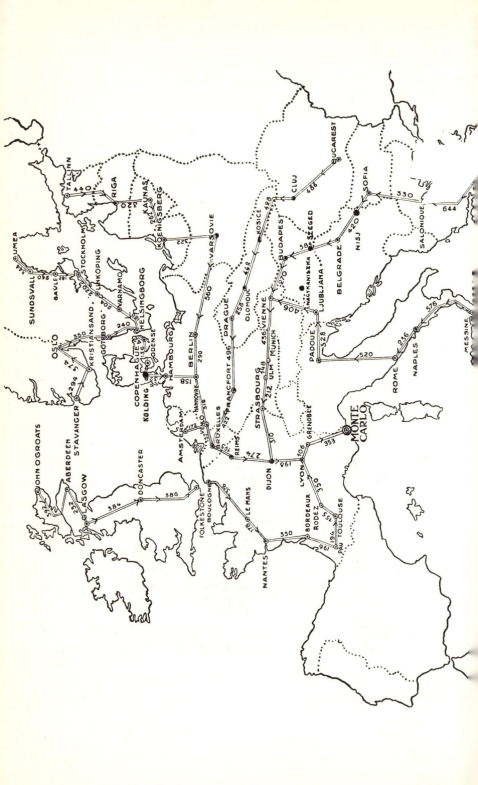

Chapter 1

Monte Carlo Rally 1936

> About my first international competition: taking a wrong turning in Holland: a very hard - but all risks insured wallop: and a Dutch victory which didn't come off.

A cold shiver runs down my spine whenever I think back to my first start in the famous Monte Carlo Rally. It wasn't easy to get a crew together for I was a mere youngster of 24, without a 'name' and with even less money, so that in assembling a crew I had to consider each potential member's ability to pay his share of the costs. Indeed, the sharing of expenses was the reason why I decided to form a three-man team, despite the extra weight being too much for the power of my little Hillman Minx, at least for rally work. Gatsonides-Van Huut-Sillevis was the crew chosen, a youthful and optimistic trio raring to become acquainted with the Monte Carlo Rally.

For some weeks before the event I drove around proudly displaying the red rally plates already fixed to the car. This sort of 'swank' in December, or February and even sometimes in March, is the sure sign of a novice! But I felt like a budding Caracciola or a Rasmussen. I spent all my spare time on what I thought was the careful preparation of the car, although it proved later that much of this time had been wasted on quite irrelevant details in so far as rallies are concerned.

Of course, we knew enough about the Monte to realize we had little chance of winning anything, and so, also taking into account the cash situation, we chose the nearby Amsterdam start. Amsterdam-Monte Carlo meant a route of only 950 miles, and meant also only 476 bonus starting points against the 500 awarded to the Athens route, and, therefore, no chance of reaching any high spots, unless the whole of Europe was snowed under. This however didn't stop me from practicing hard for the classification test which would conclude the rally. The practicing for the figure '8' in that test was done at the Dutch Ford factory in Rotterdam, and a lot of tearing around was done. In the beginning everybody was very careful, but soon the spirits began to rise, and in the end we appeared to be almost waltzing through and around the pylons. A Chevrolet and a D.K.W. overturned, to great joy of everyone but those in the two cars! I was keeping my eyes peeled to learn all I could from crack drivers like Dr. Sprenger Van Eyk - who had once won the rally - and Bakker Schut who was destined to win the Monte in 1938, compared with whom I felt almost a midget.

However, I didn't do too badly with the Minx in the 1.5-litre class, and although I got nowhere near the big fellows I still felt very satisfied returning home, even feeling obliged to exceed some speed limits on account of my new-found rally prowess.

The last few days before the 'off' went by, and almost before realizing it we were straining at the leash in dark Amsterdam, facing the 950 miles to the South. We were the last starters in the queue of cars, in which also a Kromhout-Minerva motorcoach with thirty passengers was a competitor, but such was our eagerness that it wasn't long before we took the lead. At Gorkum we crossed the river in the middle of the night by the ferry specially chartered for the Rally, and carried on to Breda where we made our first mistake with a wrong turning - an error which served to cut down our haste.

A first rally is a peculiar sensation. For although we travelled along roads I knew like the back of my hands, and which held no particular difficulties for me, a strange tension came over the crew - perhaps caused by thoughts of that far away finish - the members of which were looking at the speedometer with eyes as tense as those of the crew of a heavy bomber on a dangerous mission.

The only one spoiling the adventurous, and strangely romantic atmosphere was William Van Huut, who in a down-to-earth manner was continually asking Rar Sillevis about the condition of the foodstuff we carried. Indeed, it was on account of William's persistency that we twice stopped at petrol filling stations for cups of coffee which, he insisted, was very good at night time for the complexion.

In the darkness we crossed the Belgian frontier, continued to Antwerp and did about 65 miles per hour on our way to Brussels. There we had difficulty finding the rally control post. A couple of bleary-eyed Brussels' natives attempted hastily to clear their clouded brains in order to show us the way, uttering a series of "yes's" and "I can tell you's", but to little avail, and after wasting some time we arrived at a crossroads where each member of the crew decided on a different road. The only way in a case like that is to take the remaining road, and, as luck would have it, it did indeed lead straight to the Belgian Automobile Club. There, for the first time, we experienced the real Rally atmosphere. Competitors from the North, wearing fur hats and coats, were asleep in easy chairs. Alongside them, with their unwashed and unshaven faces, we looked and felt altogether too civilized. Co-driver William especially was fascinated by these would-be trappers, and one could almost see the wish to start from the 'Tundras' next year taking shape in his head.

Eventually our departure time for Paris arrived - 4 o'clock in the morning. A 'Pilot', mounted on an old ramshackle motorbike, guided us through the quiet streets, and then we sped along to the French Capital, arriving there with plenty of time in hand, the average required in those days only 40 k.m.h. The final 600 miles though would be at an average speed of 50 k.m.h. a much tougher proposition. We refreshed the outsides of our bodies with a hot shower in the vast building of the Automobile Club de France at the Place de la Concorde, and then our insides with cold chicken washed down with champagne, which tasted heavenly and fortified us well for the remaining laps.

From Paris via Dijon to Lyon is more than 300 miles, and the Minx tackled the long uphill slopes very nicely, and driven hard on the stretch between Dijon and Lyon even remained in front of many faster and heavier cars, with the result that at every control post we had an hour or so in hand. It was all going so smoothly that William and I began talking about who was going to receive all the trophies we intended to win, as there were several cups for the Amsterdam-starters too. But this was misplaced confidence, for when we arrived at Brignolles instead of the sunrise the rain came down in sheets, and we still faced the Estérel Mountains. I had to accelerate hard on the slippery hairpins in order to make the increased average speed, and we came across a number of competitors who had run into trouble through perhaps being over-energetic. It became worse between Nice and Monte Carlo, along the lower Corniche where it was frightfully slippery and dangerous in the numerous blind bends. For the first time we found ourselves behind schedule, and however fast we tore along, skidding and sliding, Monte Carlo failed to come into view as the minutes ticked relentlessly by. At breakneck speed we finally crossed the border into the Principality of Monaco, the final kilometre to the finish and with only a few precious minutes in hand.

Then, barely half a mile from the finish, disaster struck. Immediately before passing under the Würtemberg viaduct, where we should have turned right, two traffic policemen, who presumed that we knew our way, waved us on shouting 'avancez'. However, not in fact being sure of the way I mistook this for a signal that we should go straight ahead up the hill, and so drove merrily on. Suddenly I saw a taxi coming from the right. It must have been quite a sight when, despite my last-second swerve, the two cars embraced each other. Van Huut hit his head on the mirror, receiving a beautiful cut on his forehead. Rar Sillevis was luckier, he had been extending the legs of his camera-tripod - the points aiming at his stomach - in order to photograph our triumphant arrival, and had fortunately been warned by me a moment before not to be so stupid. I smacked into the windscreen surround.

Stranded in sight of the finish. Monte Carlo Rally 1936.

The poor old Minx looked a sorry sight. A mudguard was completely folded up, water was pouring from the radiator, and the battery was in smithereens with its acid flowing out over the hot engine. All that was of little importance as the car was 'all-risks insured', but it took years before I could get that sort of cover again for a rally! We were more concerned that we had abandoned in such a way in full view of the harbour, with a few minutes left and, it transpired, the cup for the best Amsterdam starters within our grasp.

We crawled out of the wreck, and it was a good thing the two policemen had come up for I managed to grab hold of them just as I went down on my shaking knees. I passed out just as if I had received a brilliant K.O. We were rushed to hospital by taxi, where the nurses proved to have a thorough understanding of how we felt by applying bandages to the outside and pouring a large glass of Benedictine down our throats. This bucked us up so considerably that we were able to leave almost straight-away, and set off by taxi for the finish to watch the rest of the rally.

The only real drawback now was that we had to spend all our French and Dutch money on provisional repairs to the Hillman, and William Van Huut even had to change his Dutch East Indies Guilders for francs in order to finance our journey home.

In the meantime we enjoyed ourselves by watching the final classification tests which almost resulted in a Dutch victory. It was a matter of touch-and-go between Schell, Bakker Schut, and the much-feared Rumanian driver, Christea. After the first round Bud, as we called Bakker Schut, was lying second behind Schell. Christea, who had practiced the whole test at least four hundred times in Bucharest, seemed to forget at the critical moment to make a complete figure '8'. But I was sure he did it on purpose in order not to show his hand. Bud had fixed an ingenious modification to his Ford V8, a steel cable which ran from the steering arm to the rearwheel brake levers, so that he could lock the appropriate rearwheel when turning the steering wheel (yes, these modifications were allowed in those days!) and by doing this produced masterly slides. He was betting all his cards on the second run, but unfortunately his cable construction was a little too effective. The car made an enormous overslide forcing Bud to stop right in front of a pylon. He was obliged to reverse, which cost him a few seconds and with them the first place. As it was the Rumanian Ford crew Christea-Zanfirescu-Constantinescu won the rally. Bakker Schut and co-driver Hans De Beaufort finished fourth. Well, we had seen how it should be done. And when we returned home, taking twenty-three hours from Monte Carlo to Amsterdam in the Minx which now had only three brakes working, William and I had just one wish. To do it again, and much better.

Chapter 2

Monte Carlo Rally 1937

About a solo-driven rally: snow, ice, frost: Swedish alcohol: a too-small mirror: and the largest cup of the Monte for the lowest-priced car.

It was on this rally that more than any other time in my life I experienced what it is to feel sleepy. Even now, recalling the event, blank spaces punctuate my memory, and I can feel once more the burning sensation from my red-rimmed eyes, caused by continually starring at the Scandinavian snow, the icy roads of Germany and Holland, and the endless tree-lined French Routes Nationales. Yes, that 1937 Monte would prove to be one of the toughest I have ever driven.

Still being a novice, I had entered the rally nominating Umea in Sweden as my starting point. This was the most northern, but nevertheless in my opinion the easiest starting point, and it was giving 497 bonus points that year, almost the same as the maximum 500 from Athens. I had entered with another Dutchman as my co-driver, although I hardly knew him, and, when it was too late, he proved not to have the driving abilities and capacities of endurance necessary for this hard event. Apart from that he was a nice enough chap.

Our 'warhorse' was again the Hillman Minx, my own dealership demonstration car, which had already covered almost 50,000 miles and was the same car which had suffered the nasty collision at Monte Carlo the year before. Nico Stuifbergen, my chief mechanic, had completely stripped the car down and made a very nice job of rebuilding it. It was thoroughly prepared, although no heater was fitted, such equipment at that time being an almost unknown luxury. However, a funnel rigged-up behind the radiator fan, a hose and the mouthpiece from a vacuum cleaner, would hopefully keep the windscreen free from ice and mist. Three other Dutch crews were trying their luck from Umea: Bakker Schut-Mutsaerts-Kouwenberg in a Lincoln Zephyr V12; Habnit-Burgerhout-Schouten in a Ford V8, and Cornelius with Van Rossum in a D.K.W. We had all arranged to meet in the Hotel Angleterre at Copenhagen, but making that rendez-vous was not as easy as we thought.

Plenty of snow on the route to the start at Umea. Monte Carlo Rally 1937.

A week before the 'off' I collected my co-driver from his home near Arnhem. It was cold and slippery already as we headed northwards for the start. Via Bremen we went to the frontier town of Flensburg, arriving there at 10 o'clock in the evening. Here the Customs officers informed us of a raging snowstorm over Jutland which was preventing traffic from getting through. They advised us to go back and take the ferry from Warnemünde to Copenhagen, but as the Lincoln and the Ford had already passed through we decided to attempt it too nevertheless.

Well, there was indeed a snowstorm. A cutting east wind blew the white flakes across the road, and the more we progressed the more the snow piled up. We decided to join up with a group of other cars, which were preceded by a bus and a lorry. Those heavy blighters up front were able to plough their way through the heaps of snow early on without much trouble, and their drivers were considerate enough to liberate those following cars which got struck. Even so, it became ever more difficult, and eventually the spades were in use digging out the Minx. This was a cold business, and the Bols (Dutch gin) that we carried soon came to an end.

Eventually the time came when the convoy was forced to give up, as the bus became stuck and no power on earth could move it again. There was nothing left but to leave the other cars for which the road was now blocked, and the whole lot of us set off on foot, heading towards a couple of farms situated some way down the road. Struggling through the deep snow with an icy wind biting our ears, we found it hard to believe that we were still in a habitable part of Europe. Worse was to come when we discovered that both farms and even their stables were chock-full already with other stranded travellers. There was still the possibility of some hospitality at a small hotel a few miles further on, a farmer told us. With a Polish lorry driver functioning as interpreter and guide in the lead, we headed towards a light in the distance which appeared to us as if it were at the other end of the world. And now our miseries really started.

The Gatsonides Hillman Minx stuck in deep snow on the way to the starting point at Umea. Monte Carlo Rally 1937.

We were already dog-tired from the digging, and time after time the hurricane now threw us off our balance when we came to the icy patches of road between the snowdrifts. The only thing to do was put our rug down on the road and sit down quickly each time a blast came along. Exhausted, we struggled on until my co-driver, who hadn't felt too well when we left his home, lost his courage completely. He fell down in the snow saying he could not get on. Talking to him, threatening, and explaining the danger was of no avail. I swore at him, and had to kick him to get him up again and keep him up. Otherwise of course he would have frozen to death in no time, as the temperature was minus 35 degrees celsius. Under those conditions there really is an almost uncontrollable desire to lie down in that lovely soft whiteness, and it needs all of one's willpower to prevent being found the next day as a lump of frozen meat. Finally we arrived at the guest house, but the rooms there too were all taken, and we even had difficulty in being allowed inside. Eventually inside, we warmed ourselves around the oven in the middle of the kitchen, and, after some persuasive argument, were given the bed of the daughter of the house, which, believe it or not, was still warm. And fortunately so, as during the night much snow was blown into the room through broken window panes.

Next day we faced the problem of the snowbound car. With the help of local manpower, numbering ten men, we started digging it out, and made a lane through the first snowdrift. I then had one hell of a job to get the engine to turn over. Lying in the snow under the jacked-up car, I eventually freed the starter pinion gear which had become encased in frozen snow. Finally we managed to get the Minx off the road and through a narrow opening through the hedge into the fields. We drove the car across the frozen-solid fields choosing our way carefully between the high snowdrifts. Five hours of hard work by ten men with coal shovels was needed to get the car to the guest house only two miles away. A little while afterwards with our hard working assistants we were enjoying a nice hot punch, when suddenly a very portly policeman entered. He had come on the orders of the local farmers whose wire fencing we had cut, and there was nothing for it but to pay the 10 Crowns that he demanded (about 10 shillings). Quite reasonable!

Although only three miles separated us from Kolding, it took the whole afternoon to get there, driving alternately on the road and through the fields, and again aided by the ten men with their spades.

The 'sledge' in position on the Minx, pictured on the boat to Copenhagen. Monte Carlo Rally 1937.

After Kolding conditions improved, with the eight miles to Fredericia being accomplished in two hours.

Here it was our intention to put the car on the train, but that didn't come off as the train was also snowbound in the Fünen. The only alternative was the boat to Copenhagen, for which we had to wait a whole day. That spare time was spent profitably however doing something to the front of the car in order to prevent snow from going via the front axle and collecting up in the engine compartment. At the biggest workshop in Fredericia we had a sort of sledge made, a piece of curved sheet steel running from the front bumper and continuing under the sump. This simply device worked perfectly. Now, instead of digging itself in, the front of the car received an uplift, and sub-

11

sequently I used a similar contraption in all the pre-war Monte Carlo Rallies whenever we had to traverse long stretches of similar conditions, even with our powerful Ford V8 in 1939.

Safely aboard the boat to the Danish capital, I was ready with my Contax camera as we left port preceded by an ice-breaker. I took many photos which later on were to be awarded first prize in the Photography Concours at Monte Carlo. But that was still a long way off. One of those photographs is reproduced here in this chapter.

Upon arrival at Copenhagen we learned that the other teams we intended to meet there had departed two days before. This came as a shock, and fearing that we would be too late for the start we decided against taking any rest, and continued northwards at once. We crossed the narrow channel to Sweden and went on via Jönköping, Lynnköping and Nörköping (all control points on the Rally) to Stockholm, and again had to contend with a heavy snowstorm. The continual staring ahead through the falling snowflakes illuminated in the darkness by the headlights, eventually caused almost complete snowblindness, and for many hours I was unable to proceed at much more than about six miles per hour. Luckily the roads kept reasonably clear, and to gain time we continued to motor throughout the night.

Next morning, with the snowstorm over, I let my co-driver take the wheel as much as possible to get him accustomed to driving in the snow and on the cleared, but still icy roads. I was most disappointed to discover that he was quite out of his depth in these conditions. Despite a heavy 'bumpering' as we motored through a town he didn't even realize he was driving the car along the raised centre road markers (similar to, but higher and larger than the centre cat's eyes in Britain). As he had already felt unwell when starting out he had perhaps an excuse, and the Danish adventure had certainly made things worse for him.

Driving on without a rest, we learned on the route from Stockholm to Sundsval that the others, who had stayed overnight in a hotel, were now only one hour ahead of us, and after a good hot meal at Sundsval we stepped on it with our good old Minx, and eventually caught upon with them before reaching Umea, our starting point.

During these four extremely difficult days and nights, my co-driver Cees Sanders had shown quite clearly that he was unable to cope with our Minx under these conditions. This forced me to decide that I would drive the entire rally from start to finish myself, a decision sportingly accepted by Cees.

At Umea the good life began. For the few days before the 'off' we stayed at the big Stora Hotelet, where we thoroughly spoiled ourselves. The only drawback was that if, in this strictly spirited-rationed Sweden, one wanted a drink, one had to first order a meal. As the smallest order available was for ham and eggs, the Dutch table was soon almost collapsing under the total egg-production of the Swedish chicken farms. It was said that even the geese were on overtime laying eggs to keep up with our thirst. Another advantage was that many pretty Swedish girls felt an enthusiastic admiration for the already much-travelled Dutch rally drivers, and what's more, they showed it too. We had a jolly good time there in the Swedish cold, with the Rally Ball in our hotel, ice-hockey matches and the ski-jöring seeing to it that we were far from being bored. There was drama too when our compatriot Frans Habnit forgot the Swedish left-drive traffic rule, and collided with a lorry the evening before the start. Some hard work overnight was necessary to get their Ford V8 ready for the 'off'.

The start for those 2,400 long, and slippery miles to the Rivièra took place during the afternoon. Cornelius was the first to go in his D.K.W., followed at one-minute intervals by A.C. Scott on a 1.5-litre H.R.G., and Sammy Davis with a Wolseley, racing off into snowy Sweden. McKenzie, with whom I was to drive in the Alpine Rally fourteen years later, was there with a very comfortable, but heavy Daimler. He survived a nasty skid in Denmark, continuing on to gain first place in the Concours de bonne Présentation des Moteurs at Monte Carlo. Sammy Davis won the Concours de Confort. D.H. Murray drove a Frazer Nash, and the well-known Swedish lady driver Mrs. Greta Molander, had the wheel of a big American Plymouth, with which she won the Ladies Cup.

I particularly admired the courage of those hardy Britons who went off in open sports cars. I remember the tall, red-moustached Scotsman and his co-driver in their open two-seater, both wrapped up so completely in thick fur clothing that, from a distance, they appeared to be a couple of bears in a car. Unfortunately I do not remember his name, and have since lost the entry list.

We motored behind the Swedish lady crew of Baroness von Blixen-Finecke, and in front of Greta Molander's car. At least for as long we could keep up with them, for Greta's big Plymouth went very fast indeed. She started to race with Bakker Schut, who was tearing along the icy roads at 75 m.p.h. in his Lincoln Zephyr. Greta could not quite keep up with him, but Bud, sportsman that he is, allowed her to pass

13

him as they approached Stockholm, so that she could enter the capital of her native land as number one. Between Sundsval and Stockholm I had a nasty moment when, at the end of a long straight stretch the Minx was most reluctant to go around a bend. With a strenuous effort I managed to keep it on the road, and on stopping found that the forward steering arm was caked over with frozen snow. Also, the oil in the steering box had become too thick and heavy in the intense freezing cold. At the Stockholm control I filled this up with '3-in-1' oil, after which the steering was much improved.

Whilst still driving across Sweden co-driver Van Rossum twice overturned Cornelius's D.K.W., but fortunately the small car stood up to it well in the soft snow.

At the Helsingborg control we were joined by competitors who had started from Stavanger. From various quarters we heard that several of these crews had experienced some nasty skids, with a French car having come to a stop with its front wheels over the edge of a ravine. Worse was that a Dutch driver, instead of stopping to help as did others, squeezed his car through the narrow gap, actually nudging the dangerously balanced car with his own heavier vehicle. Interestingly, during the German occupation this 'character' was one of the few of our competition drivers who proudly walked about with a Swastika on his coat lapel, so clearly underlining his sporting instincts!

Although many drivers looked like the Alaskan trappers we had seen in films, not so the French gentlemen Imbert and Franqueville who, immaculately dressed, were acting as mannequins for a French fashion house, driving a Delahaye equipped with a sleeping berth. At Monte Carlo they were to gain second prize in the Concours de Confort, the first place going as already mentioned to Sammy Davis's Wolseley which was even equipped with an on-board toilet.

From Helsingborg we crossed by the big train ferry to Helsingör in Denmark, where a strict speed limit of 65 k.m.h. - about 40 m.p.h. - was and is still enforced. Making sure that the limit was not exceeded by foolish rally drivers our cars were divided into groups of eight, each group headed by a police car. We had a car with an enormous number 'F5', and I can still see that number in my mind's eye dancing in front of me across those 450 miles in Denmark. A few miles out of Helsingör there was a potentially dangerous incident. The all-lady British crew of Vaughan and Taylor, driving a Standard Ten, were just a couple of cars ahead of us when they saw a car coming towards them on the snowbound road. Automatically reacting to the British left-drive rule (and also in Sweden from where we had just come) they swerved to the left and collided head-on with the oncoming car. It looked pretty bad for them, as although the windscreen was of safety glass, the big defroster screen was not; both girls were injured and bleeding. They were in a nasty fix, as the doors were jammed and making matters worse was smoke and a burning smell caused by an electrical short circuit. There was a lot of excitement, but nobody was actually doing anything useful, so I jumped on the roof and kicked-in the soft sunshine roof so that we could unlock the doors and get them out.

From the Danish capital we went to Odense and arrived there on the second night. I had been driving throughout and felt pretty tired, but simply dare not let my passenger have the wheel. From Odense to Flensburg and Hannover I had hoped that the cold might lessen, but not so. Outside the temperature was 35 degrees below zero, and it was minus 10 degrees Celsius inside the car. The mineral water we carried in the back froze, shattering the bottles into pieces. All windows were coated with a thick layer of frost apart from a half circle with a six-inch radius on the windscreen above my improvised defroster, which sometimes included a number of lighted candles. It was deadly tiring driving with only that small area of clear glass in front of me, and my spirit too fell below zero. At Hannover I felt like giving up; I really was fed up to the teeth. After eating a few rolls in a nightclub - no restaurant being open at this late hour - surrounded by members of the local society, I dropped of to sleep under a table, with my head on my propped-up leather coat, in which I had an alarm clock.

The journey from Hannover to Venlo surpassed everything. The road swam before my eyes, and it was only by the skin of my teeth that I avoided hitting two large deer crossing the icy road. Steering and gearchanging were done automatically as I dreamt of a beautiful warm bed, sometimes waking up and thinking "they can go to hell with their rally". Fortunately, at the Dutch frontier just before Venlo, we met up with the service car belonging to the Dutch Rootes products importers, whose occupants informed me that the Minx would be checked over and looked after for me at the control post. This boosted me a little, but when we finally arrived at the Venlo control I was so utterly tired that getting out I said "No more for me, I'm through".

Then I saw my fiancee, accompanied by Robby my cocker spaniel, who went mad at seeing me, climbing all over the bonnet of the car to get to me. The Dutch Rootes Group importers were there, and it's strange how little things like that can lift you up again. For although nobody said a word to that effect, I began thinking to myself that I simply couldn't let them all down now. After enjoying a hot meal, still tired but with a new-found enthusiasm I got into the car, which, as had been promised, had been lubricated and checked over without me having to lay my hands on it. I was determined to get through the last 700 miles to Monte Carlo, and they were not the easiest as the average was increased to 50 k.m.h. - about 31 m.p.h. The roads remained icy right through Paris, so slippery that near the Franco-Belgian border I stopped to take a photograph of a wrecked car at the other side of the road.

I don't remember much more about that drive to Paris, as I drove like a robot with a headache, correcting every skid automatically and wishing constantly that Monte Carlo was not so damned far away. Eventually I hung on to the tail of Eddy Hertzberger's Graham Paige, as I felt safer behind another car, and it also meant I didn't have to navigate either as Sanders was not even doing that correctly.

At Dijon I was sufficiently awake to point out to my friend Carol Schade, who had started from Amsterdam in his Ford V8, that his mirror was too small. But Carol, himself not feeling exactly up to the mark, answered: "I don't care a tinker's cuss". This negligence would later cost him the cup for the highest-placed Amsterdam starter.

Towards sunset on the fourth day we finally reached the last control along the route, at Avignon. I was aware of nice little ditties about the place, but I had never seen a more uninviting town. I was completely fagged. We sat and drunk awful coffee from marble-topped tables in a rotten 'bistro', and out of pure cussedness I threw a basketful of inedible hard rolls across the room. I felt as though I could stand it no more; and yet I had to, because we still had to do the regularly test of 200 kilometres - about 125 miles - from Le Muy to Monte Carlo, which had to be covered at precisely 50 k.m.h. at all times, with secret time controls. But help often comes when liquid reaches the lips, and my help now consisted of a bottle of Swedish spirits, which had been obtained in Umea with some difficulty in acquiring the special permits necessary, as alcohol was strictly rationed in Sweden. I took an enormous swig; it felt as if a bomb had exploded inside me, and lo! the birds began to sing again. Beautifully.

For the regularity test I had fitted an invention of Bakker Schut, a special average-speed clock, an ingenious apparatus which was to be found in fourteen Dutch-entered cars. It looked intricate, but worked on a simple principle using two revolving concentric circles so that at any moment you could see how you stood against the compulsory average speed. One circle driven by the clockwork mechanism went

*Bakker Schut's average speedmeter,
shown set for 50 kilometres travelled in one hour.*

round in an hour, and the other in whatever road distance had been set on the clock - 50 kilometres in this instance. It was a very handy instrument, but unfortunately for the others ours was the only one to

*Berlescu's much-modified Ford V8,
with three seats, and special snow gear fitted at one side only.*

17

function properly on the test, even that in Bakker Schut's own Lincoln failed to do the trick on this occasion due to his own miscalculations.

In the end, with a little help again from some Swedish alcohol, we arrived at Monte Carlo with a clean sheet, having completed the regularity test correctly. If you were also there in 1937, and remember seeing a thin, anaemic-looking fellow, dizzy with sleep - and alcohol - falling onto his bed like a log, you know it was me!

Isn't it lovely though, to feel the soft bed beneath you, and to let your head drop onto a clean and soft pillow when you have been driving through four days and nights without a wink of sleep? I slept for twenty-three hours non-stop! After a clear day's rest there was the final deciding test, an acceleration and braking test. Quite simply really, just 200 metres forward, stop, reverse back over the line, and then 100 metres forward over the next line with a flying finish. It was not too bad, and we had reason to feast when the final Rally results were announced. The Minx was twentieth overall in the general classification, and the highest placed British car for which we won the Barclays Bank Silver Challenger Cup, the biggest trophy on the event. And we had done it with the cheapest car of the lot, which had already cover-

The Minx achieved an excellent result on the classifying test. Monte Carlo Rally 1937.

ed nearly 50,000 miles. It had beaten those fast and expensive special sportscars which were admitted in those days. Only Innes's Riley Sprite two-seater could have threatened us, but he had received additional penalties on account of his mirror being too small. In the 1.5-litre class we had come second, being beaten only by the Fiat 1500 driven by 'Gigi' Villoresi, the great Italian racing driver. We then feasted magnificently, slept long and well, and thought of that very useful saying: "Never say die".

Chapter 3

Liège-Rome-Liège 1937

> About a mascot: ten opera stars: mountain passes in the dark: indoor mountaineering: broth and omelettes: a gate under the wheels: and a small nut in the sand.

Gradually the hunger to enter motorsport events became for me an insatiable appetite. And what event was better able to satisfy this hunger than the Liège-Rome-Liège, that legendary, long distance and so very tough Rally, about which I had heard and read with great interest. That is why, in 1937, I thought to myself: "Here goes". I had a splendid car for the purpose, the spirited Riley Kestrel Sprite, powered by an extremely strong 1.5-litre overhead-valve engine with twin high-mounted camshafts, and driving through a Wilson preselector gearbox. And to complete the picture a fine friend and colleague as codriver, William Van Huut, who most tragically lost his life later in a K.L.M. aircraft crash. William was a most sporting chap, who certainly was not averse to speeding along when required, and although he lacked experience of mountain driving routine he picked it up quickly in the Alps.

That rally was some trip! More than three thousand miles nonstop, except for checking in at forty-four time control posts, so that the possibility of having a nap was completely out of the question. The prescribed average was 50 k.m.h. (32 m.p.h) but, especially in the mountains, this could simply not be sustained, so that, inevitably, the outcome was that everybody received penalties. This, in my opinion, is a much fairer method with which to reach the final decision than classifying tests following a run of a few thousand miles, a situation found on several other major rallies. Just how tough and tiring this

21

Liège turned out to be, was plainly evident when of the thirty-four crews which started only seven arrived at the finish, and each with a sackful of penalties.

It was Wednesday, August 18th, when the two Dutch crews, Barendrecht-Klein with a Ford V8 two-seater, and ourselves, reported at the 'parc fermé' in Liège. This was one of the two points where the strict regulations of this otherwise perfectly organized rally were not being adhered to. Strictly speaking only competitors and officials were allowed to enter the 'parc fermé', and no work could be carried out on the cars. In reality, though, we were almost falling over mechanics applying the finishing touches to many cars, and even in some cases fitting new tyres.

We used this opportunity to have a good look at the other cars and discovered that numerous mirrors, mudguards and bodies didn't comply with the minimum measurements. Our Dutch sports marshall, Mr. Gerard Van Wickevoort Crommelin, soon had the organizers rather worried by pointing out that any competitor could protest against these faults, which would have resulted in several cars being disqualified before the start! But we didn't wish to spoil the show, a fact which the organizers, the 'Motor Union de Liège', much appreciated.

More importantly, we saw that the fight was going to be hard, for there were a fair number of special sports cars and even some racers. There were some engines with superchargers, although it proved later that those blown engines gave more trouble than any advantage they might have had.

At 7.30 p.m. we started in convoy for Spa, where the 'off' for this great rally was to be. Mobile police and all kinds of high authorities accompanied the procession, and at Spa we had a few hours to calm our nerves. We considered it a good omen when an elderly Dutch lady offered us her lucky mascot which, she said, had always brought her luck at the roulette tables. After making it clear that we could not be held responsible for any financial consequences of this transfer, we accepted the mascot, but only for the duration of the rally. And indeed, it was to see us home again safe en sound.

Towards 11 a.m. we got the flag, together with the Lancia Aprilia of Rogier and Rousseau, and were off on the ascent of the Côte de Malchamps, a hill familiar to us from the Dumonceau Cup Trials. Tearing up these three miles to the top we showed the Aprilia our rear lights, and headed south at a comfortable cruising speed via Luxembourg to Strasbourg. On that first stretch we met the first casualty. Mrs. Rogier, who with Mrs. Thirriot was competing in a big

Delahaye Grand Sport, had realized just a fraction too late that the 90 m.p.h. was a little too fast for a particular bend they were approaching. The two-seater left the road, cleared a ditch, and landed in the adjacent field. We stopped but could do little to help, and fortunately anyway Mrs. Rogier's husband was right behind us in the Lancia - what a rotten beginning though. Nevertheless we did appreciate it that the lady, her head still heavily bandaged, came to offer us her compliments at the finish, four days later on. That finish however was still a very long way off, more than 3000 tortuous miles. After Strasbourg came the German frontier, where for some reason we had the privilege of being allowed to leave ahead of some other competitors already there and waiting. We didn't object at all, and waving cheerfully at the drivers we shot away over the Rhine bridge via Kehl towards Ulm. From there we went to Munich and, although we hate to admit it, the traffic was extremely well controlled by the uniformed German clowns, propagating the 'Führer-Principle' with German road users, so that the rally drivers could hurry on unimpeded.

And we certainly hurried! Towards Munich the roads began to climb, and now was William's chance to master the art of negotiating hairpin bends. His training almost met an untimely end, for on the Scharnitz pass he was so pre-occupied with his cornering technique that he observed almost too late that a huge lorry and trailer was descending the mountain. We saw the high-set enormous bumper bar towering over the low Riley's bonnet, but we missed the big fellow by what must have been a fraction of an inch. After that scare he always gave a wide berth to these monsters. On that same pass a nail punctured one of our tyres, but in one minute and twenty-three seconds we had the knock-off Rudge wheel removed and the spare wheel knocked on. At Innsbruck we fitted a new inner tube, as I didn't consider it advisable to stitch patches on in an event such as this one, for with the continuous high-speed cornering the tyres get very hot and the adhesive doesn't always hold. Those handy little gadgets to vulcanize patches were not yet known then, and anyway that method would have probably taken too much time on an event like the Liège.

At the Austrian-Italian border we were treated to what amounted to a competition between the border functionaries of each country, who were still not exactly on brotherly terms due to Italian's annexation of Southern Tirol after the first World War. On the Austrian side three men managed to get our papers ready in one minute, and we were attended to before everyone else (non-competitors) who were waiting. On the Italian side they were even quicker. The whole gene-

23

ral staff of the Duce - or so it seemed - were ready to demonstrate the efficiency of the fascist paradise. Ten men, who appeared to us more like opera stars in gala uniform straight from the stage, were waiting to receive us. One was holding a rubber stamp, the second held the stamp pad, and the third grabbed our 'carnet'. For each passport there were two men on either side of the car. The foreign-exchange form, which had been filled-in during the trip by William and which as a consequence was not easily decipherable, was passed by the others. The activity in that opera-headquarters was so comical that I couldn't resist the desire to take a photo. But there was nothing doing! Six strong muscular hands seized me and quickly dumped me in the car. They were not going to have their efficient job spoiled by an 'Olandese stupido'. The papers were thrown in through the sunshine roof and we were on our way. A little way past the frontier, on the Brenner pass we came across another rally casualty. The most expensive car of the whole entry, a beautifully-bodied Alfa Romeo, on which friend Farina had spent much time, had skidded on the freshly tarred road and embraced the rocky mountain side. Another job for Farina! Luckily the crew members had escaped with hardly a scratch.

We went deeper and higher into the Dolomites, which I was seeing for the first time, and motored on to arrive at Cortina d'Ampezzo as dusk fell on the second night of the event. Driving in the dark, and through clouds over difficult and almost invisible pass-roads we could not keep up our speed, as too many perils would have faced us.

On the Pordoi pass we met our compatriots Barendrecht and Klein. The second gear of their Ford V8 had given up the struggle. And at the same point the Le Mans type Alfa Romeo of Swiss driver Hans Dreyer rested badly damaged at the bottom of a ravine. Its driver lay beside it; the poor fellow must have been killed instantly, his co-driver was badly injured. This was the first fatal accident that I had seen in my sporting career. It produced a lump in our throats, and even when considering that such an accident might also occur during an ordinary mountain drive, you have to summon up a lot of courage to carry on. The crew of a Belgian Adler-Impéria were so demoralised that they gave up, as did Desquèsnoy-Boudart with their supercharged M.G. They had simply lost all courage.

We drove on, still depressed, and with the after effects of the accident considerably decreasing our speed, but slowly our spirits rose and the accelerator was pushed down harder again. At Bormio we were thirteen minutes late, in part of course due to the sad event, and so we received our first penalties. By driving extremely fast to Gomagio we were able to make up the whole of the lost time (which was allowed in the regulations of most pre-war rallies) so that the marks lost were not repeated at the next control. Then we faced the mighty, much feared Passo di Stelvio. This ascent we had to tackle in the pitch dark and with cloud from half way up blanketing the summit.

On the climb we benefitted greatly from our foglamps, which were set so as to illuminate the road around the bends so that we never drove into a void. The Wilson preselector gearbox was also a great help. On the straight, just before a hairpin, you pre-set back to a lower gear with the lever, and then when half-way through the hairpin a kick on the gear-change pedal was all that was necessary, so enabling both hands to remain on the steering wheel throughout the turn. Cheerfully we overtook four other cars on the climb, and felt like giants. We pitied a couple of young British lads who were struggling up the climb in an antique Bentley 'long chassis' four-seat tourer. Its chassis was indeed too long for the hairpin bends, forcing them to reverse at least once on every bend. The constant heavy gear-changing must have absolutely exhausted them I thought, but they remained cheerful as we passed.

Back at Bormio we had again lost twelve minutes, following which we had to climb the Gavia pass which was little more than a miserable mule path without protective walls. As we had a strong desire to contest more rallies we climbed this pretty slowly so as not to tempt fate, and therefore we arrived at Ponte di Legno with another load of penalties. Luckily it was not so steep after leaving that control, but it still wasn't easy finding our way in the pitch dark. Furthermore we were fagged-out, by lack of sleep, our nasty experiences, and by tackling the notorious Gavia we had just left behind.

As we searched for the road to Feltre and the next control post, the sound of much Dutch bad language could be heard floating through the stillness of the night. Eventually however we came across the Venice control, which in fact was actually situated in Mestre which is on the mainland opposite that beautiful town of canals. It was daylight again and on the splendid Italian roads we soon made up our lost time. Before reaching Bologna an Italian nail created some work for a local tyre dealer, but the Rudge wheel was soon changed.

We drove across the Apennines via Florence to the Italian capital and there, to our surprise, we found that the check-point was at the top of a seven-storey garage in the centre of the town. Two wide spirals led to this 'seventh heaven', and it was amusing to race up to the top with a loud reverberating exhaust note. This indoor mountaineering for cars was easier than it might seem, as all one had to do was set the steering wheel at a fixed angle and accelerate. Some cars were already going back down, but of course they motored down the other spiral. Here, in Rome we were informed of just how tough it had been. Only nine competitors had signed in when we left this half-way control, many of the others already dropped out leaving a few still to arrive. We were pleased to hear that we had made fastest climb on the Stelvio pass, a great success for our Riley saloon in the hands of a couple of first time amateurs. An achievement which I was lucky to repeat in later years.

On our return journey to the finish at Liège, a considerable way out of Rome we met two crews still on their outward run. One were a pair of Germans in an Opel, being towed by the so-called 'voiture balay', (the rescue vehicle sometimes referred to as the broom car as it followed the rally 'sweeping up' the broken down competitors) whilst a little further on were the drivers of a Fiat 'road bug' who were sucking on their fingers in an futile attempt to cool them down. Their car, a Topolino with a special two-seater plywood body, had an overhead-valve engine with a nine-to-one compression ratio. It could do 75 m.p.h. on the flat, and rev to eight thousand r.p.m. maximum, but it required the spark plugs changing every 150 miles or so, resulting in its crew arriving at Rome with grilled fingers. Nevertheless, they continued bravely on, only to collide with a non-competing car on the final day. Like me, William was a believer in keeping well fed, and we aimed to reach every control-point with a little time for nourishment, and many times we quickly devoured a bowl of broth and an omelette or spaghetti.

On the way back through Viterbo we enjoyed peaches as big as melons. This was to the astonishment of our main competitors, the German crew Baron Huschke von Hanstein and Bundt, who had started out only three minutes ahead of us and so had witnessed our gastronomic achievements at several stops. The first meeting with Huschke was followed by many others, with an interruption of a decade due to the war. Continuing via Sienna, we shot along to Pisa, and as nightfall occurred for the third time since we set out we arrived at the Italian Riviera. It was strange watching well-dressed tourists strolling along the promenade while we, looking more like navvies, were frantically devouring mile after mile.

On the main road to La Spezia we almost came to grief. We were tearing down the lovely straight road at 80 m.p.h. when we had to dim our headlamps for an oncoming car with lamps like a lighthouse.

He too dimmed, but we still couldn't see anything. Just before passing him, Van Huut, who had the wheel, switched on our headlamps and received a nasty shock as right in front of us was an unlit horsedrawn cart. William gave the wheel a quick turn and we just shaved the large wooden cartwheel. It could have been a terrible smash, but luckily the road was wide, and so the driver of the other car too had only a fleeting glimpse of the eternal car park in the sky. Interjections such as that are a sure antidote for sleepiness!

Just before La Spezia we met tropical rain and much evidence of there have been some very dirty weather there. The roads were flooded, trees lay across them and a telephone pole hung at an angle, only held up by the cables. We managed to get under or around the obstacles, until a sudden rattling under the car aroused our worst suspicions. Stopping immediately and feeling in the water on the road under the Riley, we found a section of iron gateway in the road, totally invisible to us because of the water. What luck that our tyres had held out. We arrived nevertheless still on time in La Spezia and went on through the darkness to Genoa.

On the not particularly high, but winding Bracco pass our lights suddenly went dim, and a look at the ammeter told me that we had full discharge, a situation which again gave the opportunity to let the world know just how badly I could pronounce the Dutch language. Van Huut, who was enjoying a short spell in dreamland, received a punch in the ribs, and without stopping we planned what to do. Thanks to a clear sky and the little light we had left I was able to drive to the top of the pass. We stopped and checked the voltage regulator, but it was O.K., and therefore it must be the dynastarter, which was driven direct from the front of the crankshaft on those Rileys. So we lay down side by side on my leather coat under the radiator and after removing a clamp from the dynastarter found the problem. A little nut had come off one of the brush holders. Even to this day I am amazed at what happened next, for incredibly that little nut was lying right there in the loose sand right under our noses, it must have been working loose for some time and dropped off exactly at the time we took the clamp off. Worse though was that the wire had practically burned through, but we managed to get things fixed again. After starting the engine by the crank handle the needle on the ammeter showed 'full charge' again. We were lucky, for it might have been an armature or field failure, and then we would have been finished. Nevertheless, this 'joke' cost us twelve minutes at Genoa, from where we continued to San Remo. We had to be very careful now as the roads were very wet and slippery, and our tyres had only little tread remaining. Furthermore we were confronted by four closed level-crossings, and on arrival at San Remo we had lost a few more minutes.

After that final Italian control we had to cover a short distance to Nice, but before getting there found a stupid handicap in the form of the Italian Customs who apparently had not been informed by the Italian Automobile Club to be prepared for the rally cars. Quick as they had been when we entered Italy, now they were just the reverse. All the travellers in a couple of French coaches were being individually checked upon, and no matter how much we called out "Corso, Corso", we were refused preference. The worst was that one Customs officer was imitating Napoleon, standing there with his arms crossed over his chest, and not moving a finger to help us. When finally I got fed up and made my way to the office, this oaf became annoyed and ordered us back in the car, where we had to wait. I would have loved to have chased him down the road in the car.

Fortunately, the French equivalents were most courteous and the route Menton-Nice, which I knew like the insides of my pockets, I covered in record time. At Monte Carlo the police wished to direct us down below to the low Corniche. But I took the middle Corniche, which is much quicker and with less traffic, and a road surface offering a good grip for the tyres which would enable me to keep up a good speed in the pouring rain. With two minutes to spare we arrived at Nice. We knew that we would now be following a very difficult route, and it was at high speed that morning that we shot away into the French Maritime Alps. On the climb we saw the Italian crew Massa-Brunetto working hard under the bonnet of their Lancia Aprilia, which had lost power through a leaky valve guide. The handy Brunetto, a racing motorcycle rider, fitted a new one in thirty-five minutes. He and his companion, a doctor, were a couple of very pleasant chaps who later on at the banquet in Liège taught us all kinds of Italian limericks, but on account of their, we presumed, dubious meaning, we never recited them!

At Barcelonette we had sufficient time for a proper meal, and so were well fortified for the tough Col de Vars, a very steep and in those days narrow pass about which we had been warned a-plenty. Through France it was doubly necessary not to lose any time, as one was not allowed to make it up, and any penalties were recorded on all the following check-points until the Belgian border had been passed. So penalties accumulated, and with no chance of catching up on lost time before the route from Cambrai in France to Mons in Belgium.

The Vars was indeed tough, and the road surface terrible. Using our stopwatch we checked on how much we gained on Baron Huschke von Hanstein-Bundt, and to our satisfaction found it to be quite considerable. Every time we saw them crossing over a high bridge or taking a hairpin in front of us we started the chronometer, and stopped it when we passed the same spot. Their original advantage of three minutes dwindled down to about twenty seconds, and if the road had not been so very dusty and loose-surfaced we would have probably overtaken them. Anyhow, we made the fastest time over the Vars, and arrived only two minutes late at Guillestre. Via Briançon we ascended the following Col du Lautaret and then the formidable Galibier pass. At a height of about 8,000 feet we encountered snow, but with wild driving we managed to arrive on time in St. Michèl de Maurienne, and stormed on up the Col d'Iséran, the highest pass in Europe. There it was so cold that we put on our trousers over our summer shorts and also wore our leather coats. Even our plaids came into use. It was magnificent scenery portrayed by all those giant snow-capped mountains, but you can't enjoy it much on a rally with that high average which needs so much concentration. Leaving the road and dropping into one of the many ravines could quite literally mean being lost forever.

When leaving the Alps William took over the wheel while I went to sleep, with my poor head hanging down. It would have been wiser to have stayed awake, for after a while I woke up feeling as if I had drunk a bottle of methylated spirits. My insides felt as if a revolution was taken place there, and I thought I was going to die. My head had received so many bumps over that winding road, that it was well over an hour before I felt that my brain was back in its proper position.

At Lyon we started the final night's drive. We drove across the grape fields, territory well-known to me from the Monte and many holiday trips to the sunny Rivièra.

At Dijon we met our French friend Lahaye, who had also entered for this Liège, but whose Bugatti, in which he intended to take part had been smashed by his co-driver, the well-known racing driver Jean Pierre Wimille, the day before the start. Lahaye offered to pilot us through Dijon in his huge Monte Carlo Renault with its eight foot long bonnet. It was one o'clock in the morning, and we really made the sparks fly, with the Renault leading at 75 m.p.h. in the town, which we actually thought was quite reasonable, until at a road-crossing another car approached at a similar speed. Fearing the worst I closed my eyes, but Lahaye stood on his brakes, turned the long Renault broadside and it came to stop like a well-drilled soldier. Immediately after, this 'hard as nails' Frenchman was tearing along again just as fast, as though nothing at all had threatened him.

At Paris we had enough time in hand to enjoy an excellent breakfast before speeding away to the Belgian town of Mons, where the local people treated the few surviving cars to bunches of flowers. At Brussels we found our friend and journalist Paul Lamberts Hurrelbrink, a Monte Carlo veteran, waiting for us to tell us that we were fourth in the general results list and lying second in the 1.5-litre class. This actually disappointed us a little bit, for on the way we had discussed our penalties with Baron Huschke von Hanstein and his codriver Bundt who told us they were in total 1 hour and 45 minutes behind. In reality they had only lost an hour, while we had lost ten more minutes, and consequently the German pair won the class.

Unusually, the tail end of this rally was the easiest part, as the road from Visé to Spa, the finish, was familiar ground to us. On that stretch we saw a couple of Frenchmen cooling the brakedrums of their car with pails of water, as they had forgotten to release the handbrake when driving from the last check-point. On the final hundred miles we let our good old Kestrel Sprite fly, and we arrived at the finish

Tired, dirty, but very happy at the finish of the Liège-Rome-Liège, 1937.

dog-tired but immensely satisfied with our result, fourth place overall which - considering it was our first time - gave us not at all cause for complaint. After having the car verified in the closed park, we were filled up with champagne at the club headquarters and - teetotalers please forgive us - we enjoyed it more than ever before. Maurice Garot, the president of the organizing club, the Motor Union de Liège, apologized for not having our National Anthem available on a record, but said we would be compensated by having a male choir sing the Donkey Serenade, or something like that, when we entered the building. This was a pity. And then another mistake was made when, at the official banquet the evening after, they hoisted the flag of Holland, their neighbour, upside down! Apart from these minor lapses though the organization had been perfect - we had seen at every control throughout Europe a Belgian official from Liège, and we went home with the firm intention of never missing a future Liège-Rome-Liège for as long as we were able to compete. And what's more we had a large laurel trophy tied to the nose, and some beautiful cups in the boot of our faithful Riley Kestrel Sprite.

Chapter 4

Monte Carlo Rally 1938

> About a start from Athens: two sets of fourteen springleaves: many pistols: a broken piston: and the victory of 'Bud' the great.

Having finished two Montes, and achieved a second-in-class on the second run, I felt now that I was hard-boiled enough to go for the major awards. That meant starting from Athens, as that long route from the Greek capital was the only one offering the maximum 500 bonus points. However tough it might be, with no doubt several unpleasant Balkan surprises thrown in, if a penalty-free run could be managed to Monte Carlo the bonus points would be at least three more than would have been collected from any other starting point, putting a good final result within reach.

My friend Henk Blijdenstein was coming along as my co-driver, and the original intention was to use my Riley Kestrel Sprite as on the 1937 Liège-Rome-Liège. However, this idea was abandoned in favour of taking the Hillman Minx once again, which although not quite so roomy would be more suitable over the rough Balkan roads. During a very tough preparation the Hillman received the more powerful Rootes Group sidevalve engine from the Sunbeam Talbot. A snow sledge as had proved so successful on the previous Monte was naturally produced again, and I was able to fit twin wheels at the rear, ensuring a much better grip in the snow which we would undoubtedly meet. These additional outboard wheels were attached to drums which themselves were permanently bolted to the original wheels, with these protruding drums also able to be used as a winch should we at any time become struck. Very useful indeed with a suitable length of rope as a de-

33

ditching contraption, either for ourselves or some other competitor. I had made the rear mudguards more quickly detachable, with just four wing nuts rather than the seven hexagonal nuts normally used. It took no more than fourteen minutes to remove the wings, fit the additional rear wheels, and get the sledge on at the front to have the Minx ready for driving across deep snow. For some weeks before I had practiced this procedure repeatedly in our sand dunes, using Track-Grip tyres on the outer rear wheels. The system worked well, and the axle half-shafts proved also to cope with the extra forces. In order to encounter the least possible unpleasant surprises, accompanied by my co-driver Henk, and Han Van Der Heijden, who had entered with a Studebaker, I went to France in the Riley to scout the special routes which were to be used that year as supplementary classification tests in addition to the normal acceleration-brake-reverse test at the finish. The section Grenoble-Monte Carlo, by the route d'Hivers des Alpes, had been divided into three parts, each of which had to be covered at an average of between 50 and 60 k.m.h. (31 and 37 m.p.h). On the preceding routes to Grenoble the average was the usual 40 k.m.h. for the first half and then 50 k.m.h.

We paid special attention to the shortest, but most difficult section of only twelve kilometres between Km-stones N85-85 and N85-97, which led across the Col des Lèques with its numerous icy hairpins, of which some were without parapets. This wasn't going to be easy, but we tore along through the Alpine snow and reached the conclusion that the Minx could just do it if conditions were not too bad, and all sails were put to the mast.

We tried the acceleration-braking-reverse test at the K.N.A.C. (Royal Dutch Automobile Club) training days held at Amsterdam Airport, and when we started out from the K.N.A.C. offices at The Hague sixteen days before the 'off' in Athens, nobody could say we were not well prepared. With our pockets full of 'marks', 'drachmas', 'lires', 'dinars' and whatever other names the foreign currency (there were twelve kinds) may have, our passports full of visas, and the Minx loaded to capacity with all the necessary equipment (and some perhaps not necessary) we left the K.N.A.C. headquarters where we had received an encouraging speech from Dutch sports marshall Van Wickevoort Crommelin. We departed together with the Ford V8 of 'Bud' Bakker Schut-Karel Ton-Klaas Barendrecht, and the Han Van Der Heijden-Van Linteloo De Geer-Taverne Studebaker, all heading across the Balkans for the Athens starting point.

We had not travelled far, to be precise only the two kilometres to Van Der Heijden's filling station on the outskirts of The Hague, when we were forced to stop. Despite extra spring leaves, the overloaded Minx was almost dragging its tail along the cobbles, and there was no alternative but to unload some of the spares and equipment and leave them behind. We made it to Munich for our first night's rest, and here fitted another leaf in each of the rear springs of the still heavily-laden Minx. That was the fifth extra leaf, and it proved later that it still was not enough. When leaving Munich we had a taste of things to come. Snow lay thickly on the road to Vienna. Zigzagging carefully, doing no more than twenty miles per hour over the slippery roads, we continued until Bud managed to get into a gorgeous skid which landed the big Ford in a ditch with its front wheels resting against a pole. It was quite a wallop. The Minx too had skidded into a ditch, but there it was only soft snow and no pole. With three well-prepared crews it was an easy, albeit very cold task to get the Ford out and tow Bud to Linz, where temporary repairs were carried out to see us on to Vienna where the job could be properly finished.

We intended to get to know the various places well, and to this end we subjected the centres of enjoyment in both Vienna and Budapest to thorough investigation. The results of this research work I'll leave for those meetings of seasoned rallymen, and now take you instead along the long concrete road from Budapest to the Yugoslavian frontier. This runs for 120 miles right across the puszta, the romantic beauty of which however was completely lost to us in this cold winter season. It was along this road, at Gyon, some years earlier that Eric Fernihough attained several world-speed records with his Brough Superior motorcycle, before sadly crashing fatally on one of these attempts.

The frontier between Hungary and Yugoslavia was exactly the line that split our comfortable part of the world from the Balkans. Customs officers who emitted sounds almost unintelligible to us, seemingly to say that they didn't really believe our reasons for being there, and road signs giving all kinds of advice in a dark sort of double-Dutch, made it clear now that troubles were really about to begin. We hadn't gone more than a few yards into Yugoslavia before the mud started splashing up onto our cars. We continued through this mud along awfully bad roads which eventually led us into Belgrade. By this time we had reached the conclusion that in Yugoslavian traffic one car horn signal at a cross-roads meant 'straight ahead', two signals 'turn right', and three 'turn left'. Something to introduce at Piccadilly Circus, or in one of those interminable queues at the Bank!

We stayed overnight in Belgrade, and before leaving next day I added another leaf to our rear springs.

From Belgrade we travelled throughout the day via Nisj to the Bulgarian frontier, where we discovered that the Balkanese are not expected to visit neighboring countries after six o'clock in the evening, the frontier being effectively sealed after that time with barbed wire. We decided to return to Nisj over a short stretch of excellent new road, still under construction as part of the London-Istanbul highway. Being incomplete however it had its drawbacks, such as suddenly ceasing to exist wherever it came to a river, as the appropriate bridges had yet to be built. Because nobody was expected to use it, no warning signs were there! The technique therefore was to brake very hard, wait a-while to recover from the shock of stopping with the front wheels almost hanging over the edge, then go back a little way to find the old winding pathway to the river, which in the winter time was fortunately shallow enough to be crossed via a marked route.

Nisj was a dirty place, but with one redeeming feature in the form of a rather incongruous looking, but very modern hotel with many floors, lifts, and centrally heated rooms with easy chairs. And a plethora of neon lights on its impressive facade. It had been built by a Yugoslavian speculator, with one eye on the London-Istanbul motorhighway and the other on his purse. A complete orchestra were included in the staff, and on this night they played for the only eight guests in the hotel; eight mad Dutchmen drinking plum-brandy, and enjoying themselves immensely after abstaining for three months whilst preparating for the Rally.

Another attempt was made at entering Bulgaria next day. Still in Yugoslavia, at the frontier post of Garibrod, Bakker Schut excused himself for a moment to visit a public toilet in a restaurant, which when he entered he found to be little more than a hole in the floor, and was most perturbed when he realised there was a similar hole exactly above his head. We visitors to Bulgaria were treated with suspicion. At the frontier we encountered eight soldiers in pitoresque uniforms which reminded us of pyjamas. On their feet were shoes with long curled-up points, and colourful broad laces wound round their legs up to the knees. They were unwashed, unshaven and with unkempt hair. They were not expecting anyone, the last car across the frontier had been recorded on September 18th, almost four months before. And now there were three cars together! Very suspicious. One soldier who apparently was able to read went through our documents from end to end, whilst the others watched us continuously from the

In the ice between Nisj and Sofia, on the way to the start at Athens. On the roofrack are the snowsledge, shovels and spare wheels.

corners of their eyes; but they cheered up a little bit once they were sure we were not diplomats. One of them, heavily armed with a rifle, revolver and a knife, travelled with us in one of our cars for about fifteen miles to ensure that we didn't disorganize the Bulgarian frontier defence forces by our presence. Stopping was strictly forbidden on that stretch. Eventually we were delivered to the Orient Express station, where the Customs office was situated, and here our paperwork was carefully checked and stamped. We did not think too highly, by the way, of their Orient Express, which was no more than a glorified steam-tram passing through three times a week on a narrow-gauge track.

On the way to Sofia we saw little of the road surface which was hidden for much of the way beneath hard rutted frozen snow and lumps of ice. Driving was most unpleasant, and we became stuck on several occasions.

When we finally reached the Bulgarian capital Sofia, we enlisted the help of an official of the Automobile Club to teach us their alphabet. This was absolutely necessary as the alphabet differs in each of

Van Der Heijden's Studebaker and Bakker Schut's Ford V8 on a Greek 'Motorway'.

the Balkan countries. For instance, the letter which looks like a 'W' on its side is an 'f' in Bulgaria, and could be a question mark in Yugoslavia. As far as I can remember the same letter is an 'e' in Greece. It was most complicated.

Our departure from Bulgaria was just as jolly as our entry. From the Customs office three frontier guards, one in front of each car, took us to the barrier which was in the middle of a long, narrow wooden bridge. They had fixed bayonets, and expressions on their faces which suggested they feared that at any moment we might turn round and make a last-minute attempt to murder King Boris, or do something equally desperate. Compared with these gloomy-looking mountaineers our Western European officials are really charming. We had already been spotted from a high tower on the other side of the river, and were met by an equally miserable-looking Greek reception committee. However, we got all over the bridge alright, although it took two hours, and we left with the impression that in the year A.D. 1938 relations between countries in the Balkans were not exactly friendly.

Again bumping and swaying over the miserable road we continued to the harbour town of Saloniki, the second most important Greek port. Here we discovered, to our surprise, that firearms and ammunition could be purchased just as easily as could a tin of beans or a piece of cheese in Holland. We already each carried a hidden pistol for self-defence, but with the bargain prices for junior artillery in Mr. Papodopoulos' shop we left there armed like so many Buffalo Bills ready tackle a whole Red Indian tribe. From now on, at every 'sanitary' stop bullets would be whizzing past one's head as the opportunity would be taken for some target practice on anything we thought looked suitable, such as signposts.

Still on the way to Athens, washing the Minx in a Greek river where the bridge had been washed away by heavy rains.

After Saloniki the next stop was at Larisa, where we slept in the filthiest hotel I have ever seen. We amused ourselves shooting at the dozens of crows that were in the trees on the square in front of the hotel, befouling our cars and showing no respect at all. It became a real battle, but there wasn't a Greek who seemed to care. Quite a bullet-proof people! Notwithstanding the combined firepower of this Dutch Rally platoon we put our bed against the closed doors. All eight of us slept in two communicating rooms under the motto: 'Unity is Strength'.

Next day we arrived at Athens, where our badly shaken cars could be given a thorough check. Just to make sure, I had two more leaves fitted to the springs on our Minx, making fourteen in total which was twice as many as standard. More competitors of various nationalities came pouring in, and at the bar in the Hotel Grande Bretagne that evening one could sense that jolly sporting atmosphere which pervades any rally, and the Monte in particular.

Bakker Schut had called on the official Ford importer, where in the dungeons a very special Ford V8 was secretly being prepared. A Rumanian, Christea, who was the previous year's winner, had entered this car, but this time under the name of his co-driver, Vicomte A. De Vassal. The cunning Christea obviously didn't want to show his hand. Despite the secrecy I managed to get a look, and discovered quite a number of special items on the Ford V8 engine such as dual Weber carburettors, Vertex magneto, a switch-over installation for two grades of petrol, and the lightweight streamlined aluminium body before various heavy wrenches began to float my way, from which I deduced I was not wanted.

The nighttime start was of great interest. The unsteady light of many torches played on the marble of the Classic Amphitheatre, next to which our twentieth-century vehicles fell really out of tune. We tore off and immediately began to collect the dividends of our scouting along the way in, whereas those who had arrived by boat at Athens had now trouble in finding their way. Luckily the weather had improved slightly, but the 400 miles to Saloniki, bumping along over deep holes and ruts still kept us wide-awake, as we had to keep one eye on the road in an attempt to avoid the deepest holes, and the other to see that we didn't take a wrong turn which could lead to Heaven knows where. The Minx fared well under all those knocks, for at Athens we had also welded an extra piece of steel on the front axle, which had become rather sagged (bent) somewhere along our way to Athens.

Crossing the frontiers was easy now, as the national Automobile Clubs had posted their officials at the right spots, whilst Customs officials and the military had been fully briefed by their respective governments. Without any adventure we reached Sofia by the second evening. Lying on our backs in the mud of the frontier town of Dragoman we helped to remove a loose shock-absorber from Germaine Rouault's Matford, before carrying on again and crossing the new Morava bridge at Belgrade. On previous rallies the competitors had been inconvenienced here by having to use the river ferry.

Almost before realizing it we were driving in Hungary, again on the magnificent motorway. We were having trouble with our engine though, as the poor quality Balkan petrol didn't agree with the high-compression ratio of the Sunbeam engine in our Minx. At high revs the detonation made an awful racket, and it didn't improve matters when we were being chased by larger cars and accelerated the poor thing to keep ahead. Once over the border we faced the 120 mile long Autostrada to Budapest, along which I stood on the pedal until a nasty knocking warned that something was now seriously wrong. 'Expensive noises' as we used to say in our motorsport circle. We stopped, switched the engine off and hoped - quite without reason - that it would no longer knock when we re-started. Of course it did, and I didn't blame it at all. As it sounded like a broken valve, I removed the valve cover and promptly burned a finger on the hot exhaust.

To Yvonne Simon and other drivers who stopped to enquire what was amiss with the 'Hillman Boys' as they called us, I replied that I hoped to see them next year, for it seemed to me now that we were finished. But Han Van Der Heijden didn't think so, offering to tow us back to Szeged where there might be a chance to get the engine repaired. And the big Studebaker towed us back at 60 m.p.h.!

Thinking that we needed a new valve we stopped at a motorcycle repair shop which was advertising British motorbikes. Not considering that they had yet helped enough, our Studebaker comrades rolled up their sleeves when our engine had to be stripped. The valves however were quite sound, and so we removed the cylinder head. Then we could see the problem. One of the pistons was in halves, and very gloomily I said: "Boys, give my love to everyone at Monte Carlo". I thought I would try and get a new piston flown out from England, and that maybe with some luck I might meet up with them all again in a few days at Monte Carlo. However, the repair shop owner had a different idea. Quick as a flash he sent a boy on a bike into the village, and soon the youngster returned with two unfinished pistons. We did have a couple of hours or so to spare, and although it was far from an ideal working situation, after getting the Minx into position with its front wheels up onto a couple of stones, I laid down in mud an inch thick to remove the sump and connecting rod. I sent Henk Blijdenstein to the bank in order to change some travellers cheques, as I was expecting to have to pay out an enormous sum of Hungarian pengös.

Time was ticking away, and our Studebaker friends were forced to leave us, and I suggested that they take my co-driver Henk with them so that he could try and get our roadbook stamped on time at the Budapest control if I was too late, hoping that the Hillman's absence there would not be noticed. In those days they were not so strict with the 'closed parks' and it was possible in some cases to get the roadbook stamped without showing the car. So the three fine fellows who hadn't wanted to leave us in the lurch departed, with fourth man Henk hidden on the floor because no one except the listed crewmembers were allowed to join or replace another man.

Meanwhile the motorbike repair man was turning the cast-iron piston down to size on his lathe as if his life depended on it. Although the piston wall had become extremely thin the job proved to be a success. He fitted an oil scrapper ring, but I decided to remove it as adequate lubrication for the new piston would be vital, and I didn't care tuppence about using oil. In all we spent three and a quarter hours on the job, which I thought was pretty smart going. I filled the sump a quart above the normal level, and added about half a gallon of oil to the petrol in order to ensure plenty of top-end lubrication. After paying the very reasonable bill, I waved the motorbike man goodbye, and shot away towards Budapest with the accelerator on the floorboards. In front of me were 118 miles which had to be covered in two hours and ten minutes. I had equipped the Minx with a siren, and with that screaming out loudly I went through the crowded market place in Kecskemet like a fire engine. The poor old Minx received the hardest flogging she had ever had, averaging 57 m.p.h. for the journey to Budapest, which I entered with about ten minutes in hand, which wasn't much.

Once in the town I used the full width of the road, sometimes overtaking tramcars on the wrong side, and within minutes saw a notice: 'Parc fermé'. An approaching official said "In here", but I parked outside and ran away exclaiming that I needed to visit the toilet. I hurried into the rally offices to try to find Henk with the roadbook, only to be welcomed by the whole bunch of drivers with a loud "hurray". But that was not what I wanted. "Where is Henk?" I enquired of the Dutch contingent around a table, of whom Bud got up to help me find him. Naturally he hadn't shown himself to the other crews, but where was he hiding? At my wits' end, sensing possible failure at the last minute I jumped into the Minx, switched on the siren and drove around the park facing the Automobile Club inside which was the control post, parking just outside the 'parc fermé' with seconds to spare. Henk, who had been hiding in a small restaurant nearby, heard the siren and came running across waving the roadbook, and we got it stamped just in time.

Following these unnerving hours I had some relaxation in the back of the car while Henk drove across Austria on our way to Munich. From Ulm the required average speed increased to 50 m.p.h., but the following day went by without serious incidents for us.

At the Dijon control on the final night we met up with many compatriots who had started from Amsterdam, all looking very fresh in comparison with us. Not that they had all been without trouble. We were soon giving advice to a despairing mixed crew, Mrs. Aad Cornelius and Hans De Beaufort, whose D.K.W. had a dynamo problem. They had already bought one new battery, and were now going to have to get another. As we had suspected before the event, the second section of 12 kilometres over the Col des Lèques proved indeed to be nasty. And the Minx, with its three good, and one makeshift piston just hadn't the power to maintain the speed needed uphill, so we had to slide recklessly down the black-ice-covered slopes. We made it and arrived at the finish without having lost a mark. However, in the classification test the next day at Monte Carlo we had no chance at all. The tired engine in my poor Minx didn't have the pep for the quick acceleration vital on the test and we finished 51st overall and 16th in our 1.5-litre class.

Having done the job from the Athens start, without penalties despite our trouble, I don't need to say any more about the enjoyment we had got from this rally. For there was something else which happened that day on the Rivièra about which I want to shout. The Ford V8 of Bakker Schut-Ton-Barendrecht had also arrived at the finish penalty-free. After the first round of the two classification test runs allowed (the total time would count) our 'little giant' Bud with his ordinary everyday Ford lay second between two renowned speedsters, a Delahaye and a Hotchkiss. Fastest in that first round was Le Bègue's Delahaye which put up a formidable time, whilst the third placed Hotchkiss was driven by the well-known rally winner Jean Trévoux. The times differed only by fractions, and when the second run began the entire Dutch contingent had palpitations! Le Bègue repeated his original time, but some seconds later the loud-speakers announced that the Frenchman had missed going over a line, which meant twenty penalties which put him right out of the running. But then Trévoux went faster still than on his first run, and we thought the Dutch chances had dwindled to nil. But when Bud's turn came he simply tore along to the turning point, shot forward and then backwards in what just seemed a blur, turned for the second time and flew past again, leaving the concrete covered in thick black smears of rubber from his

Winners of the 1938 Monte Carlo Rally. L.to.R. Barendrecht, Bakker Schut, Ton. Behind ; Dutch Sports Marshall Van Wickevoort Crommelin.

tyres. Deathly silence awaited the loud-speakers now. But when the announcement came, did we shout! Bakker Schut, our little Bud, had done it! This fine driver and his crew had won the Monte Carlo Rally for Holland. And it was a double climax, with the simultaneous news of the birth of the first Dutch Princess, Princess Beatrix.

I honestly can't remember much of the fun we had that evening. Next day, at the cocktail party given by the Major of Monte Carlo in the Exotic Gardens the Dutch formed a chain from the champagne tables to hand over the bottles, the golden contents of which foamingly served to toast the victory, and our Royal Family. What a party!

Chapter 5

Liège-Rome-Liège 1938

About nails on the road: four monocles: a cannonball on the Grosz Glockner: a Royal conversation: and a painful awakening.

"What are those fellows doing there?" remarked my co-driver Klaas Barendrecht, looking astonished as he pointed to a number of cars parked on each side of the road, every one of which carried Liège-Rome-Liège plates, whilst their grim-faced crews were busy with jacks and wheelbraces. We counted about ten cars in the very early hours of that morning on the road between the Luxembourg-French border and Nancy, all with punctured tyres.

We had a nasty suspicion, which soon began to grow as our Ford V8 two-seater began to sway a little; ever so gently at first but increasing all the time until we were forced to stop with a flat tyre. We had managed to stop the car under a street light on the outskirts of Metz, and after jacking it up were immediately aware of what had happened. In the tyre we found three nails, each neatly sticking through small pieces of rubber in such a way that they would always stand up with the sharp nail end pointing upwards. Jokers, or maybe saboteurs who wanted to spoil this event, had thrown those specially-prepared nails onto the road over quite a long distance, and we were actually very lucky in having only one flat. The Italian crew Massa-Brunetto, whom we had already met the year before, had suffered five punctures and used already their entire stock of spares. This low-down trick was all the worse because garage assistance, and even help between competitors was forbidden that year under the strict new regulations of the Liège. Not surprisingly, our two Italian friends were now in prayer. It was a rotten beginning to this Liège-Rome-Liège, which would prove to be one of the most sensational in the history of this famous rally.

Klaas Barendrecht and I were amongst the fifty-six participants that year - only eighteen of whom were destined to reach the finish - using Klaas's Roadster which for the occasion had been tuned-up by fitting a pair of bronze cylinder heads, which gave a slightly raised compression-ratio and better cooling than the standard ones. The car was also equipped with heavy-duty shock-absorbers, more powerful than standard headlights, and a pair of foglights. Three other Dutch crews were on the rally: Baroness Van Tuyll Van Serooskerken-Voeteling with an M.G., which later on was forced to abandon the rally due to a broken sump sustain when driving over a pointed rock; the paring Van Der Meulen-Daniels in a completely stripped Opel Olympia; and Scheffer-Smulders with a Ford V8 Drophead Coupé.

I had been in the same class at High-School fifteen years before with Henk Scheffer, where we had been good friends and also the proud owners of a splendid terrarium, from which we sometimes livened things up by liberating snakes during lessons - but that has nothing to do with this rally.

There was only on English entry, an M.G. crewed by Anderson and McFarlane. It always surprised me that so little interest in this event was shown by British manufacturers in pre-war years, as any four-wheeled vehicle, including prototypes were eligible, and the Liège was a first-class testing ground on which the merciless terrain and impossible schedule were a combination guaranteed to find the weakness in any car. Many of the entrants were Germans. Auto-Union had sent four experimental cars, three with twin carburettor six-cylinder 2-litre engines, and one four-cylinder two-stroke of 11000 cc, all being test cars never sold to the public. Despite a formidable performance only one of these proud German cars survived to the end of this severe trial. It was a 2-litre whose driver had found out just in time that the light-alloy fuel tank could not take the weight of the full 4-gallon capacity, as this caused the metal to crack. In the end all four Auto-Unions had been beaten by the much slower Steyer driven by the likeable Viennese Peter Wessely, who always drove with a monocle in one eye, and carrying several spares - he used no less than four this rally. He was delighted that he had beaten the Germans with his standard Austrian product.

The start at Spa and the night trip through Luxembourg were not particularly exciting, and following the tin-tack interlude on our way to Nancy we cheerfully drove on to Lyon. There we found the Dutch-entered M.G. in a large pool of oil in which all its hopes had drowned.

The rally took on a more earnest atmosphere during the afternoon of the second day. We motored over the narrow winding roads from Chambéry to Val d'Isère where we arrived in considerable trouble. We were battling against a problem notorious amongst American V8 cars when in the mountains - vapour-lock in the fuel system. Only by splashing water on the petrol pump had we been able to keep the engine running, but when after the long climb we arrived at Val d'Isère, where it was terribly hot, the engine gave up completely in the slow holiday traffic in that pleasant tourist centre. There we were at the foot of Europe's highest pass, the 9221 ft Col d'Isèran. Drastic measures were needed.

Desperate necessary often results in inspiration, and we came up with a makeshift solution which involved wrapping several old rags around the carburettor and the fuel pump which were situated in the middle of the 'V' of the cylinder block. These rags were secured by wire - a most useful item in a rally! - and could be periodically soaked in cold water. For that job we had pinched a half-gallon Pernod can from a café. Fortunately there was a mountain stream close to the climb, and we stopped every fifteen minutes or so to soak the rags and refill the can. Keeping it full until the next stop was not an easy job for the co-driver who, as the car negotiated the hairpin bends, was required to place his feet firmly against the door and use his broad back to hold the driver firmly in position on the slippery leather bench seat. A tiring job in itself, never mind holding a can of water steady over rough mountain roads. Worse was when something was needed from behind the seats, maps or food for instance, which meant climbing over and reaching down, a position in which you could be feeling sick within seconds as the car hurtled on.

I looked enviously at the Auto-Unions with their full-width streamlined bodywork which allowed roomy recesses besides the seats. They could store everything there, and I introduced similar recesses into the Gatso sportscars which I designed during the war, and then put into production when the war was over. Also troubled by vapour-lock was the Scheffer-Smulders V8, and this despite them having equipped their car with an electrical fuel pump in the line feeding the mechanical one. We came across them standing at the roadside looking forlorn, and I advised them to disconnect the mechanical pump altogether, and rely on the electrical one which was in a cooler position further away from the engine. In fact I did the job for them, and they were quickly on their way. Unfortunately however they dropped out later on with engine trouble. Despite our own troubles we were still without marks lost as we now continued to Turin. Here there was drama for someone else, that magician of a driver, Trasenstèr, several times winner of this event, managed to repair a broken spring on his ten-year old 3-litre Bugatti in record time.

We continued on, through Alexandria to Genoa, and then on the way to La Spezia we played a game with a railway train along this road of seemingly a thousand railway crossings. In Pisa we threw but a glance at the Leaning Tower and went on via Sienna to Rome, where the shortest and easiest stage of the rally came to an end.

In the heat of the Italian afternoon we motored through the Apennines to Ferrara and along the east cost to Mestre. Upon reaching the next control, Cortina d'Ampezzo, we were far into the third night. There, in the Dolomites, we summoned up all our courage for what has always been the toughest part of this rally. We still had a clean sheet, but as a rule that doesn't remain so once the Stelvio and Gavia passes have been taken. We literally raced through the Alps on this night which many were going to remember for a lifetime. The Talbot Grand Sport of Carrière, who after the war became an official of the Marseilles Automobile Club which organizes the notorious French Alpine Rally, finished up in a ravine when his co-driver Bouillon fell asleep behind the wheel, and both were quite seriously injured. We brought them back to the road and stayed with them until assistance arrived. Following this accident Carrière never competed in any event again.

Our Ford was going fine, and when at Gomagio I took the wheel to tackle the Stelvio I was determined to enjoy myself. We had splendid lights on the car, two powerful French head lamps replacing the original American ones, and two fog lamps adjusted at an angle to illuminate the hairpins. That Stelvio is tough, but exciting. All the time you go at full throttle, then just before a hairpin give a quick stab at the brake pedal, change down a gear and broadside through the bend. Higher and higher, this is 'mountaineering' in a car. Under the bonnet the mighty V8 thundered, pulling the Ford to the top as if it weighed nothing, and without approaching boiling point. Looking like a white ribbon in the bright light of our lamps, the road wound to the summit, whilst below us like long fingers probing into the night we could see the lights of following competitors. Finally we arrived at the top and began the descent of the other side which, being faster, is far more difficult than the climb. But we got to Bormio with a few minutes in hand, being amongst the eight crews who had conquered the Stelvio without a penalty. Our chances looked good, and there was even a tense look on Klaas' normally placid face as he took over the wheel to do battle with the Gavia pass. Even tougher than the Stelvio, the Gavia had not yet been completed by anyone without incurring penalties. But Klaas managed splendidly. Taking bends is his specialty, and with slides which were accurate to within an inch he shot through the hairpins in his wild race against time to the top. It was absolutely rapture to sit beside him, although I had to hold on tight to keep myself, and him, inside the car. We knew it was not possible to complete this section in time; but that knowledge served only to urge Klaas on to even greater speed, and on the descent the big Ford came down as if it was being chased by a landslide.

And then, down the only straight, right at the end of the descent and already past our correct arrival time for the next control, we had to turn sharp right at a junction for Ponte di Legno. Just before the junction was a small, but rather high bridge over which it was not possible to see what was beyond. The Ford took the bridge like a ski-jumper, and at that same moment our hair stood up on end. Ahead of us right across the road was an overturned Lancia Aprilia, which had apparently taken the bridge too fast, gone straight ahead and hit a pile of stones. Klaas turned the steering wheel to the right, but as the front wheels were airborne there was no immediate effect. But when the car touched down it did indeed shoot to the right, although still not sufficiently enough as our rear left-side hit the Aprilia with a resounding bang. After having delivered that punch our Ford made a complete 'about turn' before stopping. Having engaged reverse Klaas pushed down the accelerator, but only to the accompaniment of an awful screaming noise from the rear as the car attempted to move. Trying to get out Klaas found he couldn't open his door, as the running board had been pushed upwards and was keeping it closed. Getting out myself I found that the left rear wing was pressed firmly against the tyre, which, to crown it all, was punctured. Don't you feel tremendously strong at such moments? I got hold of that mudguard and with two tugs had it clear of the wheel. Try that at any other time and you can't do it. Meanwhile Klaas had got the jack and wheelbrace out ready to change the wheel, but I told him "no". The control post was only about half a mile away and I told hem to get in and drive. Klaas took the steering wheel and we rushed into Ponte di Legno on a flat tyre, but with only ten minutes lateness to be translated into our first penalties. With our roadbook stamped only then we did attend to the tyre, after having cooled it with buckets of water. With the inner tube in a half-molten state a dirty, smelly blue smoke wafted away from it. Once it was cool enough to touch we had it removed and the spare wheel fitted in record time, and were immediately on our way to Bolzano over the Tonale and Medola passes.

At the Bolzano control we had made up the lost ten minutes, and as far as we could judge were lying fourth in the general classification. On top were the Bugatti of Trasenstèr-Breyre and the Hanomag driven by Von Hanstein-Bundt, each with four minutes lost. Third was the Kramer-Munzert 2-litre Auto-Union eight minutes down, and then us with our ten minutes late at the previous control. Well satisfied with that result in the formidable Italian Alps, we carried on to Austria where we made an almost fatal blunder.

We had to go from Heiligenblutt to Zell am See, and by mistake missed a turn to the right. As a result we tore up the wrong climb to the summit of the Grosz Glockner, and not until we got to the top near the restaurant on the Franz Josefhöhe did we realize that that way was a cul-de-sac. On that busy Saturday afternoon in the middle of August the roads were crowded with coaches, cars and motorcyclists, as we flew down again like a cannonball under the control of two maniacs. Now we had to conquer the real Grosz Glockner pass, which in fact was a mere fleabite after the Stelvio and Gavia, but nevertheless we nearly gave heart attacks to the poor holidaymakers who were

Finish Liège-Rome-Liège 1937. Left tot right: Gatso, Barendrecht (Holland), Wessely (Austria), Escalle (France), Juszezynski (Poland).

supposed to be enjoying a pleasant holiday outing over the pass. We made the Zell am See control in the nick of time.

The remainder of the journey was easy, and the Ford went just as smoothly as when we started. Through Kitzbühl, Innsbruck and Sankt Anton we motored into Germany, and on via Ulm, Stuttgart, Mannheim, Frankfurt and Coblenz to the well-known Nürburg Ring, where we had to do one lap of the circuit. Accompanied by another competitor we had a marvelous dice; so good that we were almost tempted to do another lap. But we couldn't risk spoiling our chances, and so we continued via Cologne to the first Belgian control at Visé, near the Dutch border. There we actually had some time in hand, and so took the opportunity for a quick drink. We met Joop Van Wamelen, chief editor of 'De Auto', the official magazine of our Automobile Club. Excitedly he told us we were in second place which surprised us as we still thought we were lying fourth. But Joop was quite sure; the German crews Huschke von Hanstein-Bundt, and Kramer-Munzert had lost marks in their own country, apparently due to a misunderstanding as to whether a certain stretch of Autobahn on a particular section of the route was allowed or not. Up to Visé we had been going like a couple of twenty-year-olds, but from now on we drove like a couple of pensioners with a car full of eggs that we wished to get home without cracking a shell. We almost came to a stop at every crossroad to see if anything was coming. Full of joy, but still taking great care we safely negotiated the streets of Brussels. We didn't want to lose that second place for all the tea in China. And we didn't! With the cheering of the complete Dutch contingent ringing in our ears we entered Spa. We were as proud as Punch. Just about as proud as two youngsters - together barely half a century old - can ever feel when with an ordinary Ford they have beaten 'cracks' with famous names in expensive super-sportscars. Prouder still we felt when, together with the other seventeen surviving crews, we had to wait an hour longer in the 'parc fermé' at Liège because King Leopold wished to pay his compliments to the drivers. Bareheaded in the final drizzle, the Monarch spent an

A proud moment. King Leopold of Belgium congratulates Gatso and Barendrecht. Liège-Rome-Liège 1938.

hour and a half talking to the drivers, speaking to each in their own language, Dutch with us. He wanted to know everything, and as he was a great lover of motorsport himself we just couldn't tell him enough. Naturally we reckoned that the six minutes we were behind the winners Trasenstèr-Breyre were probably accounted for by that accident just outside Ponte di Legno, but this could hardly be called bad luck, coming really under what can be considered the normal risks in such a tough rally as the Liège. Behind us with thirteen minutes difference came the Austrians Wessely-Juszezynski with their Steyer. The English M.G. crew had abandoned the event before Rome with technical trouble, as had most of the non-finishers. The French favourites, aces Trévoux-Lesurque, of Monte Carlo fame eventually arrived, but heavily penalised.

The following day was reserved for celebration. Before the banquet that day I received a phone call from the Dutch Ford factory in Amsterdam, telling me that at 12.30 p.m. the next day a reception committee, complete with pressmen would be waiting for us, and would we please take that into account. Of course, in the evening we were behaving like lunatics. I faintly remember that, dressed in tails and wearing a sun-helmet I used to wear for the Italian sun, I danced the Lambeth Walk with a dozen chorus girls. There are recollections too of ignoring 'one way street' signs in the narrow streets of old Liège, with Klaas doing another 'rally' to outrun the traffic cops.

I woke up next morning with a head weighing about a ton. I looked at Klaas, and was flabbergasted to see him asleep on top of the blankets, immaculately dressed in gala rigout and still with his shoes on. An amusing sight I thought, then scrutinized myself with no less astonishment at seeing that I was in similar attire. Looking at my watch I saw it was 10 o'clock, and suddenly realized that some hairy driving would have to be done if we were to get that reception on time. With our heads seemingly full of nails, we got into the good old Ford and made for Amsterdam. Klaas was driving but it became obvious he wasn't seeing quite clearly, as I fortunately opened my eyes just in time to see an angry Belgian Customs officer who we were quickly bearing down upon. I shouted: "Put your brakes on, you.......", and Klaas woke up, stood hard on the appropriate pedal and the situation was saved. Driving hard across Holland on the main road to Utrecht the radiator began to boil, and we had to add water. The cause remains a mystery to this day, but we were just glad it hadn't happened on the rally. A narrow escape followed on the winding road between Utrecht and Amsterdam, when just a little too late Klaas noticed that the gap between an oncoming car and two cyclists in front of us was a wee bit too small. For the next fraction of a second he was suddenly wide awake, and we survived with only a dent in our already damaged rear mudguard. Not serious, really. And so, rather tired but so very happy we arrived at the Ford factory for a belated, but marvelous reception. It had been one of the best rallies we had ever contested.

Press reception for Gatso and Barendrecht at the Amsterdam Ford factory. Liège-Rome-Liège 1938.

Chapter 6

Monte Carlo Rally 1939, the last before World War II

About howling wolves: a rammed level-crossing: detention in Hungary: three days of hard labour in the snow: and a fine success for Ford.

One snowy night a car was standing on a narrow dike in the middle of Yugoslavia, with snow on the left, the right, in front and behind. In the distance a fearsome howling began. It rose and fell, followed by ever more of those sounds joining in the mournful concert. A cutting wind blew around the closed windows of the car, and nowhere was a hospitable light to be seen.

The howling came nearer. "Blast it, wolves out there" said one of the two men in the car, adding, somewhat sarcastically, "nice little spot here". It was of course anything but a 'nice little spot' we were in. As my co-driver, Klaas Barendrecht, and I shivered there in the snow with our Ford, isolated from everyone and everything, and listening to those nice little 'pets' wailing in the distance we thought hard about what we had let ourselves in for this time. That year we had thoroughly splashed out. I was working as a mobile service representative with the Dutch Ford works and had been given an American Ford V8 for use on the job, and which I was allowed to prepare myself for competition driving. Three and a half week before the start of the Monte we departed from Holland to Athens, leaving The Hague behind us on New Year's Eve, and in the most joyous of spirits - in both senses of the word - celebrated the beginning of the new year at Montmartre. With that long, and well-lubricated night behind us, we left Paris in a rather foggy state of mind, and headed south.

A thorough reconnaissance of the critical 12 kilometres of the Col de Lèques, the first classification test on that year's rally, was carried out, and also we hid two tins of 100 octane aviation spirit in some rose bushes about two metres behind the 2 Km roadside stone from Grasse. Such high-octane petrol was impossible to obtain at that time in France, and on the rally we wanted it already in our tank for the two final speed tests, as refuelling in the closed 'parc fermé' was not allowed. Despite carefully noting the spot we had a difficult job finding it again on the rally as in just two weeks the bushes had grown considerably. We had done other crafty preparations - for instance, we had rigged up a kind of stove on the exhaust on which we could heat op tins of soup. Lovely! Following an overnight stop in Monte Carlo we headed for Budapest, a detour of about 700 miles, but decided upon because we had enjoyed such a good time there the year before that we wanted to paint the town red again. This we did, with the Dutch D.K.W. driver Cornelius and his co-driver Buyze with whom we had arranged to meet in Budapest.

It was a detour we would never forget! On the Po plain our troubles started, as 'sunny Italy' produced quantities of snow of which even the North Pole would not have been ashamed. To condition ourselves for the forthcoming event we decided to carry on through the night, and at midnight we had a quick look around Venice. We carried on, but eventually it got so beastly cold that we parked the Ford at the roadside, where we snatched a few winks of welcome, but still cold sleep. The snow continued to fall the next day and huge snowploughs pulled by no less than sixteen horses had a job to keep the roads clear.

Conditions worsened considerably once we crossed over into Yugoslavia, where with such little traffic the authorities didn't consider it worthwhile to clear away the snow, and in places it 'lay deep and crisp and even' - about two feet deep in fact. It got so bad that eventually we were forced to fit the snowchains, and the special sump sledge on the front bumper in order to get through. Also the road direction sings were extremely poor, and this played us a nasty trick when nightfall came again.

Between Slovakian Bistricia and Ptuy, we took a very narrow road which began to look more and more like a rounded-top dike, and indeed proved to be exactly that. On the right was a river, and to the left a ravine. It was snowing continuously, extremely slippery, and there was no question of turning round. For three long hours we crept forward at walking pace in bottom gear. Adding to our misery was fog, which froze on our headlights and even the radiator grille, so that despite a temperature of 20 degrees celsius below freezing point, our V8 boiled like a tea kettle. Skidding all the time we went on, saying prayers in the hope of not ending our young lives in the icy fast-running river, and stopping again and again to scout the 'road' ahead on foot for a few hundreds yards. It was there that our adventure was given that finishing touch of the howling by the hungry wolves. Neither nice nor comforting a sound when hearing it for the first time under such trying circumstances. The East European competitors though didn't care too much about wolves, for at the finish of the rally a Polish driver arrived at Monte Carlo with the carcass of a wolf, which he had despatched to the eternal hunting grounds, tied to the bumper of his Chevrolet. Unfortunately the animal had begun to decay a little, with the inevitable result, but still it was a nice trophy.

However, we eventually arrived at the frontier, which in the middle of the night was, of course, closed. After much loud knocking on the door a Yugoslavian Customs officer appeared. For a handful of dinars he was willing to forget the late hour, but on the Hungarian side it was not so easy. A rather peeved official at first showed no interest in our haste, but ten changing his brain from neutral into bottom gear he began to think. We could hear almost something whirring inside his head. With difficulty he managed to put a somewhat more friendly expression on his face and asked us: "Have you any postage stamps?" Well, we hardly had any, but when we gave him the address of a Dutch rally friend who was also a stamp collector, he cheered up noticeably and verified our papers.

With the various delays we had lost much time, but with the roads in Hungary being a little bit better we were able to push the accelerator down a bit harder now, although fog and slippery surfaces still somewhat restricted our speed, and the night's adventures were still not over. Just before reaching Nagykanizska I was driving downhill when a closed level-crossing barrier suddenly appeared in the Ford's headlights. I jammed the brakes on but the car slid onwards, hardly giving me time to warn Klaas to hold on tight. We went through the barrier to the terrific sound of splintering wood and other expensive noises. Without realizing just what I was doing I engaged reverse and accelerated. What luck that was; a second later a express train flashed by, leaving two pale and shaky Dutchmen. Fortunately the barrier was damaged more than was the Ford, of which the nose was somewhat skinned. We then realized that the crossing had a red light on at only one side - not ours! An old man appeared as if from nowhere. He turned to be the watchman, and looked sadly at the damage done. Ominously he kept the intact barrier down, only opening the pedestrian gate, and then indicating to us that he wanted our papers. We most certainly didn't understand Hungarian, and trying to explain by sign language that with no red lamp burning at our side it wasn't our fault, didn't seem to impress him. Holding a kerosene lamp he began scraping away the frozen snow from the numberplate on the back of our car. I did not like this one little bit, for Eastern Europe has always been governed according to the principle: "Two weeks in jail first, then we'll hear what you have got to say". We had to act quickly, and as I had already noticed that the car could just squeeze through the small pedestrian gates I called Klaas back into the car. We locked the doors from the inside, and with one leap the Ford was over an one-foot high ridge separating the footpath from the road. We shot through with about an inch on either side, and away we went. A few miles further on we stopped to sooth our nerves with a swig or two of brandy, having only realized by then just what the results of a collision with an express train might well have been - a sort of 'Ford sandwich Barendrecht-Gatsonides à la Tartare'.

Having decided not to risk being held up by the police further along the road we spent the night in Nagykanizska, going to the one and only hotel there after first hiding the car as well as we could. Situated over a dance hall the hotel was a shockingly dirty place, and after having eaten something unrecognizable we went to bed about three in the morning, still feeling hungry. Even then there was no rest, as a rather stout chambermaid persisted in offering us a most personal service. Eventually we managed to get her outside and closed the door, but she obviously hadn't fully understood, and back she came with a younger edition, her daughter! Sticking to our refusal we locked the door and barricaded it with our suitcases. We each put our revolvers under our pillows, and Klaas, who acted as chancellor of the exchequer, put his wallet, bulging with its nine sorts of money, under the pillow too. Shivering and dog-tired we fell sleep, and remained undisturbed.

Relieved that no robbery had taken place we sailed along the next morning until suddenly Klaas started searching his pockets, with a face like chalk he declared: "I've left the wallet". We rushed back, fearing of course that we could whistle for it, but when we pulled up outside the hotel, we were met by our chambermaid who, beaming all over her face, handed over the wallet complete with contents. And to think we had slept with pistols under our pillows. We felt pretty small.

Gratefully on our way once again we headed towards Budapest, passing the Balaton lake on which we could see many people carving large chunks of ice from the frozen water. Later we learned that these ice-blocks are stored in large caves, which serve as refrigerators throughout the summer. In Budapest as arranged we met our friends Cornelius and Buyze with their D.K.W., and despite rather dampened spirits in some quarters due to there being hundreds of soldiers about in the Hungarian capital, there because of some political disturbances, we nevertheless enjoyed ourselves very much, spending two days in the town.

Back on the road we didn't have long to wait before some incident or other intervened. On the main road to Szeged, where the year before I had changed a piston on the Minx during the rally, we saw that it was market day in the little village of Kecskemet. We stopped to buy a fur hat and boots for Klaas, but when he tried the boots on a stream of profanities left his mouth; it seems the bootmakers there don't think it necessary to flatten the nails on the insides of the soles.

Taking a few photos while we were there we included one of a couple of soldiers in uniform, with feathered hats. Cornelius, who possessed a whole battery of cameras had, quite by chance, taken similar pictures half an hour earlier. We drove on quite unaware of having done anything wrong, but at the frontier we had barely come to a stop before being arrested and our cameras confiscated. In the Customs office we were subjected to a telephone cross-examination. I'll explain. On the phone at the other end in Szeged, the nearest garrison town, was a high-ranking army officer. Over the telephone he ordered a soldier to ask us a particular question. The soldier, standing to attention, related the question to the Customs officer who, with the aid of a French dictionary, translated the question, a procedure which involved him in much head-shaking and -scratching. Our answer was translated back into Hungarian and phoned back to Szeged. After five hours of this we had apparently convinced the officials that we were not there to upset their regime, and we were given our cameras back and told to go.

There was thick snow everywhere, but the new high-lying road had been well cleared, and for the eighty miles which this road stretched, good progress was made before our miseries resumed. In some places the snow had been blown into drifts many feet high, and the little D.K.W. with its limited ground clearance and low power repeatedly became stuck. Time after time we had to force a path through the snow with our much larger Ford. Between two in the afternoon and midnight, alternately shoveling and driving we gained only a few miles. We could have got through on our own, but for the D.K.W. the situation had seemed hopeless and although Cornelius and Buyze were not happy about us being delayed on their account, we didn't want to leave them in all that snow. For some way we towed the D.K.W., with both cars taking this treatment well, but eventually the ropes broke. Then we decided to push the D.K.W. Bumper to bumper with the Ford V8 revving hard and slipping its clutch we pushed the smaller car through the snow until Cornelius said that was enough. He was concerned that we were ruining our chances by punishing our car so much, and insisted now that we carry on alone. He was right of course, but we hated leaving them in those endless snowfields with all sorts of four- and two-legged predators about.

Eventually after some difficulties ourselves we arrived at Novi Sad, from where I telegraphed the Dutch newsagency to say the D.K.W. entry could be written off. (Actually I was wrong as a few days later Cornelius was able to carry on after a remarkable change to rain and warmer weather melted the snow away. He won his class on the Rally.) That day we could not get any further, but struggled on to reach Belgrade the following day along the main road which had been cleared here and there by snowplough.

White loneliness on the way to the Athens start. Monte Carlo Rally 1939.

Then it was on to Sofia. Two days and nights battling against the elements. We could see nothing but snow, one endless white plain without any indication of where the road, the partly reconstructed London-Istanbul highway actually lay beneath the snow. Telegraph wires were the only means of following the road's general direction, but were far from ideal as they sometimes cut across the fields. Once, in the middle of the night, completely exhausted we knocked on the windows of a lonely house and blew our horn. But nobody came to the door, the inhabitants were probably sitting in their nightshirts trembling with fear, and with a shotgun at the ready. Later on we passed a small place where all the people were celebrating Serbian Sylvester - on January 9th in the Balkans!

They were all blind drunk and not interested in assisting us in any way. It was on the second night out of Bolgrade that we became hopelessly stuck. We were enjoying (!) ourselves again jumping ditches in the Ford, but this time things went wrong. We landed on the slope of a small rise, and the car slid back into the ditch and turned over onto its side. The engine stopped due to fuel starvation. We were so dead-tired that we locked the uppermost door, put our cases on the lower windows, and after having consumed a tin of tangerines went to sleep against the vertical seats. With the heater out of action due to that fu-

61

el-starved engine it was something of a miracle that we didn't freeze to death in those many degrees below zero. Awakening cold, and as stiff as planks, next morning we set off walking in the hope of finding some assistance.

In a snowy ditch on the motorway still under construction from Belgrade to Sofia. Visible are young trees planted just before the winter set in.

Eventually coming to a farm we asked the farmer - in about thirty-six languages! - if we could borrow a horse, but he didn't understand us at all. Then with my finger I drew a horse in the snow. That did the trick, and from his stable he appeared with a strong mare. Back with the car the poor animal pulled and pulled, but the Ford was too much for its strength. The farmer went to fetch a second horse while we, to keep warm, went to work with a shovel, three jacks and a plank, with which we managed to get the car half upright. At that angle the engine would run again, after which it was easy, and when the farmer returned we had the car with its four wheels on the road once again. The farmer sent the horses back to the stable on their own, and we gave him a lift back to his homestead. With much paraphernalia stowed inside the car we had to put him on the running board. It was clear that this was the first time he had ridden in - or rather on - a car, and he thoroughly enjoyed himself.

Unfortunately though he showed his inexperience of car travel when we arrived back at the farm. He simply stepped off backwards from the running board while our speeds was still some 20 miles per hour. He hit the icy ground with quite a smack, but by the time we had stopped and hurried out of the car he was on his feet again. There was some blood on his head, and we had a nasty shock when he spat something white out of his mouth. We naturally thought it was a tooth, but fortunately it was only the cigarette which Klaas had given him, and which he had almost swallowed when he fell.

Leaving the farm we were in quite good spirits again, but tiredness was catching up with us now and we faced the third night in succession without a bed. In a half-asleep state that night we took a wrong turning which eventually saw us stranded on a hillside at the end of a narrow road. Turning round was out of the question, and we had to drive it steadily in reverse, inching it back down the slippery road. Eventually we tied our long rope to it so that the other one of us could assist the driver in guiding it back.

On arrival at Sofia we felt more dead than alive. After sending an express wire to the Bata works in Holland asking for Polar snowtyres to be forwarded to Athens, we found a hotel and dropped unconscious into bed. After Sofia the situation improved. The road had been cleared, and further to the south it was warmer, and on only two mountain passes in Greece did we encounter snow and ice. Two days after our arrival at Athens we were joined by Cornelius and Buyze in the D.K.W., but we now had another worry. The Polar snowtyres had not arrived. Another wire, in stronger terms, was sent, and we awaited every K.L.M. plane landing at the airport. They eventually came in by Lufthansa only two days before he start of the rally, but we then found that Greece had an embargo on all rubber products so we couldn't get them from the Customs. The assistance of the Automobile Club, and a lawyer was sought, with the latter managing to import our tyres, provided the old ones were immediately returned to Holland. Only a matter of hours before the 'off' did we finally fit those tyres, and it is somewhat ironic that in fact we needn't have bothered with them at all. The twenty-eight snow chains we had taken with us, and practically worn-out on the trip to the start, were not used either, because the rally itself, after that 'North Pole' journey to get to Athens, was like a summer holiday ride. A thaw had set in, the roads were clear, and of course we knew our way very well. It had taken us sixty hours from Belgrade to Sofia on the outward journey, on the rally we did that return stretch in less than seven. Anything I could tell about the rally itself would be an anticlimax after the story already related. The first classification test over the Col des Lèques was a mere fleabite, and after we had recovered our aviation petrol from under those rose bushes near Grasse, we arrived at Monte Carlo with a clean sheet.

The second test, the acceleration and braking run, was driven straight away. This consisted of 200 metres forward, stopping with the front wheels over a line, back over the line, and another 50 metres forward with a flying finish. Unfortunately our brakes had suffered badly during our journey to Athens, and we took two seconds longer than the Bakker Schut-Nortier crew, who made the fastest time whilst we finished twelfth in the test. Following the clear 'rest' day during which the cars remained in 'parc fermé' the third, and final test took place, the details of which had been kept strictly secret. This was the 'Course de Côte du Col d'Eze', a hill-climb from the Middle, to the High Corniche. Klaas drove and went like the devil, faster even than Bakker Schut. But the Frenchman Trévoux, who with Lesurque drove a Hotchkiss, completed the climb in 1 minute 12.3 seconds, some 5 seconds less than our time. His fellow countrymen Paul and Contet, who in their Delahaye had done the acceleration and brake test in exactly the same time as Trévoux, now came to the line under great tension. Strange as it may seem, they once again matched Trévoux's time exactly, with the Delahaye also completing the test in 1 minute 12.3 seconds. The result of the 1939 Monte Carlo Rally was a dead heat, something which had never happened before in the long history of this famous Rally. Consequently the magnificent winner's cup was cut into halves, each of which were mounted on polished mahogany boards. The Dutch Ford competitors had done very well this time. Mutsaerts-Kouwenberg-Lamberts Hurrelbrinck had finished third, Bakker Schut-Nortier fifth, Van Der Hoek-Ton sixth, and we in seventh place overall. Only a few seconds separated these Dutch crews who between them had easily won the Team Prize, the Challenge de l'Auto. Cornelius and Buyze won the 750cc class, and these results together with Bakker Schut's victory the previous year had made the Dutch much feared, and respected Monte Carlo competitors.

Chapter 7

Sports-Car Races at Zandvoort 1939

About last-minute preparations: a very good place on the grid: and a cracked cylinder head.

When in the summer of 1939 the K.N.A.C. (Royal Dutch Automobile Club) decided to organize Sports-Car Races for the first time in The Netherlands, on a road circuit marked out at Zandvoort, all kinds of 'young' fellows (of all ages!) throughout Holland were diving under the bonnets of 'sports-cars', tools in hand. These cars varied from ordinary D.K.W. two-strokes to mighty Delahayes, with too many types in between to mention. These were old crocks looking as though they might fall to pieces if their age was whispered, but in which the mighty heart of a Bugatti beat, whilst there were new cars which looked as though they had come straight from the dealer's showrooms. All who had feverishly completed their entry forms had the same aim, a burning desire to go 'dicing' on the circuit to their heart's content. And just maybe they were dreaming of driving the victor's lap of honour before rows of thousands of spectators. That glorious sensation, though, is reserved only for the very few men clever enough to overcome all the difficulties of that most fickle of all sports, motorcar racing.

I had a special car prepared, although that shouldn't be taken too literally, as the night before we were all working liking slaves to get the thing ready in time. It was a standard Mercury (Ford) V8 chassis with a special streamlined two-seater body of my own design, and built by a Dutch coachbuilder of the highest repute. This car, which I named 'Kwik', was the result of my ideas as to what would be the ideal sportscar - fast, comfortable, and strong - for arduous long-distance events such as the Liège-Rome-Liège. It was the forerunner of my post-war Gatford, and the Gatso sportscars. With its mildly tuned 3.917cc V8 developing 110 b.h.p., Kwik went very well by the standards of the day, being able to reach 100 m.p.h. The plan at Zandvoort was to compete in two different classes: class F - standard cars up to 5-litres engine capacity, and in the unlimited open sportscar class.

In the unlimited class Kwik had to contend with three of the potent B.M.W. 328 models, of Nortier, Breeman, and De Pesters. With their very short wheelbase these German cars had a useful advantage on the winding and rather cramped circuit. (The present day circuit existed only in the dreams of Zandvoort's Burgomaster at that time.) I realized that my chances against those very fast cars were not favourable, but a race like this one didn't occur every day. During practice we had an opportunity to assess each other's capabilities, as where road-racing was concerned we were all as green as grass. This was emphasised when an over-enthusiastic chap took his Lancia Aprilia too fast into a bend. He left the road and clearly demonstrated how to somersault with a car, and was lucky in that the consequences were not serious.

The two-day practice sessions were most enjoyable, even for the old hands - and there were many - who were testing their driving skills under racing conditions for the first time, and who were attempting to hide their keenness with an overdose of jokes. In addition to those cars already mentioned, the practice sessions saw the Ford V8's of Klaas Barendrecht, Frits Diepen, Karel Ton, and others. Tielens came in a heavy, but very quick Delahaye two-seater, and there were M.G.s, Lancias, Citroëns, and a number of home-made soap-boxes on wheels, all doing lap after lap just to see if there was something which could break.

Adding interest, being there just for a demonstration were Hans Stuck's Auto-Union, and Von Brauchitsch's Mercedes record breaking car, both being so fast as to seemingly complete each lap almost before they started.

Amidst all this, in the centre of the field was the tall 'Joop' Van Wamelen, the K.N.A.C. scrutineer, walking about with micrometers, slide rules etc., and quietly giving advice where ever it was required. To be honest I must say that Kwik was far from ready, having been originally scheduled to make its first appearance in time for the Liège-Rome-Liège later that summer. In great haste I had run-in the engine a little on the bare chassis while the body was being completed. This left no time to thoroughly check out the car, and during the early practice laps a number of faults quickly announced their presence, but were attended to. I realized that it could run with a greater compression ratio, and so we machined another millimetre off the cylinder heads during the night. As expected, on the second practice day the car went much better, but after several laps with my foot hard down the engine gave up with a sigh. Investigation showed it to be suffering from petrol vapourisation, which was occurring in the fuel lines close to where I had fixed the additional exhaust pipe to give a more powerful twin-exhaust system. Other faults showed up, so there was nothing for it but to spend the second night in succession working on the car instead of having much-needed sleep. And how we worked. Realizing in the middle of the night that we wouldn't make it, my faithful mechanic Nico Stuifbergen went off to find some assistance, pulling some enthusiasts out of their beds to come and help. While two youngsters were re-fitting the cylinder heads after we had machined them down some more, Nico and I were on our backs under the car relocating the petrol feed away from the exhaust. It was an exciting night, with mechanics standing on each other's feet without realizing it, and then wondering why they weren't standing level!

When Kwik was ready and we opened the workshop doors daylight streamed in, and we were greeted by the twittering birds broadcasting the break of our 'great day'. That morning I went to bed, satisfied enough now to get a few hours rest. But that satisfaction, however, was entirely false. Unknown to me as I climbed under those blankets the race was already lost for Kwik. The gremlins had already possessed one of the assistant mechanics, who in his eagerness to do everything as perfectly as possible had bolted down the cylinder heads as tight as he could, just as he always did for cast-iron cylinder heads. But these were of aluminium, and for once his exertions were to prove to have been too much. Not suspecting anything of course on that gorgeous Saturday I arrived at the course, where thousands op people were elbowing each other behind the railings. Honestly, I felt no inclination, and really hadn't the time, to watch the early races for the smaller classes, as a thousand and one last-minute things demanded all my attention. In my big tent, which I had erected in the centre field, friends of mine were occupied applying the finishing touches to their cars, and it looked just like a beehive. Outside there was the peculiar smell of castor-oil fumes, blown into the air by the roaring exhausts, and the screaming tyres of cars hurtling through the bends announced that things had begun in earnest. Then, quicker than we expected, our class was called on the course. I donned my white racing overalls, and slowly motored along to take my place in the first row, which I had achieved as a result of putting up the third fastest practice lap. It would be untrue to say that I had a feeling of great determination. Not that I had any thoughts of danger, despite what the pessimists say, unjustly, about racing. It's just that various absurd ideas flash into your thoughts at such moments, and a sudden panic can seize you. Did you inflate the tyres correctly. Is there sufficient petrol in the tank, was the oil level checked, and so on. In vain you try to remember if all these things were attended to, as you constantly check the gauges on the instrument panel, under the gaze of thousands of spectators amongst whom in this case were hundreds of friends of mine. I felt less and less at ease, and realized that an uninhabited island can have some advantages.

Great tension in the last seconds before the 'off'. Holland's first sports-car meeting, held on the temporary road circuit at Zandvoort in 1939. Car No. 38 is Gatso's

All those thoughts disappeared when the starter dropped his flag. The roar from the engines was like thunder, and before I knew it my accelerator was on the floorboards. My splendid Kwik leaped forwards as I fought with the remainder of the field to get into the best position for the first bend, a right-hander, which came up soon after the start. Although I had started on the left side of the grid, Kwik's acceleration was such that I was able to take the right-hand bend just ahead of Tielens' powerful Delahaye, doing nothing, I might add, for the latter's ego. But it is a golden rule in motor racing that he who arrives first is first served, and when the twelve cars had rounded the bend, and flown up the short, straight stretch on the other side of the centre field I had eleven cars behind me and none in front, giving me a great feeling. A nasty right turn came up quickly, followed immediately by a left turn at which the pits were situated - on the outside of the bend! - probably with the idea that should anybody leave the course at that spot there would be plenty of mechanics around! Continuing up the slope to the boulevard, a glance at my mirror showed that Diepen's green Ford V8 two-seater was behind me, with the grey Delahaye third. At the end of the slope was another slow right-hand bend, followed by a bumpy straight stretch running parallel with the boulevard, and then we went down to the right to the left turn preceding the straight section of the course in front of the grandstand. Completing the first lap still in the lead I settled down comfortably. Kwik was running beautifully, accelerating fiercely out of every turn. Life was looking rosy. Every lap looking across the centre field I could see Tielen's Delahaye, which had now disposed of Diepen's Ford V8. But the gap between Kwik and all the others was steadily increasing. This was a state of affairs I had no wish to change, and at every bend I found a later 'cut-off' point, accelerated whenever possible to maximum revs for lap speeds of 52 m.p.h., as I was informed later on. It is difficult to put into words the pure and undiluted joy one feels when driving in a race and everything is going smoothly. The confusing, hectic first lap is over, everyone has fought for their proper positions, and from then on it goes quickly, and pleasantly by. I lapped the last two cars in the field, a Plymouth, and a Ford V8 driven by Henk Hoogeveen, with whom twelve years later I would share a drive in the famous Le Mans 24 hours. Lap after lap was ticked off, and as I started the tenth I began to think victory could well be mine. As before, Kwik flew up the slope. I turned right, and then, on the straight alongside the boulevard a strange noise suddenly came from under the bonnet. With a sickening feeling in the pit of my stomach I realized that something was wrong with the engine. I eased the accelerator to hopefully keep everything together as a thousand thoughts flew through my head, trying to grasp the cause of the noise which was

69

getting worse all the time. All that joy had vanished, and after another lap I realized I would be better to pull out rather than risk wrecking the engine altogether. It was with a heavy heart that I turned onto the centre field, to see Tielens flash by a second or so later, his Delahaye in the lead. It was a sombre Nico who confirmed my suspicions about a cracked cylinder head. The aluminium head had been unable to withstand the uneven pressure caused by the over-tightening, and I felt like tearing my hair out at my own negligence in not warning those assistants when I was busy under the car. Suddenly I thought of making an urgent phone call to the Ford dealership in nearby Haarlem, whose manager Lex Van Strien just might be able to do something about a new cylinder head in time for me to compete later on in the open sportscar race. I succeeded, and in no time a new cylinder head was brought over to Zandvoort, where we worked like mad to fit it - correctly tightened, of course!

Meanwhile out on the circuit Frits Diepen in his faithful Ford was battling with Tielens. But the Delahaye, superbly driven, was too fast for Diepen, and Tielens deservedly won the race while Diepen had to be content with the cheering he received for his heroic opposition. Kwik was ready for the final race of the day, the open sportscar class, in which things began quite differently from before. On the fist lap I had to give best to three potent B.M.W.s which straightaway took the leading positions. I did some battling with the rest of the field, but on the third lap the engine suddenly became noisier than in the first race, and it was all over as far as I was concerned. A thorough investigation later revealed that in the first race the cylinder-walls had suffered damage due to the incoming water from that cracked cylinder head. Despite everything I enjoyed watching the others fighting hard for the remainder of the sportscar race. Piet Nortier in his B.M.W. 328 held on grimly to his lead, with Breeman's similar car right on his tail throughout, followed by the third of these German cars with Charley De Pesters at the wheel. It was a hard-won victory for Nortier. Those setbacks notwithstanding, we had a lot of fun for the remainder of that day, and I had learned plenty. In the first place, that in motor racing you should never praise the day before the evening, and secondly that it is better never to leave things to somebody who cannot be expected to have the necessary competence. Pulling the hair out of your head is a painful business!

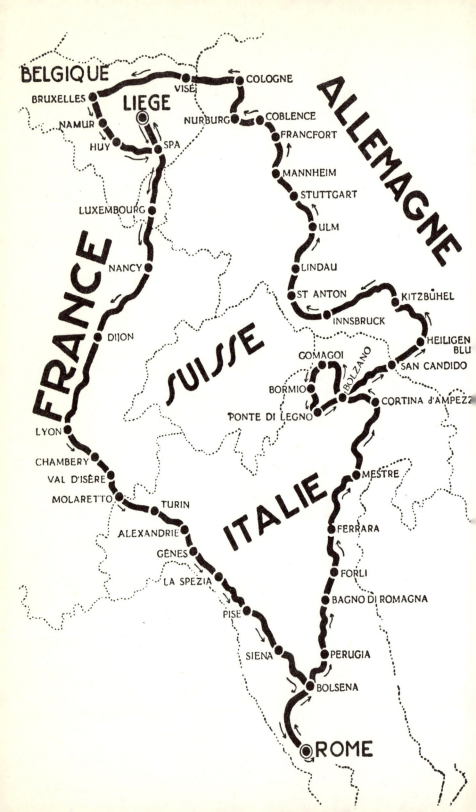

Chapter 8

Liège-Rome-Liège 1939

> About wrecked cars: a missed hairpin: an unexpected course: a mountain tragedy: petrol shortage: and a fighting Bugatti crew.

Although with our 'everyday's' Ford V8 Klaas Barendrecht and I had done quite well the year before, I was really surprised when at the start in Spa this time the voice on the loudspeaker proclaimed: "Voila Gatsonides. Il sera un bon vainqueur", as the speaker saw the low-built grey-painted Kwik come past. It would have been better had the good man kept quiet, as words like that are surely tempting fate, although I was full of hope at that moment.

As already related in the previous chapter, 'Kwik', the streamlined Mercury two-seater had been specially been built in accordance with my own ideas of what a car for tough, long distance rallies such as this one should be like. The co-driver's seat could be fully reclined, so allowing the off-duty crewmember to get some sleep, protected by a canvas tonneau-cover, and with his head under the rear bodywork, whilst his companion drove the car open. Before its engine problems in the sportscar races at Zandvoort, Kwik had proved to have an ample performance, with a speed of one hundred miles an hour available. The damaged engine had been replaced by a brand new one, once again fitted with the high-compression light-alloy cylinder heads, and very carefully and correctly run-in this time. Neither preparations nor crew were going to be suspect now. Illness in his family had caused my usual co-driver Klaas Barendrecht to cancel a fortnight before the start, but in the young Dutch driver Lex Beels, who after the war would become well known as a '500' enthusiast, I had found a co-driver who knew his job well. I had seen Lex doing almost impossible things with an ancient Fiat in the German mountains on the Harz Rally, and after he drove Kwik to get acquainted with her I knew I could start the Liège without any worries. Indeed, we were filled with keen anticipation when we left the start and drove into the darkening evening. Shooting away from Spa up the Côte de Malchamps, which I had climbed so many times before in the Dumonceau Cup Rallies, we quickly shook off the 2-litre Auto-Union of Fritsching and Tragner, who had started with us - in those days on the Liège two cars started simultaneously at three-minute intervals, a very good method in my opinion. We chased after the Hotchkiss which had left three minutes before us, crewed by the only lady team on the event, Mrs. Simon and Miss Lamberjack. We had met them before on several European events, and on one of the days prior to the start this time had accompanied them along with my Austrian friend Peter Wessely and his co-driver, Fadler, to an exhibition in Liège. I decided to stay behind them for a while in the beginning, and when they took a wrong turning, the old hairpin shortcut on the Francorchamps circuit, we caught them up within minutes and showed them the right way. Knowing we were following close behind her Madame Simon put her accelerator foot down to get further ahead, and then suddenly we lost sight of their twin rear lights. In her eagerness to stay in front she had driven far too fast for the capabilities of the Hotchkiss, which had left the road on a bend, cleared a hedge and landed on its wheels in a field. Fortunately we spotted a flicker of light from their car, and after scrambling over the hedge towards them we knew their Rally was at an end when we saw the seriously damaged car. Miss Lamberjack had lost some skin from her face, and we lifted them carefully over the hedge and into Kwik which would have to serve as an ambulance. After delivering them to a hospital in Malmédy village we continued until Lex suddenly discovered that our roadbooks and maps were missing. He remembered handing them to Miss Lamberjack when he had to sit on the rear deck of the open two-seater while the two injured girls occupied his seat. We promptly turned round and shot back up the hill to the hospital, went straight in past an astonished attendant and into the room where a doctor was attending to Miss Lamberjack who still had our papers in her hand. We snatched them and shouted goodbye as we disappeared in a flash. Driving quicker than an express train we made it to Luxembourg, the next control, only just in time.

Then for a long time nothing sensational occurred at all as we motored across eastern France, through the French Alps and into Turin.

We were very satisfied with Kwik. It was running like clockwork, had good road-holding and obeyed every command. We continued along the Autostrada to Genoa, but before reaching that Italian port came across some more wreckage. A fast French Talbot had collided with a kilometre-stone at full pelt, its driver having fallen asleep. Although he was not hurt his companion was seriously injured, and for the second time on this Rally we had to help. And a third time was still to come. Sleep is always the biggest enemy in any long-distance rally, and on the Liège in particularly you simply must relax whenever a few minutes are available. Those who boast they don't need any sleep are often hit hardest, because they don't take any opportunities which might occur for a short snap, and this has proved fatal for quite a few. We drove via Pisa, Sienna, and Bolsena to Rome. There, as we had done the year before, we spiralled to the top of a garage where the control point was situated. We had completed the first half of the event, but were facing the toughest half now, and all the more so as fatigue now really began to make itself felt.

From Rome, where we enjoyed a sandwich in the half an hour we had in hand, we went on through the Apennines, towards the most difficult sections. Yet again we came across victims of sleep, and this time in the middle of the day. Fadler, a Steyer factory mechanic and Peter Wessely's co-driver, had simply not turned the wheel in a hairpin, gone over the edge and amazingly landed on his wheels on the next hairpin some 25 feet below. The crew were uninjured, but the car's wheels had buckled badly on impact. Bidding us good-bye Peter said he would see us again next year, but to our great surprise the Steyr came wobbling in at the next control, arriving as though in the charge of a drunken sailor. A grinning Peter Wessely admitted it wasn't a joy to drive anymore, but they were going to carry on. It would have been much better if they had not. Getting into the third night we could see the eventual situation taking shape. At Cortina d'Ampezzo we were in third place overall with a few marks lost, but not without a fair chance we felt. Ahead of us in the lead were Trasenotòr and Breyère, the previous year's winners with their old but very sound Bugatti two-seater, and in second position was the Imperia-Adler driven by Paul von Guillaume and Mrs. Lotte Bahr. Chasing us were the three Auto-Unions of Müller, Tragner and Momberger, and Trévoux's Hotchkiss, so we knew we would have to continue driving hard. The control in Cortina was right in front of a night club where a party was in full swing, and we threw envious glances through the windows. Rally officials informed us that an avalanche had closed the

Costalunga pass, and that we were free to choose our route to Bolzano. Looking at the map told us immediately that the road over the Falzarégo and Pordoi passes was the shortest way. But it proved to be far from the quickest. It was a shocking road, over which I diced like a madman through nasty bends but was unable to manage more than a 34 m.p.h. average. So we arrived at Bolzano twenty minutes late, only to hear that those who had taken the longest route via Dobiacco, Bressanone and Pont all'Isarco, without mountain passes, had arrived nicely on time. Others who had travelled yet another short route over Canzi and the Passo Sèlla had, just like us fools, arrived late and been penalised. As over the half of the competitors had been penalised on this section, which under normal circumstances could easily have been done on time, there was a lot of moaning about the official's decision not to cancel this time control. Really, at Cortina, we should all have been instructed to take the same road; all the more so because by our route we found ourselves entering Bolzano from the wrong direction, which caused additional delay in finding the control as at that time, 4 o'clock in the morning, there was nobody about on the streets to tell you the way. We knew that with these penalties we had no chance left, but we motored on in the hope that the Rally officials in Liège might make a more sporting decision. We did the Stelvio and the much feared Gavia passes in record time with our low-built powerful car, before entering Austria where we were faced with the Katschberg pass, not so very high but the steepest in Europe with its

Peter Wessely's Steyer burning in a canal. L-R-L 1939.

32 percent incline. Front-wheel-drive cars have to climb this hill in reverse, and it is advisable with this to begin the ascent this way, as if an attempt to turn round is made on the severe slope there is a real risk of toppling over. On this pass near Mauterndorf an enormous 'Schlepper' is stationed, a gigantic stationary single-cylinder diesel tractor with heavy chains to tow stranded cars to the top. But we didn't need this with our mighty Kwik.

A little way past Zell am See we saw a fierce fire and huge column of black smoke rising from a canal alongside the road. Our deep foreboding was, alas, true. On its side and partly submerged was Wessely's Steyr, with its exposed side in flames and burning petrol floating all around it. It had obviously left the road at high speed, its crew presumably having at last been overcome completely by sleep. The young co-driver, Fadler, was walking to and fro on the road, unable to tell us anything as he had lost his memory. Wessely had been thrown clear and had landed in the field on the far side of the water, where we could see him sitting with both hands covering his injured head. Lex Beels ran over a bridge across the canal to help Wessely, and I raced back to Zell am See to fetch a doctor and an ambulance. On my return a grim Lex told me that he didn't think anything could be done for Wessely. That was the last time I saw or heard anything of my good friend Peter Wessely; I don't know whether he survived, but if so he must have remained an invalid. A letter I wrote to him a week later remained unanswered, and only a few days after that any chance of communication vanished with the outbreak of the war across Europe. Coming upon such an accident inevitably results in a deep depression, particularly when a friend is involved, and it was in such a state of mind that we carried on, with our pleasure in the Rally destroyed. Further along the road it began to rain heavily, but we hadn't even the will to stop and erect the hood, with the result that we arrived at Kitzbühl in Tirol completely soaked. There we were lucky to meet the sister of a Dutch friend, who greeted us enthusiastically. This cheered us up considerably. Tiredness was still a problem, and I hoped that I would remain undisturbed as I slept whilst Lex had the wheel between Mannheim and Frankfurt on the last night. But no. I was awakened by a confused Lex who explained that he kept seeing the same signs along the road again and again. Tiredness had certainly caught up with him, and I realized that somehow he must have taken a turning which had led us onto a closed circuit. This was soon confirmed as we drove past a large grandstand on our left and could see the pits on our right. There were several exits, and fortunately Lex faintly remembered the sign he had first seen, so we found the right spot and were on our way again. I decided to take over from Lex who hardly could keep his eyes open, and I had the accelerator down along the Autobahn which Lex had missed, and got into the time control with one minute to spare.

A problem was that we had no time to refuel, and although we had been warned by the organizers that in Germany we could now only get petrol from the approved suppliers at each control point (Germany was preparing to invade Poland) we carried straight on to Coblenz hoping we had enough fuel left. On the way we did an occasional attempt to get a refill at a petrol station, or garage, but the pumps were being watched by rascals in uniform who could not be persuaded. We arrived at the Coblenz control with the tank almost dry, but had time here to refuel from the official supplies.

A amazing sight greeted us in Belgium just before the finish at Spa. A competing Bugatti was parked at the roadside whilst its Belgian crew were fighting furiously with each other. It was obviously a serious disagreement, as at the finish the Bugatti finally arrived with only one driver, somewhat bloodied, who was promptly disqualified. We had to accept our fourteenth place. We had lost thirty-two minutes in total against the seven down by joint winners Trasenstèr-Breyère and Trévoux-Lesurque. Without that trouble caused by the closed road on the route to Bolzano we reckoned that at worst we would have been fourth overall. But, apart from those times of sadness surrounding the accidents we had seen, there had been much enjoyment for ourselves on this great rally. Little did I realize though at the finish that the thrills and enjoyment of this kind were over for the foreseeable future. Notwithstanding the military vehicle convoys, many large tanks, personnel carriers and troop concentrations we had seen throughout west Germany, I somehow hadn't really thought that war was imminent. But only a fortnight after this great competition between motorsports men of many European nations, people of those same nations had become bitter enemies and were vowing to kill each other. More than five very black years would ensue, during which time we would have much graver things on our minds, before better times again would mean that many of those sporting contacts would be renewed. After the war, quite understandably it was some time before the Germans were accepted back in motorsport. As late as 1948 their entry for the French Alpine Rally was turned down, but Baron Huschke von Hanstein, whom I had first met in 1937 on the Liège-Rome-Liège Rally, and again in several other pre-war events, was accepted for the 1949 Monte Carlo Rally in which he drove a Volkswagen.

After this I accepted offers from German manufacturers and private drivers to compete with their cars of various makes, these being D.K.W., Borgward, Ford of Cologne, Porsche, and B.M.W. Huschke eventually became Porsche competition manager, and when looking for a potential car for the Sestrière Rally in 1952 I asked by letter for a Porsche, his immediate reaction was a telegram of just two words: EINVERSTANDEN - HUSCHKE. The international sportsmanship was back again.

Chapter 9

Dumonceau Cup Trials

> About dust: goat paths: somersaulting Opels: scandalous behaviour: and revolutionary brake linings.

Many a complete book could be written about the Dumonceau Cup. About the fortunes and misfortunes, so fantastic, and yet always a part of this glorious trial. About the festivities afterwards, and the thousand and one things which year after year made this event so special for those connoisseurs of the competition car and motor-cycle, who were the guests of the Motor Club of South Holland in the Ardennes and other Belgian districts. Yes, in Belgium, for this 100 percent Dutch event was held in the hospitable country of our southern neighbors, because in pre-war days the staging of such events in Holland was not allowed. Into just one chapter we must now somehow cram all we wish to tell about this former annual adventure. An arduous two-day trial, named after Count Dumonceau De Berg en Dael, who had originally donated the magnificent silver cup for the best motor-cycle rider, the Dumonceau Cup Trial was held over a weekend in the summer.

In the very early hours of the Saturday morning drivers and riders, for both cars and motor-cycles took part, assembled at the start, which was usually just inside the Belgian border, in keen anticipation. The organization was in the hands of a select association of great enthusiasts, many of whom were veterans in every sense, including the three gentlemen who every year saw to almost everything, drawing upon their former experiences of competition with two wheels and four. Three stalwarts who managed to accommodate everybody, and would doubtless have accepted the devil himself had he wished to enter. Map reading wasn't necessary on this trial, for each day's three hundred mile route was marked out by chalk signs. That task was done by one of the noble three, Jan den Engelsen, who had a hole made in the floorboard of his Auburn saloon through which he dropped about 8,000 paper bags of chalk powder onto the road. A different colour was used for each day, but with dangerous sections always being marked in red. And despite Jan's appearance upon finishing the job, this method was deemed perfect, even though on one occasion the 8,000 bags had proved insufficient, causing Jan to call at a drug store and buy up all the plaster of Paris in stock. Whilst in post-war days a rally in Holland would attract more than a hundred entries, in its early years around forty contestants would start in the Dumonceau Trial, and at the peak of its popularity seventy-five dare-devils risking their two-, three- or four-wheeled vehicles on this event would be considered a lot. For it could never be denied that the Dumonceau Cup Trial was a car-breaking event. Although, of course, we are talking about those pre-war days when an old jalopy could be bought for about £ 15, and with a little 'doctoring' could be used to some effect, and if it was wrecked well the loss wasn't too bad. Nevertheless, each year in their reports the motoring magazines would write that the trial, whilst indeed sporting had also been perhaps too severe, and so suggest that it should be toned down a little next time. At this, entrants, and even the organizers would nod their heads in agreement that is was being too rough. But if you were there at the 'off' next year you would quickly find out that the devils had made it even worse! A few more 'impossible' roads would be included, and a dried up river bed, and the three schemers in charge would amuse themselves watching the proceedings, all the time wondering how many vehicles would be wrecked this time! The routes were drawn out on a Michelin map, and it was noticeable that the lines drawn were always covering those very narrow yellow or while lines indicating the miserable little side roads which, in Belgium, are just a little worse than anywhere else. As a rule one usually went straight into the Ardennes, and there the fun really started, with the route zigzagging over goat-paths - the more stones and dust the better! Once, those rascals actually sent us along a dried up river bed for ten miles. It was two hundred feet wide in places, and so you could pick your way, but the rocks on your right are always just as hard as the rocks on your left, and wherever you went it always seemed to be as bad. And then there were the special tests, increasing in number every year, so that eventually the Dumonceau Cup Trial included a whole series of speed tests and hill-climbs, with special down-hill sections too. Near Spa was the three-mile hill-climb, the Côte de Malchamps, and near Barraque Fraiture the Flying Kilometre. A race was held on the closed circuit of Siebenbrunnen, near Luxembourg, and for this we even did a Le Mans-type start. A tramline ran along part of the course, and one year the tramway authorities had not been warned. Merrily ringing his bell a tram approached from around the corner, suddenly meeting the entire class of large cars roaring along in the opposite direction. Nobody stopped. But many turned pale - including the officials too! Then there was the test down into the valley of the river Sûre. For this the average speed was increased to 45 m.p.h., quite unnecessarily, because nobody could possibly manage the normal 28 m.p.h. average down this seemingly perpendicular cattle track. The way back up was again through thickly growing broom bushes, not bad if you were driving a supercharged mountain goat. My own memories of the Dumonceau Cup are numerous and varied. I first took part in 1931, on a Belgian Saroléa motorbike. It was my first event, and I was in absolute awe of such famous cracks as Piet Nortier on an Ariel Square Four, Bakker Schut on a Rudge Ulster, Dick Eysink on his own-built Eysink Alpine Hunter, and Jaap Fijma on his well-known Ariel. I competed several more times, once on a Saroléa with a swallow sidecar specially produced for me by Bill Lyons, who of course later became famous for his Jaguar cars. Unfortunately on that occasion the front fork broke, leaving me somewhat dazed with just the handlebars in my hand.

On Sundays in the Ardennes one could often come upon an religious procession, and then had to choose between showing some respect, or speeding past. Hmm, tense moments those. Another kind of incident which I remember well occurred at the start on the Siebenbrunnen circuit, when a helpful co-driver decided to make things a little easier for Lex Van Strien. The race was driven by the entrant only, one up, and before he left the car parked ready for the Le Mans-type start, his co driver turned the ignition switch to the 'on' position. When the flag dropped Lex sprinted across to the Ford V8 two-seater, the famous 'Blue Angel' in which he competed in many events from 1934 until 1947. He leapt into the car and tried to start her, but not even with threats delivered in the most powerful language - and that came like thunderclaps from Lex's lips on such occasions - would the engine fire. He had instinctively turned the ignition switch, but this time of course from 'on' to 'off'. It took him some time before stumbling across what was wrong.

Janus Van Der Kamp's Opel after performing a half-somersault during the 1937 Dumonceau Cup Trial.

In 1937 there was a remarkable Opel demonstration. Opel's brand new 'Super Sixes' had just been put on the market, but their handling and roadholding qualities didn't match the impressive speeds they could attain. On the Dumonceau Cup that year all three of these Opels entered performed somersaults, with Janus Van Der Kamp managing this acrobatic feat twice on the same day, to the great joy of press reporter Herman De Man who was sitting in the back of the car. It was a miracle that Van Der Kamp and his passengers were unhurt, as the second display was more of a cartwheel manoeuvre with the Opel going end over end. Not so lucky was Verkamman Van Keulen driving an open-topped car. He was quite seriously injured when his Opel turned over, but thankfully recovered after receiving several blood transfusions in a Luxembourg hospital. Driving an open car is always risky in this type of trial, and really I prefer to have a steel roof over my head, especially in winter rallies such as the Monte. In 1939 Jack Van Der Meulen managed to perform a marvelous somersault, this time with an Opel Kapitän. The car almost escaped damage, only the roof suffered, receiving a large dent in it which, as it was pouring with rain, filled up with water. When the Opel was braked upon arrival at a control post about six gallons of water flew over the table and soaked the officials. Very amusing - to watch - I mean!

Miraculously though, very few of these accidents had serious long term consequences. In 1935 Rambonnet and Taverne drove in a team of three Studebaker two-seaters. Following each other almost nose to tail the second and third cars became invisible in the notorious Dumonceau Cup dust, the crews finding their way by following the treetops. Unfortunately they ran right into a large pile of stones at the side of the road, resulting in one of the cars landing upside down in a dry ditch, but without serious effects on the crew. Two gentlemen from the Shell company entered a Ford V8 coupé in 1938. They left the road at high speed, and it needed someone with excellent eyesight to spot their car about 700 feet down a slope. Nearby officials had witnessed their car rolling over about thirteen times before coming to rest, but its occupants suffered only from shock!

A premature end in the Dumonceau Cup Trial for Eddy Holman's Hudson drophead coupé.

The year prior to that I had been stopped by Eddy Holman, who we spotted in a field a little lower than the road, standing there waving his arms about. His open Hudson drophead coupé was lying upside down, and trapped beneath it was co-driver Aad Nagtegaal. With the help of a local farmer we were able to lift the car sufficiently for Aad to be pulled clear, and he was quite alright. Even so, we had been furious when a D.K.W. driver whose assistance we had called for, stopped only for a second and then just drove on. There are a surprising number of people who lack consideration when others are in trouble, perhaps they don't know the golden rule: 'Help, and you too will be helped'. That same year I had my hands full with my own car, the Hillman Minx which I had twice used on the Monte Carlo Rally. For this occasion it had been fitted with a new type of bonded brake linings of a rubberised material - as we smelled later - which had been made according to a revolutionary new process. The 'revolutionary' part as far as we were concerned was that they didn't brake at all when they became hot! At every control where we had a few minutes to spare, we removed a brake drum to get rid of handfuls of black rubber dust.

Dark glasses and a paint-spray mask help Gatso to combat hay fever on the dusty Dumonceau Cup Trial in 1938. The car is a Ford V8 borrowed from Henk Blijdenstein, who competed in Gatso's Riley Kastrel Sprite.

I suppose I have to tell the story of perhaps the most shocking behaviour ever on the Dumonceau Cup. That was when I took on the villain's role. In 1938, at the end of the first day, we went for a drink somewhere in the centre of Luxembourg city. 'We' being Klaas Barendrecht, Jan Stemerdink and myself, together with our navigators. After exchanging a few (sometimes tall) stories, the urge to do something really outrageous became irresistible. The week before I had been there with my co-driver, Paul Erens, on a reconnaissance trip, during which I had learned of a garage in the basement of the Alfa Hotel. Entry to this garage was through a very narrow passage. I made a bet with Klaas and Jan that I could shake them off in the town, and they were very pleased to accept. The six of us got into our Ford V8's, mine was a borrowed one from Henk Blijdenstein, who was driving my Riley Kestrel Sprite, and we started the 'game' racing over the Boulevard. It was so good that I turned around and we were soon racing along three abreast. I feel ashamed to admit it now, but we were doing 75 miles per hour. On a Boulevard! What we didn't know was the road led past the local Ministry of Traffic offices where a conference was being held at that moment discussing the possibility of closing the Siebenbrunnen Circuit for the following morning's race.

Right in front of the Alfa Hotel I stood on my brakes and shot into the narrow passage leading to the underground garage. The fat press photographer Gazendam was standing there obtaining some cigarettes from a slot machine. He flattened himself against the wall when he heard the thundering exhausts, trying to push his stomach in with his hands. I must have missed pulling his waistcoat buttons off by a fraction of an inch. Having just been cleaned with water, the garage floor was slippery, and the three Fords waltzed merrily around the roof support pillars and rushed out again via the same way they had come in. Off the road outside the garage was a little hairpin turn, and knowing that, I got round in one go, whereas the others had to reverse, and that was where I could get rid of them. Having lost them I began to think that this was getting too much, so I parked the Ford in a quiet street, and went off with Paul to try and get something to eat. When we got back to our hotel everybody was standing outside, gesticulating wildly as they discussed our scandalous behaviour. We tried to sneak in but were stopped by an official who exclaimed, "It's a great shame. The whole Dumonceau Cup Trial is being blamed. Someone in a Ford V8 has been speeding through the streets being chased by those two idiots Barendrecht and Stemerdink". "Yes" we replied, "That is a ......shame". Without delay we slipped upstairs to our room from where we could listen and watch the upheaval on the hotel terrace below. But at the same time we were rather ashamed. Of course we were found out, and next morning were relieved, and very pleased to learn that we were being allowed to carry on, for the supervising Dutch Automobile Club sports-marshall, Van Wickevoort Crommelin, a very formal and correct gentleman, had proposed to disqualify us. But thanks to organizer Jan den Engelsen we escaped with a twenty guilders fine (about £ 2), and an officially published rebuke regarding our scandalous behavior. We agreed of course, but felt we did have an excuse....we were still so very young! All of this didn't stop me from winning the large-car class in the borrowed Ford V8. That was all the more pleasing because although I had just joined the Dutch Ford company, I had not yet received a company car. It hadn't been an easy job, as there was strong competition from some twenty good drivers in that class, and because I was suffering badly from hay fever I had driven with a paint-spray mask, and a pair of dark glasses to avoid streaming eyes. It was my first class-win in the Dumonceau Cup, although twice I had finished second in the 1,5-litre class with the Hillman Minx.

In 1939 I drove the last Dumonceau Cup Trial to be staged, together with my friend Henk Richten. I had an old Ford V8 two-seater, purchased for £ 15, which we then reconditioned and tuned-up a little. We managed to finish second in the large-car class. On the way we were going nicely on the Kautenbach hill-climb, a stretch with many hairpin bends, when half-way round one such bend we were suddenly on a patch of loose gravel. The old Ford slid of the road and rammed a house. Henk hit his head on the windscreen wiper knob situated on the top of the windscreen frame (safety belts were unknown in those days). But we only noticed that his head was bleeding after we had freed the damaged front mudguard and wheel. In the Dumonceau Cup

With Henk Richten navigating, Gatso's Ford V8 tackles the Kautenbach hill-climb near Luxembourg in the final staging of the Dumonceau Trial.

Trials it was always a case of car repairs first, bandages for the crew afterwards. Good old Dumonceau Cup Trial!

Chapter 10

The Dripping Cock Races

> About unguarded railway crossings: invading a gipsy camp: a police visit: and ski-jumping with a Mercury saloon.

Changing the subject completely now from the big international rallies, I'm going to tell you about a pleasant little local event held each year. There is good reason for including this, as just like those major long-distance events, our Dripping Cock Races require considerable skill in the noble art of dicing. It was an event always close to my heart, not least of the reasons being its clandestine nature, as it is entirely unofficial. That was always a great attraction for the hundred or so keen young men who one night in mid-February each year would assemble outside the Dripping Cock Inn ('Cock' referring to the wooden tap of a beer barrel) at the foot of the highest sand-dune at Bloemendaal. The ancient Inn already had quite a history, stretching back to the middle ages, and now it was a focal point for these twentieth-century Dutch speedmen all looking forward to dicing through the night along the local roads, and over the surrounding rough country. No longer a race on open roads at night like it used to be, nowadays it has become a tough reliability trial in the dark, and often rainy winter's night, with some intricate map-reading being called for through some rough country terrain. But there is still the same adventurous atmosphere of the past, when not only secret control posts had to be found, but also policemen had to be avoided. I didn't compete in the first race, organized in 1933 by Carol Schade, Paul Erens and Lex Beels, but having heard so much about it I gladly accepted an invitation to take part in the second race, in 1936. I had to break up a nice birthday party to take part in it, but the lady I was making advances to at the time was enthusiastic about joining me as navigator. And we were to be accompanied by Robby my cocker spaniel, from whom I was almost inseparable. This trio, in my well-worn Hillman Minx, were to compete against famous speed machines such as Alfa Romeo and Bugatti. We didn't arrive at the start until about ten minutes before my 'off', and only then I did realize that co-driver/map-readers were not allowed. Most regrettable I thought, but at least Robbie accompanied me. From the very simple regulations, which were handed out only one minute before the start, I quickly deduced that this was going to be simply a race against the clock. Contestants were flagged away at one-minute intervals, and not until the flag dropped for each driver, was he handed his copy of the route card. It was quite simply a case of completing the route in as short a time as possible, with the route card having to be stamped at an unknown number of control points along the way, in what was a straight fight between all cars, large and small. Bearing in mind an old motto: 'If you are not strong, be cunning', I had been keeping my eyes open and my brain working hard, as the Minx, with its poor brakes and headlights could not possibly compete with those fine high-performance cars which seemed to dominate the entry. I had noticed that only thee cars with control marshalls had left the starting point, and now I saw on the route card just three unguarded railway crossings, each marked: "Dangerous. Slow down!" It didn't take long to work it out that the three marshalls would almost certainly be found at these three crossings. I looked at the map, and thought it might be worth following my hunch, and whilst everybody roared along at full speed to follow the indicated route, I drove to the first railway-crossing at Duin-en-Kruid-Berg, bypassing a long hilly section. Indeed there was the first control post! The boys were flabbergasted, and suspected a supercharged Grand-Prix engine under the Minx's bonnet, but nobody could do anything. Strengthened by this first success I calmly carried on to Fort de Lie, where as I expected I found the second control at the railway-crossing. I was well in the lead by this time. While the rest of the field was racing along the narrow roads of the Haarlemmermeer polder and the bulb district, I again carefully studied the map and route card and went via a third short-cut to railway-crossing number three, where I received the third stamp. From there to the finish was a fleabite, and I arrived back comfortably to record the fastest time. A well-used Hillman Minx had beaten the fastest cars, and all Holland's motorsports men were scratching their heads.

Naturally, on the following year's event I repeated the procedure........ The number of competitors had increased considerably, and the organizers decided to split the entry into two groups, of which the drivers once again started at one-minute intervals - in opposite directions! "Oh no", said Lex Van Strien, "driving in the same direction as those lunatics is bad enough, but fancy meeting half of them". That night they diced as never before. Carol Schade went so fast in his special Ford V8 trials car that it was boiling like mad at the finish. But, it was a little old Minx which once again got to the finish in the shortest time, taking half an hour less than the organizing official had done when he checked out the course in daylight. "How is this possible?" was the question on the lips of all the experts. How it was done came out at the party we had afterwards, when I made my victory speech and couldn't help adding something about stupid little boys who could drive fast but had apparently destroyed their grey matter in doing so. That was reason enough for them to hand over to me the organization of the next Dripping Cock race, and, although it entails a considerable amount of work, I did it with the greatest pleasure for another eight years, always including it amongst my birthday celebrations on Valentine day. Under my organization the 1938 race remained a clandestine event in the dark winter night, with each competitor again leaving the start at one-minute intervals. This time however a navigator was allowed, although such two-men crews received a handicap of some ten minutes. I remember that Paul Emons, from Arnhem, claimed to have driven his Lancia Aprilia so devishly fast over the narrow frozen corrugated roads, that he only touched the tops of the 'waves'. He finished as the outright winner, many minutes ahead of the others, but this time there was no question of cheating because I had included twenty controls on the sixty mile circuit, carefully planned to penalise anybody who took a short cut.

One of the dirtiest 'organizational' tricks on the route through the polders round Haarlem and the bulb district, was at Zwanenburg. There was an indication on the route card stating: "first road to the left". But before that road there was a 'no through road' on the left leading to a gipsy camp. In the dark almost everyone took this wrong road, arriving at the gipsy camp at speeds up to 60 m.p.h. There they had to turn around, a manoeuvre not appreciated by the inhabitants. One of the drivers, whilst reversing in a hurry, hit the post on which the camp's water tap was fixed, resulting in a splendid fountain. At this the furious gipsies began pulling out their knives - just another special attraction of the notorious Dripping Cock Race!

I had introduced classes for various engine capacities this time, with overall winner Emons of course also winning his class. Bakker Schut, who had chosen to drive without a navigator and so start with two minutes benefit, came second in his class in the same Ford V8 with which he had won the Monte Carlo Rally the previous month.

The final Dripping Cock Race of the pre-war series was beset with troubles before the start. Extremely bad weather forced a postponement to mid-March, 1940, which turned out to be only a few weeks before the Germans invaded our country. A week before the event, whilst checking over the route I found to my astonishment a deep trench right across a road that was normally not in use. An industrial railway track was being laid, which seemed to me to be too big a handicap, but the clerk of works assured me that the trench would be filled right up again before our event's start the next Saturday night. This turned out to be true, but with soft earth only, and there were problems here in the race. Aircraft builder Frits Diepen in his faithful Ford two-seater sank down deeply, hitting its sump on some concealed construction, and with such a shock that he lost his twin spare wheels. After this encounter he couldn't disengage top gear, but he carried on and eventually finished in quite a good position. However, I am running ahead somewhat, for before the event took place I ended up in hospital with concussion. Whilst carrying out a final route check two days before the race, in a small village, coming round a blind corner at about 60 m.p.h. on a slippery road, I suddenly had to choose between hitting two oncoming vehicles, a tram or a lorry. Aware of the solidity of tramcars, I chose the lorry, also because its driver should have given me priority in that street where the tramway was along the wrong side of the road. It was a nasty collision. Out of the corner of one eye I saw that my fiancee Ciska, who was sitting next to me, about to be flung right out of my Mercury two-seater. I grabbed at her, and managed to get hold of her just before she would have disappeared under the tram. I got concussion, and suffered a severe, but fortunately only temporary loss of memory. Thanks to the efforts of some friends the race went on as planned, and was won that year again by Paul Emons, this time driving a short-wheelbase Lancia Lambda. He was chased relentlessly by William Hilarius, driving a huge Opel Admiral, but when Paul realized this he shot over a tiny bump-backed bridge at top speed. The Lancia could do that, but with its soft suspension the big Opel could not. The Admiral's bumpers parted company from the car, its petrol tank was as flat as a pancake, and with a melancholy look its headlights pointed up in the sky. William was forced to give up, and so that we could commiserate with each other, he came round to see me on my sickbed. I had another visitor on the Monday after the event. A police sergeant with a suspicious look on his face, and some 'evidence' in the form of one red, and one white flag. Complaints from someone who couldn't get to sleep that night had resulted in a police investigation, during which the two flags, unfortunately left behind by one of the marshalls, had been discovered. On top of this, a newspaper published a full length race report, even mentioning the names of the prizewinners, who also were promptly visited by the police. Speed racing on roads and cart tracks open to normal traffic is forbidden in this country, like in all others, I suppose, and quite rightly too. Many summonses were issued, and no doubt we would all have been in considerable trouble with our own authorities if war had not broken out giving everyone much graver matters about which to think.

The very first motoring event to be staged in Holland after the war was the 1946 Dripping Cock Race. Organized once again by me, it was taking place at a time when all motoring was heavily restricted, and therefore secrecy was more important than ever. All the old friends from the pre-war races turned up, eager to prove that they had lost none of their skill, and looking forward also to the illicit consumption of a grilled piglet which was going to add considerably to the after-race festivities. In a strictly food-rationed post-war land these clandestine festivities would be enjoyed almost as much as the race itself. We didn't know then that it would be the last of these races in which sheer speed would be paramount, and there's no doubt that this was the most exciting of al the Dripping Cock Races. To start with, the temperature was minus 15 degrees celsius, and occasionally during the night it snowed heavily, which produced real Monte Carlo Rally conditions. My journalist friend William Leonard, the author of this book, had agreed to use his brand-new Morgan 4/4, his pride and joy, as the broom car and to assist with any breakdowns. Artist Jan Apetz went along with him, but they spent most of their time involved in keeping the Morgan in one piece, as with its minimal ground clearance the chassis was taking considerable punishment over the frozen-solid bumps and lumps on the roads along much of the route. Furthermore, these two worthy fellows drove the whole way with the hood down, and when they arrived at the finish at 3 o'clock in the morning they looked just like frozen meat. Not even the entire contents of a full bottle of brandy was sufficient to thaw them out. Incidents abounded as always. For instance, one young fellow lost his way in the vegetable prairies of South Holland, and ran about fifty miles per hour into a high stack of vegetable crates. He arrived at the finish at Zandvoort with his car still displaying wood splinters jammed into the bodywork. The most sensational adventure was reserved for Henk Blijdenstein, my co-driver in the 1938 Monte. With his wife beside him he was dicing along a narrow path in the dunes with his Mercury drophead coupé. He thought he was on the right road, but realized that was not so when suddenly he saw only a black void in front of him. Braking was no good; Henk had realized that the car was airborne. An enormous bump a few seconds later ended the short flight which had taken the Mercury from the steep dunes to the beach below. After recovering from the shock of what had just happened, Henk and his wife went to seek assistance, but after eventually locating a nearby control point they now were not sure of the way back to the car. After what seemed like endless searching we found the car on the frozen beach amidst small icebergs. There was no anti-freeze in the car, as that commodity was extremely difficult to acquire in those days, and the water in the radiator was now closing to freezing solid. The engine refused to start because of frozen condensation in the petrol feed pipe. The mechanic with the breakdown vehicle began to suck at the pump end of the fuel feed pipe, and I (wisely) blew into the tank. When the mechanic started spitting out petrol that problem was over, but it was impossible to get the car back to the top of the dunes again at that spot. It would have to be driven along the beach to the nearest point where there was a track leading off, some 15 miles distant in fact, and I warned Henk that he would have to drive across four of the German Atlantic Wall minefields to get there. I offered to go with him to show him the way, but his wife, however, said: "If he goes to heaven, I go with him". So they drove full-speed to Zandvoort over the thick ice plate underneath which were many German landmines. There they could easily get on to the boulevard and head for the after-race festivities, at which the winner Rob Hin could celebrate his victory, and once again plenty of tales could be told!

Now we are all a little older and wiser, and so indeed is the event itself, which has changed its name now to the Dripping Cock Trial. Although it remains a clandestine night-time event, it has become such a tradition that a blind eye is turned, and everybody lets it pass. High-speed dicing is no longer its principle feature. Recently we have given the competitors the task of finding a number of signposts, where at each one their card is stamped, in a fixed three-hour time limit, and many have found this task more difficult than fast driving. Those who find it too complicated however, are nevertheless usually back at the finish round 11 o'clock, even if they have only three or four stamps, rather than the full number on their card. They know only too well that after 11 o'clock a reduced tariff is charged for the drinks! So the spirits flow as those old motoring buddies get together, each and every one of them a somewhat unconventional and larger-than-life character, and for that reason all great personalities in today's rational world. As the hours pass many stories (some rather tall) are told. Legendary stories, almost all beginning with: "Do you remember", about the good old-fashioned Dripping Cock Races.

Chapter 11

French Alpine Rally 1946

> Visiting France again: a Franco-Greek in a ditch: and a very loud explosion causing bitter feelings.

'Be prepared for the worst' are the most appropriate thoughts nowadays when thinking about the Alpine Rally, for quite rightly this 'Rallye International des Alpes' had since the war gained the reputation of being extremely tough for the drivers as well as the cars. But the 'Alpine' is nevertheless most enjoyable from the motorsport enthusiast's point of view. I purposely used the words 'since the war', because before then there were so many international events through the European mountains from which the connoisseur could choose, that the French Alpine Rally remained an event almost exclusively for the French.

Now, some four years after its first post-war staging, we know pretty well what to expect, but when in 1946 the 'Automobile Club de Marseille et Provence' published the regulations for this event, most of those who entered had not the faintest idea whatsoever of what they would have to face. Certainly the compulsory high average over Alpine passes caused some head-scratching, but at that time the motto 'Don't worry before trouble troubles you' was still popular. In any case, I could face this tough event with confidence. Those long years of compulsory inactivity in so far as motorsport was concerned had certainly not been wasted by me. My own-built Gatso car, at that time named Gatford, had recently emerged, and I was quite sure that this prototype would acquit itself extremely well. Hiding under the low, grey streamlined body was a 1937 Ford V8 two-seater chassis and running gear, with the chassis frame being suitably modified to reduce the height. These were the remains of Klaas Barendrecht's car which we had used on the 1938 Liège-Rome-Liège. I had bought the car from him for £ 15 on Christmas Eve, 1940, in a damaged condition following an accident. During the war, with two of my mechanics I secretly spent a lot of time on it, even driving the naked chassis on the road (also secretly of course) and that is why in the first post-war events I was well in advance of many other competitors. The engine was the original one from Kwik, my Mercury sportscar, which had suffered a cracked block during the Zandvoort races in 1939. Without going into technical detail regarding the overhaul, I can say that this 3.9-litre V8 could safely produce 120 brake horsepower instead of the normal 95. The body had been built in my own workshop from a 1:10 scale wooden model, which was made during the German occupation, and even tested in great secrecy in a wind-tunnel.

The regulations for the Alpine Rally clearly stated 'standard cars', on which some specified modifications were allowed. I had therefore entered my Gatford as a Ford with special body. To make sure that my modifications would be accepted I had sent a series of photographs together with a complete list of all modifications on engine and chassis to the A.C.M.P., because I wanted to be sure of not being excluded at the start. This later proved to have been a good idea. When we arrived at Annécy the technical scrutineers accepted my car, whilst refusing four others. Unfortunately the modified Fiat of the Van Kempen brothers, who had driven 600 miles from Amsterdam, was excluded, as were three Simca Gordinis. On of these, entered by Madame Germaine Rouault, was a most peculiar sight with its Topolino coupé bodywork attached to the Simca 1100 chassis by wire and cord. It was astonishly fast; in the standing-start Kilometre test held before the 'off' for the road section, Madame Rouault had beaten even a supercharged 2.3-litre Alfa Romeo and Bugattis, with an average of 61 miles per hour!! Having recorded an average of 54 myself, I was astonished at this demonstration of the weaker sex's prowess. That same evening however she was informed that her car was not eligible, and she was absolutely furious. The test had been held on the quay alongside the beautiful blue Lake Annécy. The length of the quay was 150 feet longer than one kilometre. Having had the accelerator to the floorboards, the drivers were then forced to throw out all the anchors if they were to avoid ending up amongst sausages and other delicacies in the butcher's shop window which faced them at the end of the too-short runout.

My friend Henk Blijdenstein, who had accompanied me on the 1938 Monte Carlo Rally was pleased to act as navigator once again. I don't think he regretted the decision, for visiting France again after the liberation was itself more than worth the trouble. For me - as many others - La douce France has always been more or less a second home. It was really touching to experience the kindness and warm welcome with which we were met, a kindness accentuated by the embraces of my French friends demonstrating their happiness at meeting us again after seven long years of separation. We were all the more delighted as the rally dates embraced July 14th, Bastille Day. I can't remember much myself about that evening's festivities, perhaps because of that other heavenly gift of this country, le bon vin. When Henk and I arrived after dark in Annécy the whole town displayed signs of the oncoming motoring event for which all sporting Frenchman have a soft spot. We hadn't been there for two minutes when we met my old friend Pierre Fontana, a Greek living in Marseilles, whom I knew from the pre-war Liège-Rome-Liège events. After a touching reunion, I couldn't say no to Pierre taking the Gatford's wheel. I only allowed him this treat because of the pleasant meeting, for he is one of those fanatics who like to nail the accelerator to the floorboards, and consider brakes as unnecessary equipment. He didn't hide his enthusiasm, even attempting to reduce the population of Annécy when testing the suspension of my car by driving on and off the high kerbstones at sixty miles per hour. I got my revenge for these hair-raising 'jokes', but that comes later.

It all became serious on the early morning of July 13th, when the thirty-nine cars were ready to start the 300 miles of the first day, which included Europe's highest pass, the Col de l'Iséran (9,221 feet). The hangovers which some fellows were suffering after the reunion festivities had quickly changed into intense concentration, all the more because many of the competing cars would in normal times have been scrapped long before. For example, our Dutch friend Verkamman Van Keulen was driving an Opel Olympia retrieved from an army dump, and now kept together only by the will-power and magnetism of its driver. He nevertheless managed to finish the event ahead of several Lancia Aprilias in his 1.5-litre class. One of those Aprilias was driven by Joe Fry and his wife, a charming couple with whom we became good friends on that rally. Fry was a well-known rally driver who gained many successes with his self-built specials. I was very sorry to hear in 1950 of his fatal injuries in a crash with his famous Freikaiserwagen.

On that summer morning, as I drove my Gatford up the mountain slopes, Henk and I appreciated that life had many pleasing aspects. That feeling was strengthened when we caught up with the Matford of our Greek friend Fontana, who had started some minutes earlier. He was one of our strongest opponents and, knowing his fierce temperament, I made a bet with Henk that I could get him off the road within three hours. I shortened the distance between us so he could see me clearly in his mirror, and then gave him a cheerful wave. I kept on chasing him, and Pierre, always keen to accept a challenge, responded quickly by increasing his speed, mercilessly pushing the Matford even faster until bits began flying off the poor car. But no matter how hard he pushed down that accelerator I made sure that the Gatford's nose was still visible in his mirror until, after the Matford had already been in some heart-stopping skids, Pierre took it into one of those bends just a little bit too fast. The tyres screamed as they tried in vain to keep a grip on the road, and then a loud bang announced the end of Pierre's rally as the Matford landed in a dry ditch. The last thing we saw of Pierre was a brown fist shaking at us, but he had more reason to shake it at himself as nobody had told him that he must stay in front of us.

In excellent spirits we climbed the Col de l'Iséran, showing all its beauty on that summer day, surrounded by a mighty French Alpine mountain range. I'm not sure though whether 'excellent spirits' could in fact be applied to Henk, since he was not only busy with his vital task of map-reading, and feeding the driver, but he also had quite a job holding on to his seat each time the Gatford broadsided through the hairpin bends. Some fancy dicing had to be done to maintain that average of 60 kilometres (38 miles) per hour. The 'summer day' should not be taken too literally, for on the summit of the pass we were driving between walls of ice three times higher than the car, and in some places there was even snow falling, in thick fog. A few miles further and the sun was shining mercilessly again, to the delight of Henk, who was amused by the sun-helmet I wore. He wanted to return home sun-burned at any price. He did, and there was a price to pay in the form of large areas of peeling skin. We hadn't the vaguest idea that we should be 'in the running' amongst that entry of mountain specialists, but when entering Chamonix at the end of the first day's section we learned that we were in second position. We had dropped twelve minutes in total, and were only two minutes behind Huguèt in a Hotchkiss, who was leading the 'over 3-litre class'. That evening in Chamonix was one of many stories, particularly about the almost unbelievable achievements in the smallest class, for cars up to 750cc. The baby Simcas and the Fiats (the so-called roadlice) had to maintain a 46 kilometre (28 miles) per hour average, and simply couldn't climb the slopes fast enough, and in order to make that average the drivers hurtled down the mountains in their Topolinos with speeds of more than 60 miles per hour being no exception. Because they had to cover the same route mileage, they had started some hours before us, and I remember well how the Angelvin couple grumbled when they heard that they had to go off at half past four in the morning! The Angelvins were very close 'housefriends', who often visited us in Holland. Ciska and I stayed at their place when we were in Marseilles twice each year.

One of the funniest, or perhaps I should say 'oddest' experiences we had in Chamonix was in the closed park, which was in the stadium adjacent to some wooden barracks from which came a continuous singing from voices with a decidedly Teutonic accent. We learned from officials that the barracks held German Prisoners of War, who passed the time by singing songs which reminded them of the period when they thought themselves lords and masters. Nevertheless, it was an uncomfortable idea to leave your car for the night so near to people who had proved to be masters in the art of robbery and destruction. The appetizers served in the stadium's bar, also situated in the same barracks, brought up all kinds of lugubrious memories.

The following day, July 14th, National holiday, we had the second of the classifying tests, which was held on the square with the statue of the very first Conqueror of the Mont Blanc. The test consisted of an acceleration-reversing-and braking manoeuvre around the statue, and although both tests would only count in the final results as tie-breakers in the result of a draw, they were rewarded with specials prizes. I was keen to do my utmost in order to save face following the defeat which Huguèt had inflicted on me in the standing-start Kilometre test at Annécy. At one-minute intervals the competitors shot out of a narrow street into the square, stopped dead on the line, reversed until the front wheels were behind that line again, rounded the statue and stopped dead again some hundred yards further down over another line, à cheval, as they call it in France. Present in large numbers on this festive July 14th, the motorsport loving French public rewarded each driver with thundering applause.

I was one of the last to start, and had used the time to watch the others very carefully. The test had to be completed twice, with the shortest time counting. When my turn came I jumped quickly into the car, the hood of which was closed - this was compulsory - and drove for all I was worth. All went well first time, and the second run was even better. Admits resounding applause from the crowd the Gatford stopped dead first over and then again behind the first line, and with tyres screaming broadsided around the statue. I had made fastest time of day for all classes. We were awarded two cups, one of which was of such formidable circumference that it took us about a day to walk round it! Yet you could lift it easily because it was made of a gold-anodised aluminium. This result was of course reason for a great party that evening in the cosy dance-hall of Hotel Majestic. Spirits were so high that Blijdenstein, who never dances, together with Mimi Descollas demonstrated the latest jitterbug just imported from America, from which a well-trained kangaroo could have learned a lot.

The next day however it was back to serious business. We knew we had a good chance, and the good old Gatford seemed to know it too, for it shot up the slopes when we began the second and last part of the 1,050 kilometre-long Alpine Rally (in 1946 it was still a 'modest' short-distance rally). It was glorious motoring over the inter-communal country roads through the Alpes Maritimes to Marseilles. These roads appear on the large-scale Michelin maps as nicely winding yellow, and even white lines, but with their many blind bends they hold all kinds of surprising qualities when you drive over them at high speed. Occasionally we encountered broom shrubs on both sides which had grown outwards over the roadway, so that the branches brushed our faces. We didn't mind, because we were lying second, and determined to chase leader Huguèt in his Hotchkiss. At the time controls, where we had to stamp our card ourselves, using a pigeon-racing clock, Henk feverishly put bits of paper in the clock until one showed the right time, then put our card in it and jumped into the already accelerating Gatford. However, in Castellane fate delivered the first blow. We were six minutes late, and in our haste to top up the radiator from a fountain in the village square, I dropped the radiator cap, which hit the spinning fan and promptly disappeared under the engine. At such moments life indeed becomes hectic. With a piece of wire we fished in every corner of the engine compartment, burned our fingers time and time again on the red-hot engine and swore in many languages. Having wasted about seven minutes without finding the cap, we heard that Huguèt was 'only' thirteen minutes late, which meant that we now were in the lead. Deciding to risk leaving the cap wherever it was we drove off like maniacs. We just heard a shout, and braked hard to a standstill. A villager came running after us, waving the radiator cap in his hand. From that moment we were sitting on velvet, albeit velvet which was hurtling towards Marseilles at over 80 miles per hour. On the Durance valley road we made a quick stop to investigate why Joe Fry, his face and hands covered in black grease, had given up. The front suspension of his Aprilia was broken. Although the high, twisty Galibier and Lautaret passes both demanded plenty of pedal and gear-lever work they were not too bad, despite some awkwardly-placed time controls. As I automatically took every bend correctly, the Gatford proving a miracle of stability, it seemed that success would be with us all the time now as we drove on ever nearer to the finish and first prize.

On one of the very few straight and wide roads we flashed by Betty Haig's 2-litre A.C. sportscar. Then, just before St. Maximin, a thunderous explosion caused the Gatford to suddenly start zigzagging dangerously along the tree-lined road. My heart sank as I stopped the car. At 80 miles an hour the left rear tyre had exploded, leaving only bits of melted rubber sticking to the hot wheel-rim. A quick inspection of the right-hand rear tyre revealed that one also to be in a dangerous condition, worn smooth by the constant racing through corners, and also with a deep grove in it. Working like madmen we fitted our only spare wheel, losing valuable minutes. Betty Haig went past, on her way to winning the Ladies' Cup. She told us later that she had seen pieces of our inner tube over a distance of some hundred yards. Driving away we had to decide whether to risk everything and race on to the finish, or go slower with the almost certainty then that the other bad tyre would just hold out, and hopefully still finish just ahead of Huguèt. Under the circumstances, with only fifty miles to go, and the map showing the last stage to be quite easy, we had the choose the latter. We drove on at about 50 miles per hour, but soon found out that the devil can strike at the last moment. Not at all in accordance with our interpretation of the map, we found ourselves driving along the most peculiar narrow little country roads with seemingly endless numbers of curves, knowing all the time that each curve was removing more rubber from that already dangerously thin tyre. All kinds of little passes we met, of the sort we knew well in the Ardennes from the Dumonceau Cup Rally, and the broom bushes behaved twice as badly. Dirty, sunburned, and covered in red dust, we found it hard work to maintain a decent average, but as we finally arrived at the finish at Aubagne, near Marseilles, we felt sure of our victory in the unlimited class. We clocked in, and one minute later Huguèt's Hotchkiss came in to view. His co-driver almost fell out of the car to clock in, but we thought: "too late brother, too late". Then Huguèt showed us his card, and it was devishly hard for us when we saw that the clock, timing only to each full minute, had printed a total of thirty-seven minutes lateness on his card, while we were thirty-eight minutes late. The difference must have only been a few seconds, and my aggregate times from the two tests (which were to decide amongst those with equal penalties) were better than Huguèt's. It was a bitter disappointment for us, a few seconds over a distance of 1,050 kilometres is annoyingly little. The fact that I had left my second spare wheel at the start, because I wanted to avoid all unnecessary weight, certainly didn't lessen my self-reproach. After I congratulated Huguèt I wanted to be alone for a while, just to pull out a few hairs and to curse fate, which seemed to have picked on me to be the everlasting second.

Chapter 12

Lisbon Rally 1947

> About petrol and frontier troubles: a country where things were rough: a wooden head: a third position: and thieves in the night.

"It's going to be a calm, though rather long trip, but that's the way to see something of the world", I told my friend Theo Van Ellinkhuizen, when I asked him to keep me company in my Gatso on the Lisbon Rally. In 1947 this was being staged the first time as an international automobile event to celebrate the eight centenary of the capture of the Portuguese capital. It was anything but easy in 1947 to organize a sporting event like that. Foreign exchange was difficult to obtain, as were tyres, and visas for Spain, whilst arranging the passage of cars posed problems too. To crown everything we had to cross France lengthways without refuelling, as petrol was not sold there for competition purposes. Fortunately my Gatso's three tanks could hold 31 Imperial gallons, and with the additional four full jerrycans we had on board we could travel far. No less than sixteen Dutch crews had entered, while the British contingent was made up of six cars. More Dutchmen, it seemed, wanted a change of scenery than did the British. As there was still some trouble between France and Spain, the French competitors were unable to start, due to not being allowed the transit visas by their neighbours. Our chaps had all chosen Brussels as their starting point, and Theo and I left home the morning before the 'off' which took place during the very early hours of May 1st. After our car had been scrutineered and sealed by the Belgian Automobile Club, we slept that short night in Dutch cycle champion Piet Van Kempen's hotel. Piet had been a well-known and successful cycle racer about fifteen years before, and he told us a number of the 'tallest' stories about the time he and Jan 'Cannonball' Pijnenburg rode in the 'Six-days races'. Those stories were more unbelievable than any I ever heard in motorsport! He even tried to convince us that nobody would stand a chance in motorsport if he decided to take that up and compete in his Lincoln Zephyr. At 5 o'clock in the morning we took off, and only an hour later, at the border, we realized that this rally was indeed going to have other difficulties than just those of a sporting nature. The Belgian Customs officers at Bois Bourdon, near Mons, were enforcing the export prohibition rules regarding petrol. Geoff Imhof and Ken Richardson had been arguing with the officers in English, but to no avail. The officers apparently didn't understand that it was petrol brought with them from England, and therefore it was a matter of transit and no export. But the Customers wouldn't budge. I went over to help Geoff, whilst of course keeping quiet about my own four full five-gallon cans. But it was no good. More and more Rally cars arrived, eventually blocking the road completely as they parked crisscross on the roadway. Everyone spoke in his own language, or argued in one which he hadn't mastered. It was a complete shambles, and that at 6 o'clock in the morning on the first day! Suddenly one of the cars, a blue Dutch-registered Ford drophead coupé, started up, went around the mix-up and so solved the trouble in a rather unusual way. It was Carol Schade and his co-driver Robert Hin who had made up their minds, jumped in the car and guided it across a tiny ditch, over the frozen fields past all the competitors and officials, and without considering anybody worth a look disappeared in a cloud of dust in the direction of the French post half a mile away. Schade was able to do this because he didn't need a stamp on his Carnet de Route, already having a continuous triptyque for Belgium, in those years a standard international document. This astonished the Customs officers to such an extent that they instantly relented, and allowed the other competitors, except the Belgians, to pass as well. The latter were forced to leave their full jerrycans in their homeland. It was most unfortunate for Imhof, who had been first to arrive, and had just emptied his two jerrycans into other fellows tanks, and out of pure vexedness poured the remainder into the ditch besides the Customs office with the intention of setting it alight when driving away. We hurried away, and broke all records on the way to Paris, where we wanted a little time in hand in order to enjoy some French cuisine. But we had forgotten that it was May 1st, and on that day Paris is about as lively as the middle of the Sahara. Literally nothing was to be had. Our French friends Suzanne Largeot, and Quinlin, of Monte Carlo fame, had come along to the 'Automobile Club de l'Ile de France', where the control was situated, and we enlisted their help. This resulted in us being guided to a bistro, in a rather secretive way, almost as if it was an opium den. There we were treated to lemonade and sandwiches, which the restaurateur must have forgotten to throw away a week before. What a disillusion, and that in Paris!

We came to Carol Schade's assistance by getting a local friend of mine, André Claude, to repair the dynamo which had failed on Carol's Ford during the first few hundred miles. He didn't show much gratitude though. While we were standing near Carol's car a little later, he shouted from the balcony of the club "Take your dirty paws of my wireless. Do you want to ruin my battery?". In fact we hadn't touched his car at all. The music was coming from the handbag of a passing Paris beauty, who had a portable radio in it; in those days a miraculous novelty which she obviously felt had to be loudly demonstrated. Following that 'delicious' Paris lunch we set off on the 350 miles stretch to Bordeaux over the straight, endless and boring roads. We arrived there late in the evening, having been a long way round because the bridge over the Gironde, destroyed by the retreating Germans, was still under reconstruction.

We slept for an hour at the Automobile Club under a desk in the office, where it was awfully dusty, but much quieter than in the big hall. We could afford the rest, as we had several hours to spare due to the low average speed of 50 kilometres per hour on the early section of the Rally. We met Anthony Noghès there, the organizer of the Monte Carlo Rally, for the first time in eight years. He told us that the entire French entry had been cancelled, as I have already mentioned. There was some excitement amongst competitors when it was learned that on many cars the seals fixed to the engines were now missing. These and similar seals on the steering gear had been put in place by the Brussels officials, but after an investigation now by the Bordeaux club-officials all the cars were allowed to carry on, and at the finish they had no trouble.

Leaving Bordeaux we headed for the first Spanish control, at San Sebastian, along the Golf of Biscay, with a hurricane in our backs making for a 70 miles per hour average. It didn't matter as at that time of night nobody else was on the roads. Nor was there anybody on duty at the frontier when we arrived there at 4 o'clock in the morning. We hooted, shouted, knocked on and kicked the door of the office, but apparently the French Customs had not been informed and the frontier barriers stayed down. Shortly after the war it was always the same when one was the first to arrive. We kept up this night-time concerto, and eventually a sleepy French official in a night-shirt opened a window and told us that their shop didn't open until 8 o'clock. And under no circumstances before that. So there we were, facing a four hour's wait, and we had to be at the San Sebastian time control at 8.14. Fortunately, helping us to forget our miseries, we witnessed an incomparable sunrise. The white-capped Pyrenees were silhouetted majestically against the first blood red rays of the sun. We watched this phenomenon with open mouths, forgetting all thoughts of cold and sleep. At 7 o'clock a little bar at the frontier opened, where we warmed ourselves with a cup of coffee, and learned that in sunny Spain we would encounter snow on the passes leading from San Sebastian to Burgos. Meanwhile the other competitors had all arrived, and at 8 o'clock we could cross the notorious Hendaye bridge, separating France from Spain. It was not without a shiver that we thought of the thousands of Spaniards who had crossed this bridge into voluntary exile; and of the hundreds of refugees (including Dutch) who some years later, England-bound during World War II, were seized by the much-feared Spanish Blue Brigade and handed over to the Nazi hangmen over this 'bridge of a thousand sighs'. It was on this bridge that the two 'gentlemen' who had agreed on this policy - Hitler and Franco - had met, luckily without the result Adolf had expected. On the Spanish side of the river we found the Customs officials were anything but kind. One of the Dutch drivers, who had no Spanish pesetas, was shouted at in perfect Nazi style, as if he intended to attack the Caudillo. A charming welcome! The five miles to San Sebastian were soon covered, and there we were looking forward to meeting my Portuguese friend Nunos dos Santos. A charming old friend and an extremely good driver, he is as boss-eyed as a crossword puzzle, which gives him ever such a good insight of the road. I remember how he drove his B.M.W. when we did the Monte from Athens in 1939. At San Sebastian however we didn't see him, instead receiving a cable informing us that somewhere on his way from Lisbon - his starting point - his car had skidded and hit a tree, and that had finished the Rally as far as he was concerned. At the finish we did meet him, with his head in bandages but nevertheless, as always, in splendid spirits.

We carried on to Burgos, a city well-known from the Spanish civil war. From there on our way to the sunny South it was so cold that every available piece of textile was used to cover us, but we persisted in driving the Gatso open. On the passes to the Spanish plateau we

Gatso and Theo Van Ellinkhuizen at the San Sebastian control, 1947.

found ourselves driving through slush and snow about eight inches deep. We hadn't expected this and so had no snow chains with us, but we were able to skid and slide along through it, and managed to successfully tackle the long slopes.

At the Burgos time check we discovered that contrary to what we had always thought, the most spirited officials don't live in France. Oh dear, were those Spaniards excited. They ran to and fro carrying papers and stamp-pads, kept falling over the cars in their enthusiasm, and with great success managed to take three times as long as was necessary. Whilst in Burgos we took the opportunity to replenish our vitamin C shortage, as large oranges were available for a penny each. We hadn't see them in almost ten years because of the war, and so bought a large bag full. Even at that low price though they were too dear for the Spanish youngsters, and in no time our car was surrounded by underfed and scruffy little devils, most of them scarcely dressed, who obviously envied us our oranges. We began to distribute a few oranges amongst them, but then a policeman appeared and proceeded to demonstrate how to maintain order in his country. He hit the kiddies with his truncheon as hard as he could, and all our protests were in vain. We could have killed him!

Another Dutch crew, the Wittkampf brothers and their third man, actually fell foul themselves of the Spanish authorities and spent a few hours in custody. They were driving a Chevrolet, with a fifty-gallon fuel tank on the roof, and didn't need to refuel from start to finish. On the quiet main roads of the plain one could drive very fast. The tarmac was not so good, and it was dusty, but a speed of seventy was easy to maintain, although through the villages with their narrow streets we had to slow down considerably. The Wittkampf brothers were confronted by a horse-drawn cart as they were turning a blind corner in one of those narrow streets. Following the inevitable embrace, almost before realizing what happened they had a member of the Falange on the running board poking a stengun in their backs. They were taken to Salamanca, where a heavy cell door was shut behind them. This was not amusing, but fortunately they had to appear in Court the same day. Escorted by a complete regiment with fixed bayonets they arrived at Court where, still hand-cuffed, they sat down whilst the regiment took up position, looking as if they would riddle them with bullets should they make a suspicious move. The summons was read in Spanish, which conveyed nothing to them as there was no interpreter and their Spanish was limited to 'Caramba' and the beautiful song 'Valencia', which didn't help them at all. After that the local witnesses were heard, and to go by the rolling of their eyes and arm-waving gesticulations, things did not look good for the Dutchmen. Then one of the accused noticed a Spanish beauty in the Court who, from behind her mantilla, was smiling sweetly at the three blond Dutch boys. Thinking that smiling young ladies would perhaps not be coming their way again for some time, they grinned back, and after this little flirtation had lasted some time the lady suddenly whispered something in the judge's ear. He coughed and straight away announced his decision. It was a decision of which they didn't get an inkling until, with a lot of bowing and scraping, the hand-cuffs were taken off and they were escorted outside and taken to their Chevrolet. With considerable relief they continued their journey, although this judicial delay had rather spoiled the Rally for them.

Meanwhile, before Salamanca, Theo and I had managed to take the wrong turning at an un-signposted fork road crossing before Valladolid. We went on nicely at first, but eventually the road became extremely bad even by Spanish standards. We were surrounded by tundras, not a living soul to be seen, and the muddy snow we were ploughing through did nothing for our peace of mind either. As we did not want to take the same way back we tried to get to the right road by way of a little country lane, which was a mixture of red clay and snow. All the time there was the fear of getting stuck and remaining stranded for months. There were no signs at all on these secondary and tertiary roads. The only thing we knew for sure was that we were driving at a constant height of about 2,000 feet, shown on my aircraft altimeter. We couldn't be anywhere else but on the miserable and barren plateau. Luckily, with the use of a tiny pocket compass, we finally found the proper road, and carried on in pouring rain in that inhospitable land, where only once every few hours we came across a village. These usually consisted of three big houses, apparently belonging to wealthy people, whilst the remainder of the houses were indescribable slums, showing quite plainly we thought where the wealth in the three big houses came from.

How glad we were to finally turn our backs on this misery, and at last become acquainted with the warm hospitality and the courtesy of the Portuguese. At the frontier post we were welcomed by Automobile Club officials, who treated us to delicious sandwiches and port wine of excellent quality. We received a road map with the road we had to follow marked with draw-in particulars, and were invited to make use of every service that was available. After that we went down the plain in the dusk, following a narrow winding pass, where we were greatly troubled by lack of sleep. It got so bad that we stopped the car on several occasions in order to walk around and rid ourselves of the sleepy feeling. Our eyes burned and became red-rimmed due to the continuous staring at the two bright patches of our lights on the pitch dark winding road. The steady drone of the engine and the whistling of the tyres on the macadam surface became a dangerous lullaby. Close to midnight, completely fagged out, we arrived at Porto. Having made up seven hours, we promptly used these for a deep sleep on the soft cushions at the Automobile Club. Some hours later the experienced Tommy Wisdom followed our good example and also went to sleep in a comfortable chair in the hall. We didn't see the others, as they stayed at the control which was situated in an exhibition building opposite. As usual we had an alarm clock with us, and when it rang we woke up in time to see Carol Schade bringing his Ford into the park. Its crew looked more dead than alive, and had arrived with only half an hour in hand. As they came down the plains they had hardly any lights left as their dynamo had given up once more. With only their parking lights, they had followed closely the Studebaker of Mutsaerts and Kouwenberg. We, in contrast, were by now feeling as fresh as a daisy, and even had some time left in which we paid a short visit to the Motor Show, which had not yet opened to the public, where we saw the latest British and American cars of which so far we had only seen photographs.

From Porto we continued on an excellent road on which we did battle with the Jaguar SS100 of fat Fernando Mascarenhas. It became a real road race, which only finished when we had to stop at a closed level crossing. As soon as the barrier went up, I slipped my Gatso past the waiting queue, drove very fast for about a mile, and then used my little advantage to hide the car in a side street, from where we saw the fat Portuguese go flashing past at breakneck speed. We never saw him again, and can only presume that he fell off the side of the Iberian peninsular into the sea. An increased average speed of 50 kilometres (37 miles) per hour was required for the last four stages from Porto to the finish, but this was easy as the roads were splendid. Just before reaching Coimbra our horn gave up, which would have cost us some marks at the finish, so I called at a Ford garage where I had a new twin-tone horn fitted for 350 escudos (about £ 3.10s), which in our opinion was very cheap, as horns were not even available yet in our plundered country. When sounded it was so harmonious, as though some Royal personage was approaching. At Lisbon we had the time to get the car lubricated, change the oil, and have it washed. It was a shiny Gatso which arrived at the official finish at the Citadel of Lisbon. From there we went to the closed park at Estoril, the wonderful seaside resort of the Portuguese capital. Our hotel was correctly booked. What a hotel! For 14 shillings a day they gave all the luxurious comfort one could think of, with two six-course meals a day, one covered with lobster. It really was very cheap, although the prices would double a few weeks later when the season started. In the afternoon the entire Dutch contingent went to Cascais, some miles to the west, to catch lobsters at sea. Later on we eat what we had caught - and more - together with delicious port wine for just 5 shillings per head. It was paradise for us after five years of war.

In the evening we had a lovely party in the Casino, and for the first time in my life I was so stupid as to join in, and so forget all about the next morning with its classifying test. A hell of a noise woke me up, and putting my (wooden-like) head out of the window I saw that the test had already started. In practically no time I was dressed and in the car, just in time for my first test. It was a simple one, consisting of 120 metres forward from a standing start, turning right round a cone, stop, 9 metres reverse over a line, again a right turn round the same cone, and then a flying finish back to the start line. With my miserable hangover I completely spoiled the test. I put the Gatso back in the park. "Fool" I said to myself, slouching back to the hotel, thinking that I deserved a real telling-off from someone for my damn-fool behaviour the night before. Back in my room I just wanted to lay down and give up everything, and my continued self-reproach did nothing for my headache, but fortunately my good old friend Barend Van Der Hoek came in to buck me up. He gave me the telling-off I needed, then told me to get up and come with him for a good meal, after which he said he would make absolutely sure that I was in good condition for the second test. That was to be staged in the afternoon, and was a re-run of the first, with only the best time to count, so if I could recover from my self-inflicted misery there was still a chance. Barend stuffed me with hot lobster and other delicacies, all the while subjecting me to an intensive mental training, for which I am still grateful. Then, giving me a mighty wallop, he promised that if I did not do well this time I would receive another! Well, I did give the Gatso a good chance in that second test. The final result was: 1st Imhof,

The Gatso sports-car on the classification test at Estoril. Lisbon Rally 1947.

Allard; 2nd Jorge Montereal, Bentley; and 3rd Gatsonides, Gatso. My second test time was only 35 hundredths of a second slower than Imhof's fastest.

As neither of us had ever visited the Spanish capital Madrid, Theo and I decided to return home via that city, a detour which we thought would not add too much distance to the trip. That proved to be a mistake, for distances in Spain are deceptive, and when we arrived there at midnight we badly needed petrol, not to mention pesetas. To our joy we saw the B.M.W. of Barend Van Der Hoek parked outside an impressive and expensive looking restaurant, where the crew were having dinner. Chris Kok, Barend's co-driver suggested that we join them, saying everything would be alright because he knew a Sherry King there who would lend him money. Unfortunately, his Sherry friend wasn't in Madrid but could be found five hundred miles away at his mansion at the Sevilla beach. Our stomachs clamoured for food, and as we had to eat we considered it just as wise to sit where we were. After the meal though we only had enough Spanish currency left for 20 litres (about 4 gallons) of petrol, with which, we thought, we could just reach the border. Things didn't look good for our B.M.W. friends, as they hadn't enough money to buy sufficient petrol. They stayed on to try and get some currency changed, which was strictly forbidden in Spain, while Theo and I continued our trip. On that long drive through Spain we watched the fuel gauge needle move ever more close to 'Empty' as they are so apt to do. It went threateningly low, and although the frontier with France was now not far away, we knew we wouldn't make it. At such moments peculiar thoughts go through one's mind. Ours went irresistibly to a lonely petrol pump we espied on a deserted village street. We looked at each other. It had to be done. Let me hasten to add that theft was not our intention. Fair exchange is no robbery, and we were going to leave a new and very expensive fountain-pen for 20 litres of petrol. None the less, we felt like thieves in the night.

We had seen enough of Spain to know that nobody was going to help us, not even in exchange for a fountain-pen or against payment in foreign currency. I even believe they have capital punishment for the latter. Every foreigner is avoided, and helping them, especially under such abnormal circumstances as we were in, is equal to high treason. Theo stayed in the car while I began to fiddle with the pump, which was safeguarded with a kind of Yale lock. The tiniest noise sounded like a gunshot in that lonely moonlit street. Every time Theo saw a light in the distance he warned me and I jumped into the car, and we pretended to be studying the road map. When the danger was over I would start on the pump again with the uneasy feeling that a thousand eyes were prying from behind. Just when the lock was about to surrender we heard a shocking noise, filling every nook and cranny. I guess that I jumped about a yard into the air, and certainly my legs were in the running position before they touched the ground. I leapt into the car, and only then noticed it was a Spanish donkey which had almost given us heart attacks with its 'hee Haw'. Still trembling I carried on with the pump, getting the door open at last. I lifted the nozzle and was just about to move the hand-pump when Theo whispered: "Lights, coming fast". I quickly shut the pump cover and saw the headlights of a car approaching from behind. We acted like the well-known ostriches as the light shone on our necks. The car reduced speed and our hearts were making about 5.000 revs. With screaming brakes the car stopped right beside ours. "We are in real trouble" I thought. Then a rather laconic voice said: "Say boys, what are you doing". In perfect Dutch! We just collapsed and thanked our lucky stars. The voice belonged to good old Barend Van Der Hoek. My Lord, how glad we were to see him and Chris and look into the honest blue eyes of my friend. And how pleased we were to learn that they had pesetas, and a full jerrycan. They had got the money by exchanging with an agent of the Royal Dutch Airlines. Waiting in a main street in Madrid they had spotted a Dutch-registered car passing in which, they found out after having caught up with it, was a helpful agent of the K.L.M. Suddenly we were on the top of the world again. We left in a hurry and in the next place we came to found an all night filling station, the first since leaving Madrid five hours before. It was almost morning when we arrived in San Sebastian again, and feeling well pleased we decided to have a cup of coffee at a place we saw open. We were less pleased, however, when the bar-keeper charged us 16 bobs for four cups of coffee. It transpired that we were sitting on the terrace of a night club, the only place open so early in the morning. I said we wouldn't pay, but the bar-keeper didn't understand, until he realized that we were not putting any money on the table. We were so furious at this daylight robbery that we went to get a policeman, finding one who luckily spoke a little French, although he said that nothing could be done, and so we paid the bill with some rather bitter resentment. The policeman thought like us, explaining that is was more than he, with a wife and three children, earned in a week. That was our 'Good bye' to Spain, so soon after the war. Now we only had to cross France, although that was not easy. First: our francs were also finished, so that we had to live on bananas bought in Lisbon, and secondly: we were dog-tired. To stay awake that second night on our way to the French capital I smoked my first, and for the time being my last cigarette. To crown things we nearly smashed up Barend's B.M.W., when approaching a fork in the road he first turned to the right, before then braking at the very last moment and turning left. Doing eighty I couldn't brake any more and only by a quick turn of the wheel and a huge skid could I save our skins and cars. That incident served to keep us awake until we reached Paris, where we slept for some hours in a hotel.

When at last we arrived in Holland, we had done the 1,600 miles, which separated Lisbon from our homes, in sixty hours.

Chapter 13

French Alpine Rally 1947

> About sledging with a Studebaker Champion: turning, turning all the time: the speedy fitting of a cylinder-head gasket: sixteen men in a Ford: and a pail of water.

If ever I have competed in an Alpine Rally with a car not suited to that event, then it was the year I drove an American Studebaker Champion. I'm not being disrespectful to this 80 b.h.p. 2.8-litre coupé, because it simply wasn't built with such as this murderous event in the French Alps in mind. It was an apprehensive feeling taking tight corners with the hub-caps almost touching the road, and there were many corners to take! I was unable to compete in one of my Gatsos because the required minimum number had not yet been built and sold, therefore I had no other choice than to enter the Studebaker which was my own dealership demonstration car, and simply make the best of it. My co-driver was a fine young fellow, Hans Otten, a 21 year old technical student, who was most enthusiastic and very handy. Sadly, only two years later he lost his life in a motorcycle accident. Apart from increasing the compression ratio slightly, and fitting an extra petrol tank, we didn't do much to the car. We didn't have any illusions about our chances in the 3-litre category: we were competing against Tommy Wisdom's Healey, and five of the front-wheel-drive six cylinder Citroëns. There was one other Studebaker Champion, driven by Mutsaerts and Kouwenberg. Heading for the start at Marseilles we took things rather easily, as we were taking an elderly couple as passengers to Cannes. However, when for the sake of a little practice we took some passes at more like rally speed, they proved to have nerves of steel, as apparently it wasn't fast enough for them! At Cannes, where the finish was planned and the Mistral blew away our joy, we unloaded our luggage before taking the road to Marseilles, where we found a jolly atmosphere amongst many old friends. There was Geoff Imhof with his Allard, the cheery Ian Appleyard with a Jaguar SS100, and a large Dutch contingent. Lex Van Strien and Jan Erens competed with the 'Blue Angel', their famous and notorious old Ford V8, Dolf Burgerhout and Henk Sijthof presented a powerful threat with their Delahaye, Verkamman Van Keulen and his wife started with a Ford Taunus, and last but by no means least Kees Kruit was there with his own-built Fiat special, and had his book-keeper with him as co-driver. Due to a lack of foreign exchange they were forced to sleep in a tent on the Rally. Rumour had it that these Fiat friends were fiddling with their car day and night, and they certainly looked like a couple of chimney-sweeps as the Rally progressed. Kees had in fact encountered much trouble in getting his car accepted. The Vertex-magneto was allowed only after hours of discussion, but his extra petrol tanks had to be rendered useless by drilling holes in them. Then we saw old hands from pre-war days, Peter Van Dijk and Janus Van Der Kamp. Both were driving Ford V8's with which they hoped to conquer the Alps. We had no problems in the closed park on the Cannebière, because, as it was non-standard, we had already removed the extra petrol tanks at Cannes. After the scrutineering in the burning sun, the Pernod offered as a toast by the Automobile Club of Marseilles tasted very well indeed. In the evening we started cheerfully on the fist stage, to Cannes, through the Estérel mountains. Trouble, always in abundance on an Alpine Rally, began straight away. A Dutch Lancia left the road on a curve in a little village, shot over a high kerb.....and the drivers could make preparations for their return journey by train. At Cannes both the Ford V8 crews of Van Dijk and Van Der Kamp retired due to fuel vapourisation. This rarely happens at night but the temperature was tropical, and the Fords once again demonstrated this notorious fault of theirs. At Cannes our erstwhile passengers the elderly couple provided us with lots of nice things to eat, and away we went into the mountains heading for Barcelonette. Now we really had a taste of what was facing us with the Studebaker. It sailed through the curves as if it were drunk, protesting loudly with screaming tyres, and it was proving difficult to keep it on the winding secondary roads.

    Kees Kruit was having far more serious trouble. In pitch dark he suffered an enforced stop with a failed cylinder-head gasket. At such times normal people would give up, but not the Kruit crew who knew every part of their Fiat like the insides of their own pockets. A new gasket was fitted within a matter of minutes, that's all. Taking the cylinder-head off could be 'done in a jiffy' according to Kees. Even worse problems faced him, when on a nasty narrow and winding little road between the famous red rocks of the Gorges de Cians, the car's lightning gave up. But that didn't result in surrender, as Kees simply handed a torch to his co-driver and they carried on. The persistence of these two enthusiastic youngsters is almost unbelievable, and apart from that they are really nice chaps, who with modest means but immodest spirits only give up if their car literally disintegrates into bits and pieces. This time again Kees managed to struggle through, eventually arriving at Barcelonette as though nothing had happened, but of course loaded down with penalties.

Kees Kruit and co-driver looking rather travel-stained on the Alpine Rally, 1947.

Daylight was just beginning as we left Barcelonette, setting course for Grenoble and covering the distance so quickly that we had time left for a cup of coffee. From Grenoble we went to Aix-les-Bains, over the Col de Porte, Col de Granier, and Col de Cucheron over all sorts of miserable little mountain roads. Aix-les-Bains is a well-known rather 'stuck up' spa resort, where everywhere very old, almost antique, ex-beauties were taking the waters. Gradually my arms became very tired from steering, as for every bend I had to turn the wheel almost as many revolutions as the engine, before the Champion would obey. To achieve anything worthwhile at all with this car in so far as cornering was concerned I had to inflate the front tyres twice as hard as the rear ones. In this 2,000 kilometre Rally we wore six tyres down to the canvas. However, at Aix we had covered the first lap, and were still without marks lost. In the afternoon we had a classifying test. This involved flinging the car round a couple of markers, and stopping dead between two lines. Mistakes were made by many drivers, with only Ian Appleyard in the SS100 giving a really polished display to show just how it should be done. The next day was an early start for everyone. The smallest class, in which our friends the Angelvin husband and wife team courageously fought the mighty Alps in their little Simca, started at 4 o'clock in the morning. Fortunately we in the large cars didn't have to leave until 06.30. We refuelled in a hurry because that was included in the driving time, and shot away to climb the Iséran on the way to Chamonix. We really did give the Studebaker a thrashing, but I have to say she took it well. On one ear she slid through the curves, and under the bonnet the brave side-valver had to call upon all her horses to arrive on time. It was dicing again, and Hans Otten had the difficult task of holding on with both hands and feet, meanwhile providing his captain with food and drink. But we made it, and, considerably relieved, we went to the hotel, where many (sometimes tall) stories were circulating. Ian Appleyard told how when he was descending the Iséran his not-so-slow SS100 was suddenly overtaken by a blue cannonball. It was Jan Erens who had reminded his car, the Ford 'Blue Angel' that he was in a hurry. "They came down like a bomb" said Ian, speaking almost in awe. Jan Erens hadn't things all his own way though, as the old-type mechanical braking system of 'Blue Angel' was neither responsive, nor had the crew had time to carry out a re-adjustment. Broadsiding they could come down the slope, but on a long straight stretch Jan accelerated to gain some time when suddenly in the distance they saw a large removal van parked blocking nearly all the road. Jan check-braked, but he might just as well have whistled. Now he pushed the pedal down hard, but it made little difference, and with that cheerfulness peculiar to him he told Lex, "We are going to hit it, boy", and began to pull up the handbrake lever. Well, 'Blue Angel' slowed a little, but 50 miles per hour is still considerable if you hit a big truck. Jan tried two hands but still the Ford wouldn't stop. Then, Lex the giant put one great mutton-chop hand on that handbrake lever, said "Whoa", and the Blue Angel stopped about a yard away from the truck. As big Lex muttered something about people with no strength, Jan got out shyly to adjust the brakes. Everyone was full of respect for these two prewar cracks who, driving a 1934 Ford fitted with a new 100 brake horsepower V8 engine, managed so well, although Lex remarked to Jan: "I'd rather lend you my prayer book than my car".

In the afternoon we started for Annécy, via a different route over the small, but steep Col de la Forclaz, which was a narrow road right above the main road. It was chock-full of broom brushes again, and so narrow that overtaking was almost impossible. When we followed a Peugeot its French driver was sporting enough to put his car well into the bushes to give us room to get through, an example of sportsmanship which might be copied in our country, for it happens quite often that clearly faster cars are not allowed to pass by those in front. It would teach those drivers a lesson if they were to take part in the small-class at Le Mans, where the big boys chasing each other are going about 50 miles per hour faster.

It was still burning hot that day, and things were not helped when about twelve miles before Annécy a farmer threw a bucket full of manure at the Studebaker's open window as we passed. He was, quite understandably furious, as one of his loose-walking pigs had been killed by another competitor's car a few moments before. At Annécy, in the hotel we found Kouwenberg and Mutsaerts with faces about a mile long. Downheartedly they explained that they had no more brakes.

With great wisdom I predicted that the following day they would have brakes again. They didn't trust this prophecy, but fortunately I was right, having suspected vapour-lock in the braking system due to the overheating which can be caused by too much braking. My suspicion proved true after their brakes had cooled down after the overnight stop.

That evening we had an opportunity to check up on the positions, and it transpired that the Dutchmen were doing quite well. In our class four cars, Wisdom's Healey, Roeloffzen's Opel, and the two Studs were still penalty free. The Citroëns, for various reasons, had been unable to manage it. In the unlimited class were still held some trumps, with the following having a clean sheet: Imhof (Allard), Van Strien (Ford), Potter (Allard), Burgerhout (Delahaye) and Huguèt (Hotchkiss). That was worth celebrating, so a party was quickly arranged in a hotel on the other side of the lake. As our own cars were all in the closed park, sixteen of us all went in Piet Feitz's Ford V8 two-seater, which had already retired from the Rally. If you looked very carefully you could just spot bits of the car. Piet treated us to a blind-driving demonstration, guided by those who could see ahead. We had a swim in the ever-warm lake, and did some water ski-ing with Ian Appleyard, which we could do for an hour for a cost of three 10-litre petrol coupons.

The next day was the July 14th holiday, and we only had the Standing Start Kilometre test to do. When leaving the closed park for the test next day we quickly realized that Tommy Wisdom, our strongest opponent, was in trouble. He switched the engine off every time he had to stop. A water hose had burst and the Healey was without cooling. He was in possession of a spare, which he would be able to fit the following morning after leaving the closed park for the next stage of the event. On the Kilometre test Imhof provided the drama. Accelerating fiercely, he changed from first gear straight into reverse, and expensive noises, which must have sounded like music to the ears of his opponents, announced that the Allard's gear box had disintegrated. Kees Kruit provided the sensation of the day by driving his Fiat special over the Kilometre in the fastest time for the 1,100cc class. We took 37.1 seconds, for an average of 60 miles per hour from the standing start. That may not seem too fast, but the Kilometre on this occasion was marked out on an uphill slope. With the test completed we began the July 14th celebrations, only to be rudely interrupted by a protest. On the previous stage a control post had been set up late, and there was uncertainty about whether all drivers had taken the difficult road over the Col de la Forclaz. All competitors were called together for a discussion in the Rally Headquarters, where the chief marshall, Monsieur De Laval, made a speech saying that if the protest was handed to the A.C.F. the whole event would have to be cancelled. He openly admitted the mistake, but appealed to the sportsmanship of the drivers not to spoil everything. His speech, translated perfectly by Imhof's Swiss wife Gina, impressed to such an extent those who had submitted the protest, that to everyone's relief they withdrew it. And so we faced the final, hardest day. Almost all the cars had suffered badly, yet much hard work remained if we were to keep our clean sheets. From Annécy we tore along at full speed on a splendid road to La Chambre, where a prediction that Tom Wisdom wouldn't come through proved not to be true. On the Col de la Croix de Fer our Alpine Rally particularly, and maybe all our future events, nearly came to an untimely end. Just as you have to do in an Alpine Rally, I flashed into the inside of a curve, and notwithstanding a warning which had been given to oncoming traffic that the road was closed, we met an enormous truck. On the left was the mountainside, on the right a ravine, and ahead an almighty bump. How in the world it was possible I still don't know to this day, but apparently there was a gap through which a Studebaker Champion could just squeeze. Our hair was standing on end, shivers were running down our backs, but our spirits had not been downed and we carried on hell-bent. On the top of the Galibier was a time control post well-positioned to give anybody who had not yet collected any, a sizeable portion of bad marks. However fast we diced that Studebaker across those mountain roads and through the hairpin bends we could not make the average. We were ten minutes late, and collected one hundred penalty marks. Wisdom was only two minutes late with his Healey. After that the run was easy, compared with what was now behind us. We were bumped about a little on the road over the Izoard, but only one more shock when, quite near Grasse, a tyre burst which caused the Studebaker to skid right across the road. The wheel was soon changed, and we arrived at Cannes, quite content to be second-in-class behind Tom's Healey. Mutsaerts-Kouwenberg (230 marks) were third and in fact only other survivor in this class, as Roeloeffzen had eventually retired as the result of a damaged bearing. The largest class had supplied a fine Dutch victory. Burgerhout and Sijthof finished first with only 10 penalties (1 minute late), whilst Lex Van Strien and Jan Erens were second having dropped just two minutes overall. Despite all his bad luck, Kees Kruit had managed fourth in the 1,100cc class.

Hans Otten and I were quite satisfied with our result, and before celebrating all the victories we patted the bonnet of that faithful Studebaker, which, protesting, screaming and skidding had brought us across the mountain passes at a mad average of 36 miles per hour. But it was a more a feat of tobogganing than fast driving. Whatever, the American car had proved to be a strong one, whilst more than 50 percent of the competitors had been forced to retire.

Jan Erens (left) and Lex Van Strien with their notorious old Ford V8 'Blue Angel', having gained second place on the Alpine Rally, 1947.

International friendship in motorsport. 5 Frenchmen (one of which was a naturalised Austrian), 3 British, and 6 Dutch at the prizegiving. French Alpine Rally 1951.

Chapter 14

First Dutch Post-War Sports-Car Races, 1947 and 1949.

>About dicing on airfield runways: lack of power: and an expensive little cork gasket.

Sports-car racing in Holland had only just taken its first rather hesitant steps when we were forced into five years of compulsory 'hospitality' to our Eastern neighbours. During those years, many of the cars which had managed to escape the grabbing Teutonic hands had inevitably deteriorated as a result of 'storage' in hayricks and other agricultural corners throughout the duration. Despite everything, some owners had spent many hours working in secret on their cars throughout those bitter years, driving away sombre thoughts and dreaming of the wonderful moment when they would get behind the wheel again and drive to their heart's content. When the long-longed for liberation came, there were naturally more pressing matters than sports-car races at first, and it was perhaps a little later than many of those dreamers expected when it was announced that on July 21st, 1947, more than two years after our liberation, the runways of Leeuwarden airport were to be used for Holland's first post-war sports-car race. At this news all the old pre-war motorsports men who had indeed managed to keep something in the shape of a car from the invader's hands were jumping for joy, and began preparations at once. I myself had nothing to worry about, as the Gatso had already proved itself, although unfortunately in my case a thorough preparation for the race was out of the question, as I had only returned home the night before from the French Alpine Rally with my Studebaker Champion. However, my mechanics Nico Stuifbergen and Co Wijmenga had been expending loving care on the Gatso while I was away, and so we started happily for the North that Saturday morning. Not everyone was so well prepared, as on the way, near the Zuidersea dyke, we saw Kees Kruit in his Fiat 1100, driving at great speed in a direction which certainly didn't lead to Leeuwarden and who, as he told us later, was busy giving his car a last-minute test. Luckily I had the opportunity for some practice, all the more welcome as the circuit was rather complicated and contained some nasty bumps and holes.

Several people had cancelled their entries, and my arrival pleased the organizers so much that they allowed me a few practice laps between the motorcycle races which were a part of the day's programme. I had a rather peculiar sensation when, having lost a couple of wheel discs in the first curve, I noticed a soldier waiting for me a few hundred yards ahead with the discs in his hand. I thought I had found a ghost, but the circuit at that spot was O-shaped and he had simply walked across from one runway to the other. Unfortunately the 3-litre and over class in which I had entered was poorly represented, there being only three cars at the start. Piet Nortier's Alfa Romeo had bearing trouble, and Pril's Mercedes failed to arrive. This left only the Delahaye belonging to Blom, but driven by Molenaar, and Jan Stemerdink's 1934 Ford V8 two-seater (with a 100 b.h.p. engine) alongside my Gatso. Although I had done a couple of laps I didn't know the details of the circuit yet as the runways were extremely wide and ran through vast fields of airport grass. But I knew that Jan Stemerdink was very keen to pinch the curve to the right. In fact, he was so keen that his clutch was already in when the flag had gone down about an eighth of an inch. It would be nice to be able to say that this gave me such a shock that I also started, but honesty compels me to admit that I hardly waited for the second eight of an inch. Side by side we shot forward to that first curve, but just as the public rose to miss nothing of the seemingly inevitable collision, the old Ford gave way a little so as not to make the show too spectacular. From that moment on it was an unequal battle. The Gatso was considerably faster than the other two cars, which served to lower the tension not only for ourselves, but also the public who had come from all over the country. In order to give the spectators a show I decreased my speed to allow the Delahaye to catch up a little. Rather stupid really, as I soon realized that should I get any mechanical trouble this 'show' could be costly, so I returned to my senses again. This was a good thing, as Molenaar had almost beaten me for the fastest lap. As it was I cheerfully cake-walked through the remaining laps (6 kilometres each) and the Gatso's grey nose was first to finish having made an average of 61 m.p.h.

The lack of tension, however, was more than made up by the pleasant atmosphere surrounding the handful of drivers who saw their dreams fulfilled, at least to a great extent. There was the greatest enthusiast of them all, Hans Hugenholtz (who would later manage the new Zandvoort circuit) with his faithful old Riley 1100 of which the cigar shape brought back memories of the grand old days. It proudly bore the name Casque as a token of honour to the crack British driver, Sammy Davis. Resplendent in white overalls, Hans, who during the war had considered that missing The Autocar was even worse than the chronic food shortages, was as happy as a child as he walked around his Riley. He was so engrossed in the proceedings that in a great panic he suddenly asked my wife Ciska if she had a wire brush with her, as if things like that are usually found in ladies' handbags. When it came to the actual racing, and Hans had changed his blue 'walking tie' for a yellow 'racing ditto', he gave the Riley such hard treatment that everyone expected to see the car fall apart at any moment. Actually, the courageous Riley heart carried on until the last lap before sighing and giving up, the engine having seized. Concerned that Hans had not arrived, my wife and I ran through the grass at the side of the tarmac until half a mile distant from the finish we saw a red Riley, a white figure beside it with arms raised in dismay. It was a downhearted man who, completely beaten, at first refused to answer our questions, but in the end, with what would one would have thought was his last breath, groaned: "And this is what I have waited for, for nine long years".

When we next saw Hans on a racing circuit, the situation in the Dutch racing world had improved considerably. It was in July, 1949, when the new Zandvoort circuit, of which Hans Hugenholtz was the first manager, had just been completed and so created many new and exciting possibilities for racing in Holland. Not only for Grand Prix races, which for the time being were not for Dutch drivers, but also for our no less exciting battles with sports cars, for which this winding circuit with its splendid tarmac is ideally suited. Of course in 1949 the number of sports cars in our country was not great, and the quality was not top class. Nevertheless, much 'doctoring' and importing parts from England and France had been done, and Hans Hugenholtz had plenty of reason to be pleased about the races organized by the Royal Dutch Automobile Club (K.N.A.C.) on 'his' circuit. An exclusive sportscar day was not yet considered possible, and so these were again combined meetings in co-operation with the Royal Dutch Motorcycle Club (K.N.M.V.) Junior's Day. This meant that due to time restrictions, the

1,100cc and 750cc classes started together, as did the 1,500 and 2,000cc classes. We hadn't been sitting still with our Gatsos. In addition to the 4-litre model we had developed a prototype 1-litre car on a very much modified Fiat six-cylinder chassis. This had a beautifully-streamlined duraluminium body, designed with the help of Jan Apetz, and made by ourselves. The car however - and I know my story gets monotonous - was not quite ready. The chassis, in so far as roadholding was concerned, and the body for its minimum wind-resistance, were all that I could wish for, but the engine had not yet been tuned sufficiently. There was no possibility of obtaining a special cylinder head from Italy, and so we came to the start with an engine barely run-in and still equipped with a single carburettor. Obviously it wasn't wise to start with this un-prepared prototype, but the temptation was just too great. As long as one does these things for the sport only, a lost race is not all bad, being good experience and often very enlightening. In any case, Klaas Barendrecht, my good friend in many tough rallies, was there to defend our colours with his 4-litre Gatso, and so we were full of hope in showing off this new make which was now on the Dutch market. At the practice the 1.5-litre proved to be a troublesome baby. Most peculiar was that with a cold engine it pro-

duced top performance, but by the time the engine was really hot she had lost power. Just what we did experimenting with the car, and trying different wheels in order to find the most favourable gearing, over those two days really defies description. But it could not take away from me the thought that the two most serious competitors in the 1.5-litre class, Richardson with an Alfa Romeo, and Molenaar with an M.G., would prove to be faster, although during practice - with a cold engine! - I had made the fastest lap. Richardson's Alfa Romeo was originally a type Zagato, which had been brought down to 1.5-litres, and in place of the prohibited supercharger it now featured six motor-cycle carburettors. That was a clever piece of 'doctoring', and the blue Alfa with its young but talented driver was very fast. Molenaar's M.G. was a brand new TC model, its engine sounding very spirited and robust.

In the large class, Klaas with his 4-litre Gatso was keen to avenge his defeat in 1939 at the hands of Tielens, who this time had entered a similar but even faster Delahaye. Supporting Klaas was Kees Bloem in my old Gatso roadster. Klaas' Aero-coupé however was the faster of the two, and as he is a top-ranker where dicing is concerned I didn't worry much about him. The night preceding races we worked like slaves, and as in addition to the three Gatsos there was also faithful old 'Smoke' (Piet Nortier's B.M.W.) and Johnny Knegtel's Ford V8 in my workshop, we were extremely busy. Well, the next day told again that nothing is so uncertain as car racing, but I won't anticipate the event now.

Tens of thousands of people had come to the circuit, and the nervous tension in the pits quickly rose to that pitch where nobody can find the wrench he wants, everybody stands on someone else's toes and strong words drown out the noise of exhausts. When eventually we went out for the start, and Richardson, Molenaar and I lined up on the front row, we had barely enough patience to wait for sports marshall Jan Van Haaren's flag to go down. The final seconds went and so did the flag. The spirited rumbling of the engines gave way to thundering exhausts, and we were 'off' as if we had been catapulted. With one eye on the ever so close mudguard belonging to the M.G., and the other on my rev-counter, I accelerated all-out to the most favourable position before entering the Tarzan curve, the first hairpin bend following the start and Molenaar, not expecting so much in the way of fireworks, could only watch my tail - at least for the moment. Leading, I took the Tarzan curve, came out of it broadsiding, accelerated again at full throttle to the nasty little bend behind the pits, took the second hairpin in third and, going up the slope, began to feel a lack of power as the red M.G. flashed past me, followed by the gloriously-humming Alfa Romeo. That's when I realized my chances were not exactly favourable. Nevertheless, I managed to get into the Alfa's slipstream, its suction helping me along very nicely so that on the straight before the grandstand I was able to draw level with them both. The public sensed a battle, and even above the thunder of three exhausts as we shot close together towards the Tarzan curve I could hear the crowd roaring. Again I was leading into the Tarzan, and continued to do so for a little while. But in that nasty little curve behind the pits an overdose of fighting spirit cost me dearly. I went just that bit too fast, and the Gatso skidded broadside. Quick opposite-lock put things right again, but Richardson and Molenaar, who had skillfully avoided me, were by that time yards in front of me. I did what I could in that race, but to no avail. As the engine became hotter and hotter the car became ever slower. With every lap I saw the other two far ahead of me, and I can give everyone the assurance that it is a rotten feeling when you are short of that little bit of extra power with which to keep up with your competitors. I could have kicked the pedal through the floorboards, but that helps little and costs money. There was nothing left for me except to enjoy myself keeping ahead of the remainder of the field, consisting of considerably slower cars. I was even able to lap some of the smaller ones. Richardson, who indeed had the fastest car, stuck nicely to Molenaar's tail until receiving the signal 'full speed' from his pit. He gave the Alfa a little more throttle, and was rewarded with first prize for a first race driven with admirable skill. Molenaar was second and the Gatso third. Laps of 66 m.p.h had been made. There was nothing left but to go to the pits from where I could watch and encourage Klaas Barendrecht and Kees Bloem. Klaas stood on his accelerator and had the lead before anyone realized it. To believe it one needed to have seen the way my pal took that heavy car through the curves. Even in the hairpins the Gatso did not slide an inch further out of line than the driver intended, and as the grey car stormed up the hill there was joy and satisfaction in the Gatso pit. It took another two-and-a-half minutes before the grey car appeared again at the beginning of the straight. Or rather: a grey car, for it was not Klaas' Gatso which was in the lead, but Tielen's grey Delahaye triumphantly in front. Gone was our joy, and everyone was stretching his neck to see if the next approaching dot in the distance was the Gatso. But the Gatso had vanished, and remained so as our initial disappointment quickly turned to worry. Thousands of questions raced through our minds. Somersault, left the track at a bend, collision, fire......? All are possibilities, and the worst of it is that you can't go and find out what's wrong. One simply has to wait with the cruel uncertainty inside. Nobody in the pits wants to show their worry at such a moment, but everyone's face is an open book. The mood in the grandstand too was excitable, and although Piet Nortier continued to talk cheerfully over the microphone, we could see him watching that far-away curve from where the cars appeared. Minutes went by and still no news, then from the grandstand, where the occupants had a better view, a cheering rose, a relieved cheering. Fifteen seconds later Barendrecht flashed by as if the devil and all his disciples were chasing him. But as he passed the pits at 105 m.p.h. he found time to shake his fist and point to the bonnet. Our brief joy and relief was inevitably tempered with disappointment, it really is hard to bear when some silly little fault spoils a race for your stable. Nevertheless, Klaas, hopelessly behind, didn't give up. He fought like a lion, and at least had the satisfaction of establishing the fastest lap of the day at an average of 69 m.p.h.

Even so, after the race it was a very sad Klaas who came to the infield. He got out, lifted the bonnet without saying a word and pointed to the fuel filter glass. This had a cork gasket, which had been leaking because it had not been screwed down tightly enough. But even such a small fault needs time to be found. Klaas told us of his fury when, half way through the first lap the Gatso suddenly spluttered and stopped. One of a thousand-and-one small, but fatal traps which can so easily cause the driver to stumble and lose the race. It was little consolation that Van Der Tuyn, driving in the 2-litre class, and who had fought for and gained an excellent position then saw his chances disappear. He had simply forgotten to take of a cloth which he had draped over the radiator of his B.M.W. for the pre-race warming up lap, and in the race he was forced into the pits with an overheated engine. "It's all in the game", as they say.

The Gatso 1500 'Flatty' with Gatso himself at the wheel, establishing a Dutch one-hour endurance record for 1.5-litre cars, at the Zandvoort circuit in November 1949. 'Flatty' covered 63.7 miles in the hour, with a fastest lap speed of 65.4 m.p.h.

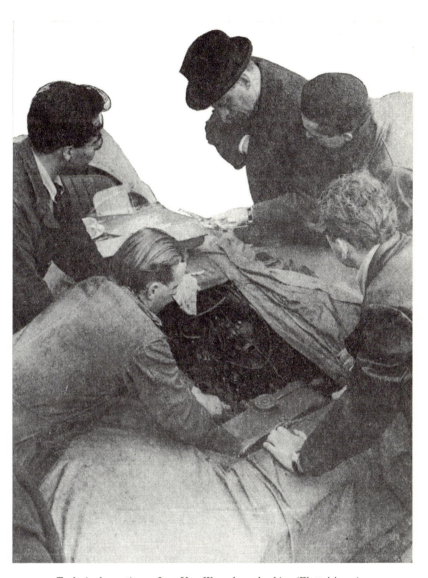

Technical scrutineer Joop Van Wamelen, checking 'Flatty's' engine cylinder capacity after establishing the one-hour record at Zandvoort.

Chapter 15

Monte Carlo Rally 1949, the first after World War II

> About a valuable intuition: a bad stomach: eel sandwiches: a first prize: and a cup which had to be returned.

It was not until 1949 that the Monte Carlo Rally reawakened from the deep sleep it had been in throughout the war. It had taken an additional four long years before the political situation had become conducive to the staging of such an event once again. Four years before foreign exchange, and other restrictions were relaxed sufficiently enough so that Mr. Anthony Noghès felt confident that it could at last take place. During those four years many enthusiasts at home and abroad had been restless indeed, spending much time recalling the good old wild and carefree days, when car spares were ten a penny and the costs of the damage to the cars incurred in numerous incidents on the glorious rallies from Athens and Umea were hardly counted. Damage of all kinds was most liberally handed-out by the Holy St. Christopher in those pre-war Montes, which at that time were indeed Grandes Epreuves de Tourisme, and of which that fascinating name of the most important of all rallies - although it was not actually quite the hardest - was truly deserved on the bumpy desert roads of Greece, or the barren ice-fields of the North. In 1949 all of that was no more. The Iron Curtain was in place, effectively cutting off for the time being our former motorsport friends in Czechoslovakia, Poland, Yugoslavia and the more distant countries which had now come under communist rule. Only Prague could still be used as a starting point, apart from which the Rally was restricted entirely to Western Europe. The shortening now of the pre-war 3,600 kilometre distance also excluded

Umea, and so, beforehand, it could be seen that this Rally was likely to be little more than a rather tough pleasure trip, or perhaps just a classifying test after a 3,000 kilometre run. This could be seen in the quality of the entry list, which appeared to be rather too civilized in parts, with all kinds of people who would not have known what to do in an ordinary map-reading trial, now thirsting for some post-war adventure. That didn't stop us from having great pleasure making careful preparations for our trip to the sunny south. When I say 'us' I mean my faithful rally mate Klaas Barendrecht and myself, who were keen to know how far we would get with our new Hillman Minx. I had of course tuned it up somewhat, and although only of 1,185cc it had now become a quite spirited, albeit rather thirsty little Minx, for that little acceleration and top speeds was duly represented on the fuel bill.

Although this time we were denied the extra points and the adventures of a Balkans' start, it was with considerable pleasure that we left in convoy for Monte Carlo and the start. It was indeed quite a procession as in addition to the Minx and our luggage car, a Chevrolet, we had joined up with a 1.5-litre Riley crewed by Gijs Pollé, Henk Luyting, Han Van Splunter, and Captain Adriaan Van Splunter. They didn't mind all competing together in one car, but the Riley was less happy about the situation, its undersides almost touching the ground under the weight of four men and plenty of rally luggage. I had advised them not to go four up, but they didn't want one of them left behind. On arrival at Monte Carlo however they had realized it could not be done, and so drew lots for someone to stay behind. Henk Luyting was the unlucky one, who sportingly accepted the decision, and despite not being able to speak French did in fact thoroughly enjoy his forced stay in the casino town. The Riley crew gained a lot of experience on the journey from Holland to Monte Carlo, as we let them find the way by studying their maps and driving in front of us. This is a recommendable procedure.

Once there we found that atmosphere peculiar to rallies. All the pre-ware aces were present again, and that was reason enough to organize many festivities, although even all those pleasures were not able to take our attention away from the great event about to take place. And when, on that glorious night, it became our turn to start, we immediately had the unique feeling once again of actually being 'in' the Rally. It is a strange feeling brought on by the knowledge that human beings and machines are about to be severely tested along the 3,000 kilometre route lying ahead. For the next few days a thousand

and one little things are waiting to spoil the broth, and you can be absolutely sure that some of them will come right to you. But against that you know you will be able to count on your team-mate throughout the forthcoming tiring days and sleepless nights. And above all there is that adventurous tingling inside you, and the adventure is beckoning both novice and veteran alike. Then there is the hope that you will make good, so that at the end on that dirt-streaked muddy bonnet which you have seen in front of you for seemingly endless hours, there will be hung a laurel trophy, a trophy which will never be won by the faint-hearted.

It was exactly twenty-three minutes past midnight when with a pleasant exhaust rumble our Minx shot away into the dark night. It was unseasonably mild weather, and so I was only lightly dressed, which is always stupid in a rally, and this time resulted in me catching a cold which nearly caused our failure. Climbing from Grasse into the Maritime Alpes we quickly realized that the roads were already slippery with ice, so that we had to be careful now not to end the Rally, and indeed ourselves prematurely, as a drop into a ravine can quickly shut a lot of doors behind one, sometimes even that of the family grave.

It was not without a dark foreboding that, when topping a slope, we saw a fierce burning. "That's one burning", we said simultaneously, and down went the accelerator of the Hillman as we raced forward to offer first aid. We went faster and faster, but the red glow always seemed to be one mountain further ahead. It was a relief to our helpful souls to find out in the end that the expected burning wreck was the Northern Lights playing a trick on us. Later though, a little further along we could exercise our desire to always give help, when alongside the road we saw the stricken Delahaye of Yvonne Simon and Germaine Rouault. The engine of the Delahaye was not receiving any petrol, and of course we searched diligently for the trouble in the hope of getting the girls going again. In the end we fitted a complete new fuel pump. Germaine and Yvonne, who had their eyes on the Coupe des Dames, were frightened out of their wits that some other competitor might see them receiving male assistance and give the game away. Each time another car approached they went into a chorus of French yelling and we played 'hide and seek'. However, without petrol they would definitely not win the cup, although it later proved that they would not anyway, for it went to Holland's Duchess Van Limburg Stirum. It was noticeable to us, by the way, that there was very little urge in other male drivers to assist those damsels in distress. The whole affair had cost us eighteen minutes, and we had to dice like mad in order to arrive at Digne on time. There had been no time left to refuel our car, so that after checking in at the control, we went back to a pump situated just before there. After refuelling we turned round and drove past the control again, causing some shouting from those who hadn't realized what we had done, and who thought that only those stupid Dutch could miss a well-marked control point!

At Grenoble we had plenty of time again. From there we carried on via Annécy (oh, sweet memories of the sunny Alpine Rally) to the frontier, but before crossing it we stopped for ten minutes at the monastery La Grande Chartreuse, which was another sweet memory itself. It was regrettable, but certainly not advisable to combine the liquid produced there by the monks with the driving required for the Rally average. At Geneva we met the Florence starters, who had not had things particularly easy. At some forsaken Italian spot several trucks had collided and completely blocked the snowy road. British crack drivers including Tommy Wisdom, Donald Healey, and Geoff Imhof had been stuck there and lost so much time that they were forced to drop out. Meanwhile we were beginning to find that it really was winter. To save weight we had no heater in the car, and were now learning something of what it must be like on an Antarctic expedition.

We continued to Strasbourg via Bern, where a couple of over-zealous French officials nearly spoilt everything for us. At the control we went as usual to the restaurant where the control is situated, and where hungry and thirsty souls are being revived. As on this section we had gained some time we parked the Hillman Minx between the 'parc fermé' and the control post, which was not in accordance with the ideas of the officials who said that as we had arrived we should hand over our route card. However as we had gained more time than the maximum average allowed I kept tight hold of the card, and pointed out that I had not crossed any line or been in the closed park, and therefore had not officially arrived yet. The Frenchmen got quite cross, threatening us with all kinds of recriminations, including disqualification. But we stuck to our guns, and so the situation developed into one of those lively discussions which make life in France so attractive, and we eventually won the argument. On the second night of the Rally we went from Strasbourg to Luxembourg over roads which only in France seem so long. At Thionville we were cheered up when we saw in our headlights a big Swiss-registered Kaiser standing horselike, with its four wheels across a dry ditch. How it got there was not clear, neither was how it would get out of the situation, which is always the most troublesome part. We couldn't solve it, for our Hillman simply wasn't suitable for such tractor jobs. It was certainly a peculiar sight for one could walk underneath it, which we did of course.

At Luxembourg we learned that the starters from Britain were late. But we started on time for our trip now through the Ardennes, which with their winding and undulating roads keep the sleep out of your eyes. Our lights swept over the ruined houses of Bastogne and La Houffalize, where the Americans held out against the furious onslaught of the Nazi regime. At that moment we remembered the time not so very long before, when the noise of the exhausts of the big G.M.C. American trucks, full of tired but brave G.I.s echoed against the walls of these Ardennes villages. Even as a rally driver, one suddenly felt very small indeed. Black ice was encountered on the road just before Liège, but the slippery conditions didn't kill our joy. We usually hurried whenever approaching Liège because at the Motor Union de Liège Klaas and I always enjoyed looking at the photographs there taken during the pre-war Liège-Rome-Liège rallies, from which we have such sweet memories. Friend Maurice Garot and his staff almost overloaded us with sandwiches and drinks. It was all very cosy, but the time soon came for us to be hurrying onwards to Holland. Through Visé and Venlo we made our way to Amsterdam. We were followed in by several competing French cars, and also the Tatra of our pre-war Czechoslovakian friend Formaneck. We were able to assist the Czech crews and officials with their language difficulties etc., and built up much goodwill between us. (This goodwill was to prove beneficial the following year, resulting me in driving a Czechoslovakian-entered Aéro Minor in the Le Mans 24 hours race: the full story is in chapter 18.) It was daylight when we arrived in Amsterdam, and I saw my son Tommy, who with his rally step parents (Ciska was waiting in Monte Carlo) had risen early to encourage his dad. At the control point at the Apollo Hall the Van Splunter Brothers told me they were pulling out due to clutch failure on their Riley. I advised them to immediately get in touch with the Riley importer, who managed things for them so quickly that the Riley arrived at the Brussels control dead on time. Over the very slippery Dutch roads - two French ladies managed to land their car in a ditch near Utrecht - we went on to The Hague, where Klaas' family was waiting for us with a carload of food. Also there was our friend Theo Van Ellinkhuizen who seemed to have bought the whole country's egg production, and so much salt that we had enough to keep our screen ice-free for the remainder of the Rally. No less than eight men from the Hillman importer in The

Hague were there to lubricate and wash our Minx, before we rushed off to the Belgian frontier. There, at Wernhout, the Customs officers with whom by this time I was quite familiar, promised us a brass band if we should return with a prize. At Brussels we had a few minutes to visit the Gatso stand at the Motor Show, and shake hand with Jan Apetz and his three assistants manning the stand.

We reached Reims with still more time in hand, and were able to enjoy the warm welcome by the Automobile Club de Champagne, which did honour to its name. Over long straight roads, but with many climbs and descents, we went to Paris, where many competitors had difficulty in finding the control in the centre of the town and arrived too late.

From Paris Klaas took the wheel for the first turn of the last long stretch to Monte Carlo, and in the bitter cold we faced the South for a stage which not for the first time held a few unpleasant surprises. These started at Nevers, where the always badly organized control post was besieged by a crowd of rally drivers whose nerves were badly frayed due to tiredness, cold and discomfort. It was a proper push and elbowing party in the narrow passage as everyone was attempting to get his roadbook stamped in time. It became even more unpleasant when I began to feel sick with fever, shivering like a dog. I felt colder than an ice-cream, and sitting shivering under a rug I damned the Rally and all its organizers. Back on the road my stomach continually showed signs of a desire to turn itself inside out. My feelings of wanting to vomit grew worse when Klaas became hungry for eggs. If I remember correctly he ate thirteen of them, and I had to hide them from him. Wow, under those circumstances does a hard boiled egg smell!! All the time I was praying to heaven that he wouldn't get an appetite for the smoked eel sandwiches. I prayed in vain. But when he asked for a smoked eel sandwich I simply felt too rotten to grab a monkey wrench. However, those eggs and eels seemed to have given Klaas wings, as he skillfully drove the Hillman right across the Massif Central to Lyon. Just before Lyon came another 'treat' in the form of a thick fog which quickly froze to the windscreen. Although I know the town very well we passed the control on the Saône quay three times before eventually finding it in that pea soup. We didn't even see the river, and continued round and round having no idea of where we were. Even Klaas' resilience came to an end, and with the courage of the condemned I took the wheel for the last lap. A miracle (aided by a Pervitine pill) happened. Bitter necessity stopped my stomach from further acrobatics, and feeling lots better I began the difficult task.

Kitchen salt and newspapers keeping two small spots free from the freezing rain.

And difficult it was! Immediately outside Lyon the windscreen wipers froze to the thick layer of ice on the screen. We took the right-side wiper off to give the other a little more power, and using our salt managed to keep two small spots free of ice. It was a hell of a job driving to schedule, and was sometimes only possible in that freezing fog by keeping the wipers going with our heads out of the side windows. This way we passed many competitors who then tried to hang to our tail, and so we came to the Rhône Valley, which lay below us under a thick layer of cloud. Above this, at the top of the hills the sun was shining, but we had to get down through the clouds to the valley below, a descent which for us was like blind-flying in a car. It was something which I was not keen about having to do ever again, although many times in the future we would indeed be faced with a similar descent. It was not until the control at Valence that our sufferings were at last behind us, and from there it was only a fleabite to Monte Carlo. Across the Col de Cabre we flew to the Digne time control, and then over the Col des Lègues via Grasse to Monte Carlo. Before the finish our wives were waiting for us with the Chevrolet luggage-car on the Moyenne Corniche. We put all that we could spare now into the Chevrolet, in order to arrive at the closed park with the Minx as lightly loaded as possible in readiness for the classifying test. Sunny Monte Carlo smiled at us, but as I was suffering from some form of reaction following my temporary revival, I went to bed with a shipload of quinine in my stomach in the hope of being somewhat fitter for the test.

 I had already had a brainwave about this test even before the start in Monte Carlo. The particulars issued about the secret circuit stated that it was 17.1 kilometres long, that it had to be driven three times, and that enough petrol for 75 kilometres had to be in the tank. The first time round the circuit was for reconnaissance and not timed. The circuit was split into three sections of respectively 3.5, 3.5, and 10.1 kilometres, and on the second and third times round the 3.5. km sections were timed in 10ths of second, and had to be covered as quickly as possible, but also in equal times. The third section had a larger margin which did not influence the penalties. In bed I had been thinking where that route might be. After studying a detailed map I reached the conclusion that it had to be on the Mont des Mules. As the Minx was of course locked away in the closed park, we went to the Mont des Mules in the Chevrolet and practiced diligently in every curve. My intuition hadn't deceived me. The time controls were almost to within a yard of where I had thought they might be. I decided - again purely to save weight - to drive the test unaccompanied, ours being the only crew out of the best 100 finishers from the road section to do this on the test. However, it was a decision which I'm afraid did rather upset Klaas. But saving weight was vital if I wanted to have any chance against the much faster Lancias, Jowett Javelins and some other potential winners in the same 1.5-litre class. I took with me my precious piece of wood with the three chronometers attached, which I would have to handle myself during the test. Well during the practice lap I did the most difficult of the two special 3.5 kilometre sections in 4 minutes and 10 seconds, and so decided to set myself at 4 minutes 8 seconds in the actual test.

There isn't really much to tell about it - I succeeded beyond expectation. With hands and eyes being distributed equally over the steering wheel and clocks I started, and away went the little sidevalve Hillman. I can only remember that I drove as never before. The faster I diced through the curves of the Mont des Mules, the more the French public enjoyed it. The first, and easiest of the two 3.5 kilometre sections I did in 3 minutes 12 seconds, and so stopped before the line. I waited until the chronometer showed 4 minutes and 3 seconds and then drove off again over the line. This was repeated in the following 3.5 km section, and then once again in the next round. When it was all over I had made 4 minutes 7 seconds, 4.8, 4.7, and 4.8. I was well satisfied with that, as to judge by what the others were saying it was plain they were not so consistent. It was late in the evening before the test had been completed by all the qualifiers, and not until late the next day before the results - some of which would unfortunately later prove to be incorrect - were announced. You can be sure that I am not usually a tearful type, but when the news came through that the team Gatsonides-Barendrecht in a Hillman Minx had won first prize in the 1.5-litre class I went out alone to swallow the lump in my throat. This, you see, was one dream fulfilled. Probably not so very important, but at the same time absolutely marvelous, as I was so proud to have done this in a class in which our car was somewhat prematurely considered to have no chance at all. We were presented with a genuine-silver cup by the Prince of Monaco, together with a decent sum of money. With our French friends the Angelvins, who had won first prize in the 750cc class, for celebration purposes we exchanged the money for champagne in the Sporting Club.

The next day however not only our heads whirled (champagne), but that also of the Rally Organizers (protests). It had just simply rained protests! Soon it became apparent that the organization of this first post-war Monte Carlo Rally was considerably flawed. With every new protest lodged, competitors names went up and down the results list in great leaps. The calculations were almost completely wrong and practically every protest was accepted. Some who claimed they had been classified too low went up ten places on the list.

Next morning, after we had loaded our luggage and enjoyed a last coffee before departing we received a phone call from Anthony Noghès, informing us that the British Jowett Javelin driver, Tom Wise, had protested against the decision in the 1.5-litre class. We were told that we would have to hand the cup back, and I thought it darned lucky that the money was already spent. Noghès had been forced to agree with the important leading official Charles Faroux who had decided in Wise's favour. When we told him that it was not right to ask for the return of a prize already given out, after consulting a no longer valid copy of the Code Sportif (dated 1937, instead of the revised edition of 1939) Faroux still maintained the trophy had to go to Wise.

The use by Faroux of the wrong edition of the Sporting Code was only found out later by the Dutch sports marshall Jan Van Haaren, who, unfortunately for us, had already left Monte Carlo for Holland on the day after the Rally results were announced, and so was not able to act on our behalf when the protest, which according to the regulations was too late, eventually came. (In the regulations for every international event the procedure is clearly noted, giving competitors usually a period of between 6 and 24 hours within which to enter a protest following the publication of the provisional results, after which the results cannot be changed.)

Some weeks later at home in Bentveld we heard from our Automobile Club that they had received a letter from Anthony Noghès in which he openly stated that his decision had been wrong: "But now it is really too late" he wrote. But we did not wish now to appeal at the

French Automobile Club, because although Wise had lodged his protest outside the time limit, it transpired that he had indeed made the best test.

After being presented with the Silver Cup for 1st place in the 1.5-litre class Gatso is interviewed by B.B.C. reporter, Peter Stevens. The presentation was made by Prince Rainier of Monaco, who can be seen seated at the top left of the picture. At the top right is Charles Faroux, who intervened the following day. Incorrectly according to the FINA rules.

An advertisement by the Dutch Rootes car importers for the Hillman Minx following the 1949 Monte Carlo Rally.

Chapter 16

Monte Carlo Rally 1950

Through snow and ice, fog and gale to the sunny South.

It was no doubt due to the success Klaas and I had with my Hillman Minx in the Monte Carlo Rally in 1949, that Rootes suggested that I take a Humber Super Snipe saloon on the 1950 Monte. With its tough mountain classifying tests, the Rally had gradually become a matter of power-to-weight ratio, and in all fairness the comfortable Super Snipe, with its great weight (36 cwt unladen) propelled by a 4-litre sidevalve engine of 95 b.h.p. couldn't be expected to compete with special prepared, much lighter and more powerful cars. Quite honestly, I mentally prepared both myself and Humber's director Loyd Dixon for jus a reasonable result, and to have only a look from some distance at the many desirable cups which were meant to go to the favourites. However, providence and the Weather Gods were to decree otherwise in the end, although of course we didn't know that beforehand, which was all for the best.

I must begin however by introducing the car and crew. The Humber Super Snipe was an absolutely standard rather majestic looking 1950 model, without any special accessories, and with its engine in the catalogued state of tune. It only carried a limited rally outfit, and the most important instrument we felt was the large alarm clock which would serve to wake the crew when it was time to start from the controls. On each side of its long nose the Humber displayed a small English and a Dutch flag. The English one being in honour of Bobby Spencer, an enthusiastic 19 year old apprentice at the Rootes factory in Coventry, whom I had invited to join Klaas Barendrecht and myself who made up the rest of the crew. Because of continuing

151

foreign currency exchange difficulties even in 1950, we decided to tow a caravan down to Monte Carlo in which our ladies could live for the four days whilst we were away on the Rally. A fancy-dress head piece which we fixed to the door of the caravan resulted in it being christened 'The Bull's Head', and the whole caravan idea would have been very practical if only Monte Carlo had blessed us with its normal climate. Unfortunately though it turned out to be so beastly cold that the ladies were soon forced to move to a (rather cheap) nearby hotel. The fact that we chose Monte Carlo itself again as our starting point had nothing at all to do with the Casino.

Although once again 'secret', we guessed the final classifying test would be held over the same 17 kilometre route including de Monte des Mules, where the previous year we had gained much experience with the Hillman Minx. Naturally we did some practicing through the hairpin curves to see how the big Super Snipe would take them, and the experience we gained to the detriment of our tyres, was nevertheless to prove extremely useful later on because the classifying test was indeed again staged over the same circuit. It was a clean and nicely polished Humber which checked in at the start during the night of January 20th for what was to prove the toughest Monte Carlo Rally so far. We were warmly dressed, and had plenty of faith that this Rally would end well. The weather was dry, and we had no worries as our big comfortable car began the long trip which would stretch to some 2,000 miles.

One crew who did have early worries were our fellow countrymen, Prins, and Van Herk, whose Jaguar collided with another, non-competing car, which crossed in front of them in Nice, only fifteen miles from the start. We stopped to see if something could be done, but one look underneath the front of the Jaguar revealed a bent steering wheel. Carrying on again, we occasionally encountered rather nasty slippery little bits of road in the mountains. It didn't bother Betty Haig in her M.G., for she passed us at a speed suggesting she was late to catch the last train! This devil-may-care driving however was to be her ondoing on one of the icy northern slopes. We found her M.G. balanced precariously on a wall separating the road from a ravine. With some difficulty, even with the help of a long tow-rope, we managed to pull the M.G. back onto the road again. But that skid had finished Betty Haig's Rally, as the car had a broken kingpin, which is not a spare part usually carried in one's pocket. There was nothing else to do but wish her a pleasant holiday in Monte Carlo.

Dutch class-winners Hans Van Der Heyden and Ies Langestraat with their Panhard at the Monte Carlo start.
These small Panhards won their class in several events during 1950.

Without further incident we reached Digne. That was the first time-control, with the inevitable French black coffee which resembles real coffee in so far as colour is concerned. After that Klaas took the wheel for the drive to Grenoble. However pleasant driving along good smooth roads may be, we soon had a longing for some rougher going such as we had been forced to contend with immediately in our two pre-war starts from Athens. Now, crossing the Swiss frontier we didn't even have to stop, which was very decent of the officials concerned.

The next stop was in Geneva where at the Automobile Club passage control we were presented with a very hospitable breakfast. This consisted of soup, rolls, a world famous brand of chocolate, and coffee. On the Quay de Mont Blanc it must be admitted that the bitter cold of that dark winter morning offset the gastronomic pleasures just a little. Later that day we arrived at the time control in Bern, where we had plenty of time which we used to have special snow grooves cut into our rear tyres, and of which we would benefit greatly later on. Driving on into France the Super Snipe tirelessly covered more than 100 kilometres in an hour over the long straight road to Strasbourg. Klaas and I took turns to sleep, but not so Bobby Spencer who was finding everything so fascinating on this, his first rally. Even our threatening to send him to sleep with the aid of a wrench didn't have any effect. He would regret it later.

At around 4 o'clock we entered Strasbourg, where a lovely meal of snails, and wines from the Alsace region awaited us. Perhaps all this talk about food and drink seems out of the place in the story of such a tough event as the Monte. But I can assure the reader that the man who keeps his stomach well-filled and who can snatch some sleep whenever he gets the chance, even when his team-mate is driving at sixty miles per hour or more along winding roads, is half way there to a successful outcome. At Luxembourg we met the Glasgow contingent, and had to endure some friendly teasing from the Rootes team members in Sunbeam Talbots. They respectfully, but not without a little scepticism, doffed their caps to big brother Humber, which they expected not to arrive at Monte Carlo until a few weeks later. "A very nice car", someone said appreciatingly, "I'll buy one when I am eighty". Within a week he would be making enquiries about its price, but that's another story.

From Luxembourg we drove along the winding roads through the dark forests of the Ardennes, with the broad sweeps from the headlights finding the way to Liège for the big Humber. At the Motor Union de Liège we once again had a little spiritual uplift, refreshing our memories by looking at the photos of the glorious long-gone days of the pre-war Liège-Rome-Liège rallies. The Belgian Rootes organization welcomed us with extensive service facilities, which we didn't really need as the Humber was running like a precision watch. Refreshed again, we carried on to Holland.

Although the Customs are perhaps a little more strict than elsewhere, crossing the border into Holland is always one of the most pleasant moments of the Rally. One feels on familiar ground again, and all the Dutch crews drive flat out trying to be the first to reach Amsterdam. Also spurred on by that desire we made the disgraceful average of 63 m.p.h., but it was of no avail as our countryman Verkamman Van Keulen, who had in fact started twenty-five minutes ahead of us, had pushed his Vauxhall hard enough to arrive there a few minutes before us. It was fortunate indeed that the Amsterdam police had kept their eyes closed to the speed excesses. A warm cheering from the many who had braved the bitter cold of the night greeted the drivers at the Apollo Hotel, and it took some time to get through the crowd of well-wishers, some known to us but many not, who surrounded the control post. My children, watching the gathering with big sleepy eyes were there with their rally step parents, son Tommy was already counting the eleven years separating him from the age of 18 when he can have his driving licence. When we got in to the restaurant Bobby Spencer finally succumbed to the enemy - sleep. He was busily engaged tucking into a large portion of ham and eggs when suddenly his eyelids, which he had somehow kept open for 36 hours, dropped firmly shut. It happened to him with a mouth full of food, but that didn't stop him snoring loudly enough to make the building tremble. Leaving Amsterdam at daybreak we took the familiar arterial road to The Hague. It was there, so close to home, that I reflected on the seeming absurdity of first driving from Holland to Monte Carlo, then back to Holland, back again to Monte Carlo, and finally to return home to Holland again all within a fortnight.

At The Hague control we had a short rest during which car and crew were both lubricated. Then we pointed the green nose of the Super Snipe towards Brussels, where Mr. R. Spencer senior, Rootes Continental Director, was waiting to boost the crew's spirits with cold chicken and Vienna steak, enquiring at the same time if dear 'sonny' was any trouble. So far the monotony of this chapter does I'm afraid reflect the monotony of the Rally. It may be very nice to drive through half of Europe, shaking hands with all sorts of friends old and new, without meeting any more serious a problem than sleeping under a rug which is a few feet too short. But that kind of rally driving is hardly worth the trouble of getting red-rimmed eyes for. However, that situation was about to change. Hardly had we been guided through Paris by motor-cycle 'flics' (police) with their screaming whistles, when we heard the first rumours that heavy snow was expected. Not yet knowing how bad it was going to be, we cheerfully poked each other in the ribs. All the time we had been waiting for bad weather conditions which we hoped would make many competitors' clean sheets rather dirty. And indeed, by the time we arrived at the Nevers control-post the roads were becoming slippery. Many rally cars were skidding on the frozen cobbles which led to the café where two nervous officials were beleaguered by a crowd of drivers who themselves were hurriedly becoming nervous. With Klaas at the wheel I felt safe enough to have a little nap.

Half an hour later I was rudely awakened by a couple of punches in the ribs of which Joe Louis would have been proud. An incredulous Klaas was looking ahead, muttering "It looks like a blinking Christmas tree". It certainly did. On the slope some way ahead the road was illuminated by dozens of red lights, but they didn't invoke any festive feelings. On the contrary, we pretty soon realized they were the tail lights of many rally cars which had become well and truly struck in the snow on that hill. Klaas, who is the last person to give up in such situations, simply put his foot down hard and accelerated the Super Snipe, which shot up the hill past fifteen or so stranded cars before our joy was ended by two cars completely blocking the road. He braked to a stop, but that didn't last long, as the heavy Humber immediately began sliding backwards and came to rest with one wheel in a ditch. We quickly got out our snow chains and lengths of rope which I also carried to tie round the wheels for better grip. But we had neglected to do any practices as regards fitting them, and in the difficult situation the car was in it took us about 55 minutes of hard work and bad language before getting going again. And it hadn't been pleasant work either. The drivers of other cars which had got going from below didn't seem to notice the assortment of Dutch and British legs sticking out into the road from underneath the Humber. Wet, cold and dirty, we climbed back into the car again, and Klaas calmly announced that he was going to catch up some lost time. That was sufficient reason for me to close my eyes again, but not for want of sleep this time. The way in which Klaas raced that huge car over the snowy and icy roads at a speed which didn't drop below 65 miles per hour was of course well worth watching, but not from the passenger seat! With his hands lightly on the wheel, and his right foot on the floorboard he whisked the car over snow and ice as if it were a sports car.

One of the many which dropped out between Nevers and Grasse.

With his face beaming as though he were on a pleasant cycling trip, time and again he shot past slower moving cars.

Eventually, making the situation a little more difficult, despite the fact that we had fixed an additional screen heater strip next to the usual defroster, we now got ice forming on the windscreen. That was when I praised the British sunshine roof, because through the open roof, with my cap turned backwards, I could reach out and with wetted newspaper rub salt on to the screen without Klaas having to reduce speed. It was no joke though to poke one's head out of the top at that speed and temperature.

Well, Klaas pulled it off. We arrived in Lyon with seven minutes to spare, and the wild ride had been such that when Klaas removed his flying suit clouds of steam hid his happy face. Then it was my turn to prove something in that Polar-like night, and I took over for another drive which I shall never forget. On the main road from Lyon to Valence endless queues of trucks in both directions were struggling between Paris and Marseilles, and rally driving became a matter of dodging them. In the light of our headlamps we saw many overturned cars, and occasionally a sonorous rumble announced another victim. In one way or another most of the time I managed to keep to the centre of the road and out of trouble. We had half an hour in hand at Digne, but whilst there made a disappointing discovery. The snow chains, which had been treated unmercifully for almost 400 kilometres were jus about worn out, and we were forced to remove them rather than risk a breakage on the road and have them wrapped around some vital part underneath. There was a furious snowstorm that winter morning, and never had Monte Carlo seemed so far away.

The big Humber making good progress, going as fast as possible on the frozen snow between Nevers and Grasse.

Under those conditions we ascended the mountains with millions of snowflakes swirling towards us in a never ending chase. Visibility became so bad that we couldn't see the road signs, and as the kilometre stones were also covered it was impossible to know where we were, and how far it was to Grasse. At such moments we would have gladly traded all we had for a little security, because the only thing we knew of for sure were the ravines, sometimes on both sides of the road. In those circumstances we couldn't go fast. Up the Col de Lègues we did little more than about 25 miles per hour, which was seven below the required average. Fortunately, due to excellent grip and the perfect brakes on the Humber, we were able to come down much faster, reaching 65 miles per hour along the straight stretches. The fact that we were almost ahead of the Rally queue satisfied us a little, although the big snowploughs clearing the roads made a totally carefree drive impossible. A very happy crew arrived at the Grasse control with two minutes in hand as one of only six remaining penalty-free cars. And from there to Monte Carlo was only the proverbial fleabite. Nevertheless, when we came to the finish still without loss of marks, we somehow felt no reason to boast. As others came in we saw and heard just how difficult it had been for many participants. The number of dented and damaged cars was countless and we heard the most awful stories. Many had been forced to give up between Nevers and Grasse. The Delahaye of a Dutch couple dropped into a ravine, and after falling forty yards down it came to rest against a tree just long enough to enable the car crew to get out. After they left the car did slid down another two hundred yards, having reduced itself to scrap before finally coming to rest. Even a crack like Chiron, whom to his fury we had overtaken on the inside of the last hairpin just before

B.B.C. reporter Peter Stevens interviews Gatso after his toughest ever Monte drive, in an 'unsuitable' car.

Grasse, didn't finish with a clean sheet. Then we heard that only five crews had survived to Monte Carlo unpenalised. Of the six still penalty-free cars at Grasse, Sidney Allard, who was destined to win the Monte two years later (1952) had suffered engine trouble on the last easy stage, resulting in 'expensive' lost marks.

We certainly had plenty of reasons to be satisfied, and this satisfaction grew when Klaas managed to make the fastest time of the 'clean sheeters' in the brake-acceleration test (22.7 secs.). He could have done better if I had not delayed him by doubting whether he had passed the line or not. Whilst practicing the identical manoeuvre at Zandvoort before the Rally Klaas had consistently produced times of 21 seconds. Not once however did our satisfaction turn into optimism. A child could work out that the Humber, with its 95 b.h.p. sidevalve engine and 36cwt unladen weight, was no match for the Hotchkiss Grand Sport of Becquart and Secrèt, who had 150 b.h.p. with which to propel their 30cwt car. There was the possibility also of course that the other three unpenalised cars, three fast, much lighter and more

Left to right: Henri Secrèt and Marcel Becquart (winners), Klaas Barendrecht and Maurice Gatsonides ('moral winners'), and Pierre Lahaye (former winner) discussing who will win in 1950.

agile Simca Sports, driven by experts Scaron, Quinlin, and Angelvin, could beat the large Super Snipe in the speed and regularity test on the Mont des Mules. We knew that Becquart had been practicing all year for this one Rally, and that his organization was well nigh perfect. And yet that one spark of hope remained in our hearts that the Hotchkiss crew might just drop a stitch in the test. Personally I felt pretty certain of our performance, for where this test was concerned I had left nothing to chance. That spark of hope (I should have known better) was still with me when I went to bed that night, tired, but happy. Could we win the Rally?

The next day there was a fine drizzle, and Monte Carlo looked rather miserable when the only five cars in the huge closed park left to tackle the Mont des Mules. My concentration was like never before. The tension was terrific. Friends came from all directions to wish us the luck which we needed badly. The cars set off at one-minute intervals, and the moment came at last when the Hotchkiss started. When I saw the Frenchman shooting away up to the hill to do a faultless test I knew we were beaten, and that our hopes for that 'one little mistake' had been in vain. I did my utmost on that wet mountain circuit, and the Humber gave all it had. But it wasn't enough. Becquart had covered the four deciding sections in 3.32, 3.36., 3.34, and 3.36 respectively, whilst our Super Snipe did the same in 3.54, 3.56., 3.55, and 3.55. Naturally at such moments a thousand 'ifs' enter one's mind. If we had done the brake-acceleration test in our Zandvoort practice time we would have won the Rally. And if......but we hadn't. We simply lost the first place. And we couldn't really complain about the co-operation from Lady Luck even though she hadn't supplied us with the 1 point we were short on Becquart's total of 45.2. However, there was one thing to comfort us even more than the huge Barclays Bank Cup (for the highest-placed British car) and the numerous other cups and prizes which were stacked of us. A French pal, André Claude, sent us a telegram which read: "Congratulations on your second place, being worth more than many easy victories". We were very proud also at the prize giving ceremony, when in an unprecedented gesture towards a second-place crew, the organizers arranged for the playing of the Dutch National Anthem, in recognition of our achievement with what everybody knew was really a most unlikely rally car. For me this result would prove to be a great help in regards future contacts with - mainly British - car manufacturers.

RALLYE DE MONTE CARLO 1950:

1e in het algemeen klassement de heren Bequart en Secret met

HOTCHKISS de auto die de Rallyes wint.

Zes maal werd de Hotchkiss overwinnaar in de belangrijkste der internationale automobielwedstrijden, de Rallye de Monte Carlo.

     2 × 3 OVERWINNINGEN

IN SUCCESSIE

Importeur:
H. C. L. SIEBERG N.V. Stadhouderskade 143 Amsterdam, Tel. 28400 (5 lijnen)

Wij importeren tevens: Willys Overland, Jeep, Javelin, Bradford, Thornycroft, Scammell, D.B.

The 1950 win for Hotchkiss meant that for the second time this famous French make of car had won the Monte three times in succession. Right Henri Secrèt, left Marcel Becquart who became one of Gatso's best friends and co-driver in many rallies and Le Mans races in the following years until 1959

Gatso's second-placed Humber Super Snipe was equipped with Dutch Vredestein tyres.

Advertisement exclaiming that 'SPECIALISTS PREFER LODGE', and showing Gatso, in his 'inseparable' farmer's hat, working on 'Flatty'.

Chapter 17

Sports Car Races, Zandvoort, 1950

About great expectation: special French wheels: and a whistling kettle.

Once you are familiar with the motor racing world to such an extent that the grey faces of the drivers and mechanics on the morning of a race are not longer put down to an overdose of intoxicating liquid, but are indeed recognized as the consequence of a night in which the poor devils saw plenty of spanners and wretches, but no bed, that is undoubtedly the time that you'll see them as people who, in the Spanish way say: "Manana por la manana", which means they prefer to postpone until tomorrow what they should have done three weeks ago. But really, those poor subjects of St. Christopher who sacrifice their soul, money, peace of mind, marital happiness, and even their business to attend to all the thousand and one things which enable them to fight it out at the wheel on a race track for a glorious half hour, are not lazy men.

It so happens that a racing car can always somehow be made to run a little faster than it already does. But against this there is always a secret little army of 'Gremlins' searching for any opportunity to sabotage the job. Gradually I am beginning to believe that somewhere there is one very clever little Gremlin always shadowing me carefully and watching just how everything is working out, and waiting until I think everything is looking rosy before then giving me a knock. That belief grew considerably when, only six weeks before the K.N.A.C. sports-car races on the Zandvoort circuit in 1950, I ruined the engine of the 1.5-litre Gatso in which I was determined to get my revenge this year for the defeat I had suffered the year before. The engine compartment of my precious 'Flatty' (nicknamed so because of its extremely low build, less than one metre high) suddenly began producing the most terrible 'expensive' noises. There was nothing I could do but to take the engine out and have it reconditioned. All that wouldn't have been so bad if a rebuilt engine didn't need running-in for a few thousand miles. And even that job could have been properly completed if it had not been for the fact that a brand new 4-litre Gatso was also waiting for me, its powerful engine not yet having done a single stroke only eight days before the race. When I say 'brand-new', please don't get any ideas of a beautifully polished shining car straight out of a showroom, as in this case much of the equipment and accessories normally found on such a car were either very rudimentary, or lacking. From the driver's seat one had a splendid view onto the road beneath the car, as there was no floorboard as yet in this 120 m.p.h. model. Taking it altogether it was indeed a rather airy affair, and offering little privacy as neither doors or windows were present. Originally I really hadn't thought there would be a possibility of getting the 4-litre on the starting grid, but we got on so well with the job that about a fortnight before the race some daring part of my brain began to act, and consequently I entered the non-upholstered body on a freshly-painted chassis. By doing so I had accepted a lot more work for my mechanics and myself than even I had first suspected. What I did understand was that the so often repeated determination to have everything in order weeks beforehand was once again put to shame by the facts. It was a feverish week. A week during which all my spare time - for after all I had to earn my daily bread - was spent taking out the 1.5-litre to get the engine run-in. Normal running-in, such as advised by the manufacturers on those nice little transparent notices they kindly fix on the windscreen, was out of the question. It boiled down to revving the engine to just below the point where it would seize. This was alright in the early stages, but became more difficult on the roads as the engine loosened up. When it could reach 4,500 revs it was sometimes rather precarious when maintaining 80 m.p.h. on the country roads, as I must shame-facedly admit that during this running-in period several fowls paid with their life. The car was ready in time, but I must be honest and admit that 90 percent of the credit was due to the mechanics at my workshop. Without any grumbles, indeed on the contrary with genuine enthusiasm, they sweated until the early hours of the morning with only one desire: to witness a Gatso victory.

Whereas 'Flatty' was practically finished, although still requiring a sensitive touch so as not to overtax it, the same could not be said about the 4-litre Gatso on which much overtime was being spent. Many were the times we thought we would never get it done, but every tightened nut was a step nearer. By the Thursday evening before the race we had progressed sufficiently to take the three Gatsos - Klaas was driving the previous year's Gatso 4000 - to the Zandvoort circuit for a try-out. Well, that new 4-litre Gatso was a revelation. After just one lap with Klaas at the wheel, the passenger, our journalist friend William Leonard, was positively white around the gills as he got out of the car, which he described as 'unearthly'. It certainly was. Weighing in at 21cwt, and with 155 b.h.p. from its hotted-up V8 engine, its acceleration was wicked. Only a slight pressure was needed on the acceleration pedal for it to seem as if a giant hand was pushing the Gatso forward with a mighty force. And this was with a strict rev-limit as the engine was not yet run-in. As 2,500 revs won't win a race, my friend Geert Hoogeveen, enthusiastic sportsman that he is, agreed to drive the car throughout the night until the next morning in order to loosen up the engine. Bearing in mind the draughty nature of the un-finished bodywork Geert was risking pneumonia, but we reckoned the sheer pleasure of driving this big Gatso would be such as to not notice the cold. The first official practice laps on the Friday were used for further loosening up, whilst the worst holes in the body were now covered with plywood and aluminium sheet. The first practice laps with 'Flatty' on the Friday afternoon showed the small Gatso to be quicker than the M.G. T.D. models, unlike the previous year when these British thoroughbreds had out-accelerated our car. Our Fiat engine had been tuned up considerably, and the replacement of the two S.U. carburettors with a pair of ordinary American down-draught Strombergs was another improvement. We thought we had solved the wheel size/gearing problem with the fitting of a set of special-made aluminium wheels from France, and which looked really classy too. It was most important to be faster than last year as I had six T.D.s to contend with, of which four, belonging to Dries Van Der Lof, Wally Kühne, Joop Molenaar, and Gerd Roeloffzen were extremely fast. Even faster than the M.G. with which Molenaar had beaten me the year before, 'Flatty' did well in practice, and friends handling stopwatches were soon telling me that I was faster than Dries Van Der Lof, who at first could not get under 2 minutes 23 seconds. I made 2 minutes 20 seconds with something still in reserve, as I was certainly not going to let my hard-boiled M.G. friends know just how fast I really could go.

During practice for the big class Klaas supplied the sensation by wiping the boards clean with his Gatso in 2 minutes 9 seconds, which was 6 seconds under the record and much faster than the Jaguar XK 120 of Van Dieten, and even the feared Delahaye of our old rival Tielens. Van Dieten was a wild fellow who apparently didn't mind at all the possibility of skidding off the road in the dangerous curves opposite the stands. I didn't risk fully opening the throttle on the new Gatso 400 Coupé during practice, and so achieved third starting position behind Klaas Barendrecht and Van Dieten, but ahead of Tielens who never puts all his cards on the table in practice. Throughout the practice laps the Gatso went like a whistle. Unfortunately in the race it was more like a whistling kettle. Of this and other forthcoming disappointments we knew nothing on that sunny Sunday morning before the racing. Once again in the paddock there was that indescribable atmosphere. All kinds of people, dressed in all kinds of overalls, stooping over all kinds of cars, passing all kinds of remarks about the cars of everyone on the course. The flags flying cheerfully in the wind. The loudspeakers playing rousing marches for the thousands of spectators. Tension began to rise, occasionally accentuated by the deep rumble of a powerful engine, revving up to its four or five thousand revolutions. Before I realized it the 1.5-litre class was called to the start by Piet Nortier. Piet of course just couldn't refrain from cracking a joke about my Gallic farmer's hat from which I was inseparable, apart from in the actual races of course! There I was, more or less by myself amongst the crowd of healthy-sounding M.G.s. On the right, Dries Van Der Lof, who in his final practice lap had made 2 minutes 19 seconds. On the left was Wally Kühne in his yellow M.G., still considered a novice but with his heart definitely in the right (racing) place. Behind me were Joop Molenaar and Gerd Roeloffzen, both old hands who wouldn't make things easy for me. Beating healthily beneath the streamlined nose of my small orange-coloured Gatso was the stout heart of the hotted-up Fiat six-cylinder engine, reacting to the merest touch on the accelerator with a growl like an infuriated panther. Nevertheless, I was just a fraction too late when starting marshall Van Haaren's flag went down. As we shot away Dries Van Der Lof managed to beat me over the first few yards, enabling him to enter the Tarzan hairpin bend first. However, I stuck close to his tail, and wasn't one yard behind him when we went through the bend opposite the grandstand. Side by side we entered the Hunze hairpin, and the gap was just big enough for me to get past the M.G. going up the slope. Dries immediately got into my slipstream and managed to hang on

'Flatty' leading Dries Van Der Lof's M.G. in the Tarzan bend, Zandvoort 1950.

there throughout the first lap. Still mindful of the new engine I didn't dare yet to open the throttle fully, but we nevertheless went so fast that Dries and I had pulled about half a mile in front of the field of chasing M.G.s in the second lap. After losing

Dries from my slipstream I gradually became certain that I could beat him, and after he had mounted several more attacks he seemed to realize there was nowhere on the circuit where he could beat me, and he now had simply to satisfy himself by chasing me from a short distance. As I had no desire to lose the race through over-revving the engine I also cooled off a little, and settled down comfortably to enjoy the marvelous drive on the winding Zandvoort circuit. 'Flatty' was running like clockwork, its healthy exhaust note spurring me on to greater achievements. Everything went smoothly. Following exactly the same line in every bend, and lifting my foot always on the same spot, braking and changing gear we sped over the course. Silently to myself I began to sing out that this time all those hectic hours of preparation had not been for nothing. Lap after lap went by without incident. Although Van Der Lof stayed close to my tail I knew the M.G.

......and suddenly the left rear wheel collapsed.

needed just a little more power to be of any danger. Jan Apetz and Jan Erens signalled from our pit that I was gaining 2 seconds per lap, and like that, averaging 67.5 m.p.h. we entered the sixth lap. It all went exactly to schedule. Right on the outside into the Tarzan hairpin, sharp across the inside, and almost sliding out again. Then maximum acceleration in third gear to fly to the next hairpin. But that would be no longer possible. Hardly out of the bend I felt a sickening bump behind me on the left. Immediately the thought "puncture" flashed into my mind. I steered 'Flatty' from the road into the loose sand at the bottom of the Hunze hill, throwing up a cloud of dust before coming to rest with the car sitting at an angle.

I saw Dries Van Der Lof flashing by up the Hunze hill to a certain victory. When I had recovered a little from the blow it took only a glance to show me what had gone wrong. One of those very special French aluminium wheels, that fitted to the left rear, had given up the ghost, the rim having broken away from its centre. "Just fancy", I thought, "going all the way to France for a set of specially-made wheels which then fool you at Zandvoort". Thoroughly downhearted I walked to the paddock, feeling once again that victory had slipped through my fingers because of sheer bad luck. Some consolation did come from the many people in the motoring world who came up to me just especially to offer their commiseration, which meant more to me than any speech might have done. In such a furious state of mind due to the actions of my 'bad-luck Gremlin', I almost kicked the pedal through the floorboards of the new 4-litre Gatso when the starting flag dropped in the race for the big car-class. Right from the start I was involved in a monumental battle with Van Dieten's black Jaguar XK 120. On the first stretch up to the Hunze hill we were more or less side by side. Going up the hill

I was delighted that my new Gatso Coupé accelerated faster than the XK 120. For the second time that day I took the lead, although with some unease in my heart, knowing that also somewhere behind me was Tielens in his Delahaye. Always the tactician, Tielens would wait patiently for a chance, which when it came he would usually seize. It was true that the Jaguar was the car right behind me. It gave me a nasty shock in the Tarzan curve going at 80 m.p.h., but I feared it much less because the inexperienced Van Dieten was in fact driving his first race, in which he was bound to make some mistakes. With each lap my worries decreased as the opposition seemed to recede further into the distance every time I looked into the rear view mirror. In the beginning I was only a few yards ahead, extending this to about 20 yards on the third lap, and by something like 250 yards on the fifth. I felt quiet safe at this distance, all the more so really as I still had some power to spare. I was lapping at 72 m.p.h. And believe me, that is pretty fast going on the winding Zandvoort circuit, which at that sort of speed doesn't give a moment's relaxation for either car of driver. Not that I was wanting any relaxation. For anyone who ever felt that strange desire for speed, this race must have been the ultimate in dicing. In the mighty exhaust roar the 150 horses were singing their powerful song, to the accompaniment of the tyre's high-pitched scream on the tarmac. Every time I accelerated again after a curve I felt that enormous strength of the 4-litre V8 engine pressing me into the back of the seat as the car shot forward as if there was no law of inertia. Then, nearing the end of the sixth lap a discordant note crept into this high-speed symphony, and slowly but surely the engine temperature began to rise. The needle moved ever nearer towards boiling point. On entering the seventh lap the engine began to misfire. Loosing speed I saw the Jaguar come past, and the Delahaye and Klaas' Gatso approaching quickly. Not even ten prayers to St. Christopher were any help. The engine boiled merrily, and on the winding stretch in the wood the other competitors passed by so fast that it looked as though I was standing still. The only thing I could do was to stop at the pits, where Jan Apetz had to quickly jump aside to escape the jet of steam and boiling water when he removed the radiator cap.

Van Dieten's Jaguar with Gatso's new 4000 Coupé right behind. Following them are Tielens (Delahaye) and Klaas Barendrecht in the other Gatso 4-litre.

It felt as though there was a lead weight in the pit of my stomach as I slowly drove the Gatso into the paddock. That feeling became stronger as I realized I had made a miscalculation. I had driven without a fan (which requires 3 b.p.h.), because the Gatso had run perfectly without its fan during three successive practice laps. But in the hectic rush of the overnight work my mechanics had forgotten to remove the thermostats, one of which apparently jammed closed at high temperature and restricted the water circulation. Wherever human beings work, mistakes will always be made. Of course it is wrong to save the car when practising, it should always be made to do its utmost so that if anything happens repairs can probably made before the race. Without its fan the Gatso's engine, still not completely run-in, had withstood three practice laps without signs of trouble, but was unable to cover more than seven laps in the race. Such things always fill me with the hope that someday I will have learned something from these lessons. All mistakes are lessons from which we should learn in this unreliable game. I had already learned many lessons, but every new event brings along new ones. Still, for a change it would be nice, and handy if in a race I could only have to face the problems which I already knew about. These thoughts from this and other races were in my mind as I watched the rest of the race from the pits. A race in which Klaas could not play a leading part this time, because his Gatso, which in practice had been faster than ever, was now just missing that maximum power needed to give him the lead, again caused by one of the hundreds of little setbacks which can occur. We saw Tielens' third Zandvoort victory in succession. A Tielens who, steering his Delahaye with incredible accuracy always placed his car exactly where it ought to be. He had no trouble with the wild-driving Van Dieten. The latter, although he could not hear it, was warned about his driving by Piet Nortier speaking through the public address microphone. Third was Klaas who, though not so fast, treated the public to a display of cornering as only he can do. It was a shame though, that Tielens yet again didn't get a real honest chance to show just what he was worth, as he would have had to do had it been a matter of 'touch and go'.

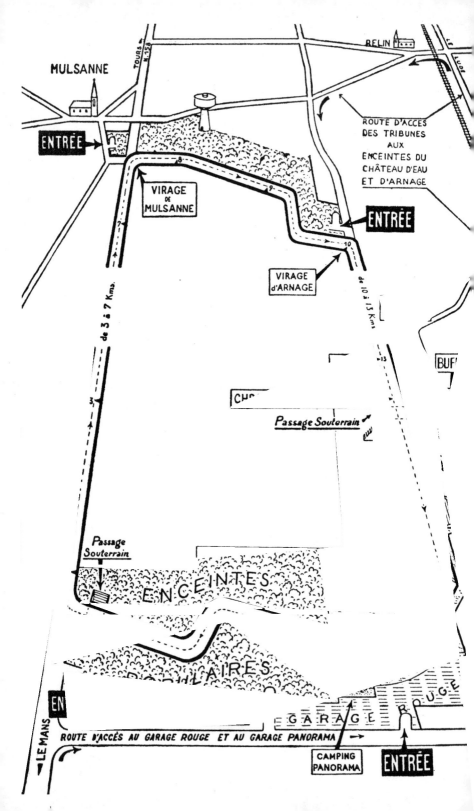

Chapter 18

The 1950 Le Mans 24 Hours Race

About 'Smokey', small but brave in a legendary race: parts that were and were not on board: fog in the night: and five scrap pieces of roadwheel.

"So this is Le Mans" I said to myself, feeling humble and not without respect. I planted my feet firmly on the road of 'Le Circuit Permanent de la Sarthe'. As I had called at a place only 30 miles from Le Mans to collect some special aluminium wheels ordered for my Gatso 1500, 'Flatty', I couldn't resist the temptation to have a look at that sanctuary of automobile sport where for years the '24 Heures du Mans' had been held. A sports-car race lasting 24 hours, which is about the ultimate in endurance for both man and car. I had a go on the famous circuit, taking the bends at Mulsanne, Arnage, and Tertre Rouge. Names which cause many true drivers to tremble with emotion, because they bring back memories of long gone years when those heavy Bentleys thundered over the circuit to take victory after victory. Times when sports-cars with almost forgotten names such as Chenard-Walker, La Lorraine, Corre-Licorne, Aris, Stutz and other makes of car whose names are indeed now forgotten, tore along averaging 65 m.p.h. Stories can still be heard of heroic battles, with failing brakes but a never failing spirit. Those were the days when battles were fought for the honour of the 'marque'. Battles in which the driver's success counted less than that of the team. Who doesn't remember the tale of Sammy Davis from those times? During the night, swinging his heavy Bentley round a corner, he saw in the beams of his headlights the horrible 'debris' of five cars in a 'pile up' which his Bentley could not possibly miss. But as was normal in those days he went on, driving his car through the wreckage to continue even though now he could hardly keep his car on the road. At the pit stop, where grim face were all around, there wasn't a living soul with the courage to look underneath the car. Everyone feared the damage would so bad as to force the withdrawal of the car from the race. But with his spirit undiminished Sammy carried on and won. Only then the car was examined. The steering rod hung on only one bolt, and even that was broken half way through. Such recollections were going through my mind as I drove 'Flatty' a little faster around that famous track.

I could well imagine that tales still circulate about mysterious, ghostly races in the night in which Le Mans cracks, whose whereabouts now had long since been decided by a higher power, once more raced through the bends to the accompaniment of screaming tyres and roaring exhausts. Whilst driving back to Holland the desire to just once join in that wild chase, gradually became a irresistible one. And I even had a faint idea of how that desire was going to materialize. Had not the Aéro Minor of Czechs Kratner and Mikula finished second in the Index of Performance category (a handicap result) last year behind the Ferrari of Chinetti and Lord Selsdon? And didn't it jus also happen that young and talented Dutch driver Henk Hoogeveen, who lived only two miles away from me, had made a Minor sports car which had proved at Zandvoort to be quite fast and very reliable? He and his father had prepared the car with considerably skill and ambition, building a lightweight aluminium body specially for it. At home I immediately contacted Henk. Both he and his father, who is well known in the Dutch motorsports world, were enthusiastic about my proposals, and that same day an application to enter was telegraphed to Le Mans. It was about three months before the race, and we were not really surprised that no answer came. There were 132 applications, of which only 60 could be accepted. However, luck was on our side. The Hague-based Dutch importers of the Minor, Messrs. Englebert, learned of our plans. It so happened that they were informed by the Czechoslovakian factory that their drivers Kratner and Mikula were not being allowed by their government to leave the country that year. This was as a result of the failure of the famous Czech athlete Emil Zatopek to return home after his world record marathon race win in the recent Olympic Games, instead seeking political asylum in the West. This meant that the factory's Aéro Minor, which had already qualified as an entrant for the so-called 'Coupe Biennale', a competition over two successive years, because of its excellent result in the previous year, would now have to be withdrawn. Mr. Englebert however suggested that we would like to drive the car, and the factory agreed. We were jumping sky-high for joy. The only condition I made was that the car must first come to Holland, in order that we could thoroughly prepare it to our requirements. It did indeed come, but arrived rather late, being delivered by a train to the Dutch border railway station at Oldenzaal on June 17th, which was only eight days before the race. Aster some searching, Geert Hoogeveen located it at midnight on the Saturday. From there on everyone co-operated. The loading master and the Customs official left their beds at that late hour to help right away. As we had to drive this Czech car under Dutch numberplates, our K.N.A.C. marshall Van Haaren did his utmost on the Sunday to get the documentation organized for temporary importation into Holland, and at the Ministry of Finance they were also prepared to do anything they could. With its very dull aluminium finish the Aéro Minor looked as though it had spent all year in a dusty loft, and when we got it into the Hoogeveen's workshop on the Monday, we quickly realized that it needed plenty of work before the race if it was to last more than a few laps. For example the silencer and exhaust pipe were connected by a rubber hose which burned through within a matter of minutes. Whilst I rushed to and fro getting all the customs and other formalities fixed up, Aéro Minor experts Henk and Geert had their sleeves rolled up and worked feverishly until the early hours of the morning sorting out the car. It was a hell of a job, but our three-car procession was able to head for Le Mans on the Tuesday before the race. Henk and I were the two race drivers, and accompanying us as pit assistants were Geert Hoogeveen and the Czech car importer's son, Guy Englebert, who was a most even tempered likeable sort of chap. We also asked Jan Apetz to join us, as in an event like Le Mans Jan's sunny disposition and absolute refusal to become downhearted come what may would be worth its weight in platinum. Five Dutchmen whose knowledge about competing at Le Mans amounted to about as much as a canary would know about swimming the channel, would between them somehow have to cope with whatever situation arose.

As usual the first difficulty came at the border, where we had problems about taking our spare engine and other spare parts for the car abroad. Luckily we managed to convince the officials of what we were about. Henk and I alternately took the wheel of the Aéro Minor which, with its twin-cylinder two-stroke engine and front-wheel-drive was something quite strange to me, and therefore it was essential that I got used to it in the short time before the race. We had christened it 'Smokey' because of the enormous amount of blue exhaust smoke it always trailed behind it in typical two-stroke fashion. It really looked a miserable little thing, its drabness relieved only by the roughly painted Czechoslovakian blue-white-red racing stripes on its nose. But on the flat it could take to its heels, although uphill we noticed it wasn't exactly potent. The first night we stayed at Laôn, and went on via Paris to Le Mans the next day. There was excitement everywhere in that small town, and even had we not known the way to scrutineering at the old cavalry barracks at Cavaignac we certainly couldn't have missed it. Crowds of sportily-dressed Frenchmen, with a burning enthusiasm in their hearts for anything to do with racing cars, were heading for the barracks to witness the scrutineering. At about 4 o'clock in the afternoon our 'Smokey' arrived there, accompanied by five rather embarrassed Dutchmen, who felt a little quivery at their Aéro Minor being amongst all those scintillating stars, such as Talbots, Ferraris, Aston Martins, Gordini Simcas and so on. Amongst the drivers walking around were some real aces: Sommèr, Chinetti, Rosiér, Fangio, Trintignant, Gonzalès and Manzon. An attraction of Le Mans is that in that mixture of drivers, officials, reporters, photographers and enthusiasts, one is immediately accepted as one of the family. Never mind whether you are a crack with a Grand Prix reputation or an ordinary little Dutchman of whom only a few people may have heard.

When we drove 'Smokey' into the large hall behind Tonny Rolt's Nash-engined Healey we noticed that some tempers were frayed. It was an animated scene. Raymond Sommèr was walking about grumbling at the officials who were insisting that a mudguard on his Ferrari was a fraction too short, and therefore couldn't be accepted. Quite a shouting match developed between them, with the officials pointing out that Sommèr was just a poor driver who had better hold his tongue, whilst he retorted that he doubted if any of them actually knew the difference between a spark plug and an exhaust pipe. With that parting shot he drove away to have a piece of sheet metal rivetted to his mudguard. When our Aéro Minor was examined several discrepancies were found. Our front mudguards were also too short, but with five inches of aluminium sheet we quickly corrected this. The mirror was too small, which also wasn't much of a problem. Worse was that we had no certificate from our insurance company that we ourselves had valid personal accident/life insurance cover for the race. A telegram to Holland resulted in confirmation that the race risk was indeed included on our life and accident policies. To come back to the scrutineering, we were astonished to see some of the competing cars which were there: the Allard of Sidney Allard and Tom Cole, with its tuned-up 5-litre Cadillac engine; the Cadillac tank-biscuit-tin of Briggs Cunningham, which had four Stromberg downdraught carburettors; no less than five Ferraris, two of which were fantastic Le Mans Coupés; and six Gordini Simcas, two with supercharged 1.5-litre engines, and all entered by Amedé Gordini himself to be driven by cracks like Trintignant, Manzon, Fangio, and Gonzalès. What a crowd!

Our first priority after the scrutineering was to have a good meal. Then we found the local Jawa (Czechoslovakian) agent's workshop where we could do plenty of work on the car. We had been introduced to this workshop by the mechanic, Jean, working on the only other Aéro Minor in the race, driven by Frenchmen Poch and Mouche. A most helpful fellow, Jean even let us have some carburettor jets from their stock of spares. Fortunately we were able to help the French Aéro Minor crew later on with a drive shaft.

Following another nice meal we went in search of somewhere were we could find a bed, having not been able to make a hotel or guest house reservation because our entry was so late. From the Automobile Club de l'Ouest, the event organizers, and possibly the oldest Automobile Club in the world, we were sent to a few private addresses. The first house on the list proved to be in a shocking slum area, and crawling with bugs, nasty little red things. And anyway there was only one single bed available, and with five of us that was not good at all. Without having reserved any shelter for the night we returned to the track, where practising was taking place between 9 p.m. until 1 a.m. Our pit assistants took possession of their quarters and realized immediately that our pit organization was hopeless. All the others had tables, chairs, lamps, and cases full of foodstuff, while our poor boys had to sit on either hard benches or the floor. Not the slightest comforts were provided, and feeling cold and miserable they swore at themselves for forgetting about such things. Also our signalling device between pits and driver was very antiquated. The Ferrari pit had a splendid signal-board, made of white glass with many small lights at the back, enabling them to keep their drivers informed about their position even at night. We had to use a primitive, but actually rather effective system. Jan Apetz, in his white overall and wearing a straw hat, stood in the bright light of the pit holding a blackboard in front of him on which the latest news was chalked. Our only comforts were two air-mattresses in a large tent behind the pit, but one mattress was of course for the drivers. Our worst discovery though was that our pit was seriously under-manned. We needed more people, and asked a friend if he knew a couple of youngsters who might help. Two Frenchmen promptly arrived, but they had such a funny idea about the sport that they wanted payment, and no small amount either. We decided to manage after all with our own people, and they really did do just fine, although after the race they were more exhausted than the two drivers, Henk and myself. As far as practising was concerned I must say it was a funny experience being mixed in between all those giants with our tiny Aéro Minor. Giants that flashed by at more than 130 miles per hour on the straight stretches. Through the bends especially it could be sometimes a precarious business, for when the headlight beams of a Ferrari or Talbot tickled the back of your neck some pretty quick guess-work was required to prevent them from running into the rear of your car. Only when we found out that little front-wheel-driven 'Smokey' was just as fast in the bends as the big ones, in fact in some cases even faster did we feel a little better. Apart from that it was pure joy to roar around the circuit in the dark. Past the pits, opposite the grandstand, one had to pass under the enormous Dunlop bridge shaped like half a gigantic tyre. Go up the slope and then into the S-curve between the pine trees. On account of 'Smokey's' front-wheel-drive this curve at first gave us a new sensation. Coming down the slope at 90 m.p.h., braking to 60: then accelerating fully to take the first half of the bend at 70 and the next part at 80 m.p.h. Once I braked a little too hard there and skidded right across the road. That was most unpleasant, and although I quickly got 'Smokey' back on line it was fortunate that nobody was behind me. At some forty yards from the Tertre Rouge corner I had to brake again, change down to third, and accelerate fully to go through at 70 m.p.h. That was by far the trickiest corner of all, and most of the accidents happened there. Leaving that curve I continued accelerating flat out, changed into top gear and settled myself down as low as possible in the seat for the four mile straight, keeping close to the shielded side of the road because 'Smokey' didn't like side or head winds. In the Tertre Rouge curve during practice the Delahaye driven by Frenchman Veuillet flew out of the curve, somersaulted and landed on the sandbank. That was the first time the ambulance went out. Even so, with his head heavily bandaged Veuillet came to the start of the race; but that is another story.

At the end of that four miles of straight road from Le Mans to Tours there were little lines across the road at 100 metres distance,

Whilst practising before the race Veuillet's Delahaye ended up in the protective sandbank at the side of the notorious Tertre Rouge corner.

and signals by the side to warn drivers of the approach of the Mulsanne curve. This had to be taken carefully, for it was more than 75 degrees and you were coming from a wide road into a narrow one, sometimes with large cars following like express trains. Just before Mulsanne you had to change back to third, brake a little and down into second to take the two 90 degrees curves at Arnage, from where with renewed courage, having almost completed a lap, you went up the slope towards the pits to start the whole thing all over again. I lapped at 70 m.p.h. which equated to around 7 minutes 8 seconds to 7.10. Just once, doing my utmost I managed 6 minutes 58 seconds, which was 72.2 m.p.h. With that first practice session over, at 2 o'clock in the morning with our ice-cold pit assistants we went in search of a hotel in the town. Somebody gave us the tip to try the famous Hotel de l'Hippodrome, near the circuit, where each year many British drivers stay, but we were unsuccessful. However we found a hotel opposite the station, which proved very nice and not expensive. The food was delicious, and more importantly it had room for all five of us. That must have been something of a miracle at Le Mans at a time when not one bed remains unoccupied due to the tens of thousands who arrive from all over France to this normally so quiet little town, just to see the race.

1950 - Le Mans at night. On the left the pits, with spectators on the roof. Grandstands on the right.

Some 30,000 spectators lined the circuit during the night time practice sessions, and this number swelled to 200,000 for the actual race. On Sunday there are open air church services, and inside the circuit an enormous fair, with many cafés and stalls where all the specialties of the district can be bought.

On the second day we had new worries regarding our little aluminium stepchild. Despite what we understood to be a binding arrangement the Czechoslovakian Barum tyre factory didn't supply the promised new tyres. We were lucky to get hold of some Belgian Engleberts which were reserved for the Svenska Champion which George Trouïs had entered. That car however didn't turn up, and we were able to have the five tyres, which were not exactly our size, but quite usable. Another problem we encountered was that after about three hours of practising the starter motor would not restart the engine. I suggested fitting an ammeter, and sure enough that indicated a battery discharge when the headlights and foglights were all in use. Obviously the generator was not of sufficient capacity, but we were able to alleviate the problem by adjusting the headlights slightly to the outside, and using one foglight only set to illuminate the right hand corners. Saving the battery power was essential as at pit stops during the race the engine had to be switched off, and using the starting handle or also pushing the car to restart the engine was not allowed.

But the worst thing really was that the little engine absolutely refused to reach maximum revolutions. Our competitors Poch and Mouche had bought one of last year's class-winning Aéro Minors, and had come to the practising on Thursday night. They completed a few laps in well under 7 minutes and didn't show up any more. Their lovely pale blue Aéro Minor gave the impression of being perfectly prepared. 'Smoky' on the other hand was just not quick enough, and we worked incessantly trying to find out why. Only at the last moment did we began to doubt the carburettor jets. The manufacturers had advised us to try Nos. 130 and 180, but when we were allowed to experiment with jets from the abundance of spare ones in Poch and Mouche's jet box, we soon concluded that Nos. 230 and 280 were what was needed, which was quite some difference. And indeed, when we fitted these larger jets 'Smoky' went much better, although still not quite so fast as its blue twin brother. During the last two evenings we practiced to our hearts content, but were not the only ones. Drivers like Rosiér, Meyrat and Mairesse for instance, who knew the circuit like their own pockets, each night covered 200 miles just to get into the routine. Doing it in a different way were Briggs Cunningham and his co-driver with their biscuit-tin-shaped Cadillac. They immediately began so fast as to leave the hard road in every curve. They soon knew all the trees (even saluting them in the end) and eventually knew exactly where all the dangerous spots were. One of them looked astonished when I passed him on the inside of the Tertre Rouge right-hander.

Our poor pit slaves had spent the first night with only their toolbox, some spark plugs, a note book and pencil, and a blackboard and chalk. But they had learned a lot, as on the following night you could hear them chewing gum as one came around the Arnage curve. That was not all they copied from the other pits, there being many other little things. But still their organization could not possible compare with Cunningham's Cadillac team, with their two-way radio system between car and pit never before seen in an European race. Sommèr worked in a totally different fashion. He did it the French way. He would write something on a slip of paper whilst travelling at 130 m.p.h., roll it into a ball and fling it to his assistants as he passed the pits.

Those feverish practice days during which we looked like greasy rags, particularly Geert Hoogeveen and his son Henk who both worked tirelessly, quickly came to an end. A last attempt to extend our too-small pit crew with some Dutchmen we met failed because they preferred to watch the race from the grandstand. Perhaps that proved that being actively involved in racing simply didn't appeal to them, and if so they wouldn't have been much use to us in the pit. Our pit was in fact well organized between the three. Guy had the important but not so easy task of race administration, a full twenty-four hour job which he did perfectly throughout with not a minute's rest. On that memorable morning of June 24th we were up very early, awakened by a kind ray of sunshine shining right into our room. "Lovely weather", Jan said, watching from the window. "As far as I'm concerned, I'd prefer fog", was my reply. Little did I know the granting of that wish would come to help us. The streets of Le Mans were already crowded almost to capacity, with hordes of enthusiastic spectators who wanted to watch the whole twenty-four hours. They knew the exact capacities of every car and could tell you the B.H.P.s and all such details. With the whole convoy, 'Smoky', Guy's Panhard, and the station wagon which was loaded with crates of various soft drinks and lots of lovely food, we went to the circuit. People were arriving from all directions to watch the race, sometimes from the most 'impossible' places (some would sit for twenty-four hours in the trees at Tertre Rouge) quite willing to face heat, cold, fog and lack of sleep. Fathers who had probably never driven a car; wealthy-looking types with Valentino haircuts and hand-made suits; eccentrics; judges and dustbin men; public notories and boys from the slums, all with their heads absolutely full of the race.

We ourselves felt very small as the hands of the clock crept slowly towards the afternoon, and 4 o'clock. We consumed another hot meal at the very good restaurant at the paddock, and I spoiled myself with snails, which were refused by Hoogeveen, saying he didn't want to die yet. We had a large swig of wine for dessert, and felt that we were able to accomplish great things. Whilst eating we in fact carefully calculated our chances, not that our expectations were too high. Obviously we hadn't come here for the 'Coupe de la Distance' for which one simply had to cover the longest distance. What we were definitely aiming at was the 'Coupe de l'Indice de Performance', the Performance Index for which according to a complicated formula cars with a small engine capacity were supposed to have just as much a chance as the big ones. Of course we were also competing in the 750cc class in which we might be successful. After lunch it seemed as if the hands of the clock moved faster. At 1 o'clock we had to be present to drain the fuel tank, after which it was filled again with the official compulsory petrol and sealed. Then things went very fast. Everybody seemed to be running about having something to attend to. I had a little talk with Tommy Wisdom, who I had met many times already, even before the war. There were four bluebottles on his cap, and only when I tried to flick them away did I realise they were sewn on! Gradually things were sorting themselves out in this hive of activity, and the first cars began to go up to their starting places on the gentle slope in front of the pits. At the start only the two drivers were permitted to be near the cars. Henk, who was taking the first turn, and I took 'Smoky' to our starting spot which was some way from our pit, and there we waited for things to happen. At ten minutes to four all engines had to be stopped, and the exhaust noise died away. It was an impressive and colourful sight to behold, that line-up of sixty cars with their drivers standing alongside in overalls of white, blue, and green. From the huge stands flags fluttered in the wind, and thousands of those colourful caps with publicity slogans produced a sea of colour in the sunshine. Spectators seemed in danger of falling from the stand roofs, and the roofs of the pits almost collapsed under the weight of the people who wanted to see it all. Five more minutes to go. Slowly one of the drivers of each car walked to his circle marked on the opposite side of the road, from where he would sprint across to his car the moment the starter dropped his flag. "Encore une minute" the loudspeaker proclaimed. You could have almost heard a pin drop as a hundred thousand spectators held their breath, with only the singing of the birds to punctuate the silence. In the middle of the road stood just one man, Charles Faroux, holding the flag. Standing behind our car in that uncanny silence I looked at my chronometer, and could feel my heart in my mouth. Thirty seconds, twenty, ten, five.....down went the flag. The long row of drivers began to move, those towards the front row first, the others I could not see so well, and Henk, who had jumped to start a fraction before the flag moved, went back, afraid he would be too early. "Run, Henk. Run" I shouted. And Henk ran, jumped into the Aéro Minor and started the engine. Le 24 Heures du Mans had begun.

And what a beginning! Engines began to roar ever louder, until at last every other sound was lost in that almost unbearable thunder which had exploded out of the terrific build-up of pre-start tension. Sidney Allard in the make of car bearing his name was the first one to shoot away, accompanied by the deep drone of the four-carburettor Cadillac engine. Then the furious scream of Sommèr's 12-cylinder Ferrari, the deeper thunder of Rosiér's mighty 6-cylinder Talbot, the fierce whistle of an M.G., and the sinister hiss of Tony Rolt's Healey. Amongst that cacophony of a thousand horsepower 'Smoky' with Henk at the wheel shot away like a tightly coiled spring. Not in the least over-awed, Henk manoeuvred amongst the criss-cross of cars to find a clear way ahead. A push on the accelerator and at full speed the little aluminium car went up the slope, its tail glinting in the sun. When all the noise had died away two or three cars were left forlornly in the quietness which had descended but would soon to be replaced by the chattering from the stand. Veuillet's Delahaye which had been done up nicely again after its excursion during practice, could not be started by its driver who had taken over the wheel from the injured Veuillet. It had to be pushed away after half an hour, to the sound of many sighs of pity from the public. In the middle of the track was Juan Manuel Fangio. The engine of his Gordini had cut out after only a few hundred yards. The quick Argentinian jumped up and down in the narrow seat, pushed and pulled every button and looked flabbergasted at the dashboard, only realizing after a while that the ignition switch had not been pushed in far enough. Then he, too, shot up the hill in a thick cloud of smoke produced by the fearful wheelspin.

Feeling quite at ease I walked back to the pits, but there I found Geert shouting and swearing in the most bad-tempered manner. He was not at all pleased with his son Henk who, Geert thought, had been too much gentlemanly at the start of the race by going back just as everyone else began to run for their cars. However his temper cooled considerably when the tall Guy Englebert, who with his stopwatches had settled down on the corner of the pit counter, shouted: "Seven minutes, fifty-eight seconds". Old Geert jumped forward and just managed to glimpse 'Smoky's' tail. "Damnit, that's not bad from a standing start", he said, now shining with pride! Indeed, Henk was doing fine. Regular as a clock 'Smoky' appeared amongst all those express trains, which were already tearing along as if they were making for the finish. You could bet your last penny that it would not take more than 7 minutes 30 seconds for Henk to reappear on every lap. Each time he passed the pit he gave us the 'thumbs up', indicating that all was well. I went to the tent to get some sleep during the 30 times 7 minutes which Henk had been ordered to drive.

Now that all had settled down the pit crew had only to put out the blackboard every lap, carefully note down the time, and every now and then check up on the position. This was done by sending a request to the timing calculation room, from which were received by return details of the exact position of a quarter of an hour before. This service between the pits and timing room was provided by a group of friendly Boy Scouts acting as runners. Meanwhile everybody was being thrilled by a fierce three-cornered scrap between Rosiér, Sommèr, and Chinetti, who were busy destroying all existing records. Finally it was Rosiér who with his Talbot completed a lap at 165 k.m.h. (102.5 m.p.h.), which wiped out the 1939 record of Mazaud by 10 k.m.h. Henk, and the competing Dyna Panhards, Monopoles and Renaults were lapping at a calmer pace. These 'babies' still had a long way to go. By the time our Aéro Minor was approaching its 30th lap the pit crew brought me back to life by the effective method of pulling my nose. Blinking my eyes in the light I made my way to the pit. A meal had been prepared for Henk. Tools had been made ready for the pit stop. Cans of engine oil, wheelblocks, clean goggles, seven caps for the pit crew, and two soft leather helmets for me were laid out on the counter. All under the watchful eyes of an official, one of whom was stationed in each pit, and whose task it was to observe that only the official fuel was put into the tank, and that no additional spare parts were taken on board. (Out on the circuit repairs were only allowed using parts and tools already carried in the car at the start of the race, a rule strictly enforced, but still not always obeyed at Le Mans.)

Smoky' leading Briggs Cunningham's 'Le Tank' between the Arnage corners (one left- and one right-hander).

As soon as 'Smoky' came in two new spark plugs were fitted, the tank was filled, and within two minutes I was out on the track.

The Minor was going like clockwork. Exactly in accordance with the lessons learned in practice I shot under the Dunlop bridge, up the hill, down into the S-curve right under the nose of a Ferrari. Next a change of gear for the Tertre Rouge right-hander, and out of there almost on the verge of a skid. Now getting myself as low as possible in the cockpit for the long straight stretch where 'Smoky', with its two miserable little cylinders, managed to attain 135 k.m.h. (84 m.p.h.) maximum speed. How fast the Jaguars, Ferraris, Aston Martins and most others drove on that straight I simply couldn't guess. They were so fast as to give the impression that I could easily have stepped out of my car, as it seemed as if I was standing still. In that way I continued lap after lap. Mulsanne, Arnage, up the hill to the pits. 'Thumbs up' to the pit crew and perhaps a glance toward the crowded grandstand, and pass again under the Dunlop bridge.

Meanwhile, before settling down to some sleep, Henk was taking the opportunity to tell the others in the pit about his experiences during the first hectic rounds, in which a cool head had been needed throughout as a variety of incidents were occurring all around. First time round Briggs Cunningham's 'biscuit-tin' Cadillac shot off the road in the Mulsanne corner, and again in the Arnage bend. A small Deutsch-Bonnet had somersaulted right in front of 'Smoky's' nose. During the next lap the Ferrari coupé of Madame Yvonne Simon, a good friend of mine from Monte and Liège-Rome-Liège rallies, became stuck in the sandhill on the outside of the Mulsanne corner. Two kilometres further on Briggs Cunningham's Cadillac had left the track for the third time. While Henk was no doubt enjoying a good sleep, I was wide awaken and enjoying myself too turning 'Smoky's' steering wheel. A twenty-four hour race is totally different from a half-hour fight over only a few laps at Zandvoort. After a while, having become familiar with all the bends, you feel quite at home and can settle down to a constant routine. Occasionally you try lifting you accelerator foot a little later, braking a little later, making yourself more comfortable, whilst all the time keeping one ear sharply tuned for the first hint of any potentially expensive noise, which of course can come from under the bonnet at any moment. But the Aéro Minor carried on nicely, and when the rather tiring twighlight period had given way to the dark night, with the headlight beams illuminating the road everything was quite alright. With a broad sweep the lamps lit up the pine trees at Tertre Rouge, as I concentrated fully on everything before me. Coming from Arnage the hill up ahead was a sea of light which I drove right through between the grandstand and the pits, where Jan Apetz in his white overalls was holding the blackboard against his stomach for me to see. Above the noise of the car I could detect the noise of the spectators as I continued on by and then into the quiet darkness once again. At about 11 o'clock, above the regular humming of the engine I heard an ominous ticking, which experience told me was coming from the fan belt. Although it worried me a little I carried on. Approaching midnight 'Smoky' was thirsting for more fuel, and I was ready for another nap. So, the pit suddenly got busy, and after refuelling Henk took over the wheel and quickly disappeared into the darkness. I enjoyed some chicken soup with rice. After learning that we were thirtieth in the distance classification and thirteenth in the Performance Index, I settled down contentedly under the blankets. After eight hours the classifications certainly looked hopeful, although, at Le Mans, one should never praise the day before the evening. This means not before you have passed beneath the Dunlop bridge for the last time. Ample proving that statement was a formidable list of cars which had given up, amongst which were all seven Gordini Simcas, an Aston Martin, three Ferraris, the M.A.P.-Diesel, and sundry Renaults and Panhards. Half an hour past midnight came the drama of our neighbours Poch and Mouche, with whom we got on so well. Their Aéro Minor was leading in the Performance Index classification and everyone in their pit was well satisfied until suddenly their 'Smoky' didn't come past any more. Necks were stretched towards the darkness which enveloped the track, but whoever passed by there was no Mouche. Exasperatingly slowly the minutes accumulated until after a terrible half an hour the pit had given up hope. But then, a murmuring from the grandstand grew into applause as Mouche appeared in the lights, standing next to his car in an exhausted state after obviously having pushed it for some quite considerable distance. Two mechanics ran towards him, but other than offer him encouragement were unable to assist physically, as to do that would mean disqualification under the Le Mans rules. Gasping for breath, seeming near to collapse, after a short rest poor Mouche started pushing again, with the sympathetic crowd willing him on, whilst everyone in his pit remained silent. They simply couldn't bring themselves to urge him on any harder in the exhausted condition he was in. Yard by yard the stricken Aéro Minor came nearer, as other cars flashed closely by on the track right next to him. Twenty yards from the pit he stopped for one more rest. Perspiration was streaming down his face, and we thought he would collapse. But summoning up all his courage he began pushing once again whilst his two mechanics could do nothing but stand alongside him and watch. It was terrible to see the poor chap having to continue when he was so near collapsing. Inch by inch, pushing more with his dead-weight than any strength, he shoved the car into the pit and fell down into his wife's arms, more dead than alive. What had happened was that at Arnage corner the Aéro Minor had run out of petrol, whilst at the same time its lights had become almost extinguished due to insufficient charge from the generator. Mouche had wisely then turned off the lamps to save the battery for an eventual restart, and then in the pitch dark bravely started to push, and sometime pull the car (using the belt from his overalls) the two miles uphill to the pits, to eventually become almost totally exhausted within sight of his goal. It was a tragic episode. For a whole year Poch and Mouche had worked on this car with a determination to win the Index of Performance classification. But the Aéro Minor stayed in the race. After refuelling the engine started up alright, and Poch shot away in an effort to try and make up some of that lost time. That is a Le Mans tradition. Amongst the vocabulary of numerous powerful terms and phrases applicable to this race, 'giving up', is almost unknown. Although their 'Smoky' had lost eighteen places in the Index classification, Poch battled hard to pull them back, and by daybreak had regained twelve of those places to put the Aéro Minor into sixth position in that classification.

Meanwhile, as Poch's fight was going on, fog had begun to form around midnight. In thick white clouds it drifted across the roads, getting denser all the time and finally becoming a solid white wall. I didn't know anything about this because I was nicely asleep, and was absolutely furious when my nose was pulled again to awaken me after spending only an hour on our folding bed in the tent. Father Geert was worried because 'Smoky' had slowed down, now taking about 7 minutes and 40 seconds per lap. He knew that I have the strange ability of being able to see about as twice as far as anyone else in the fog (maybe something to do with my eyes picking up infra-red rays). He realized that this was our chance to climb the ladder. Jan Apetz said: "Next week you can sleep, now you are going to drive; you wanted fog, well here, you have it!" He signalled Henk to come into the pits, and meanwhile I quickly had a little something to eat before going back out on to the track. The fog was indeed thick, but I could see the road well enough to maintain the speed required for the 7 minutes 10 seconds lap times we wanted. At this speed we climbed four places on the Index classification, but then another problem occurred. The dynamo had become loose, and I was forced to stop in order to tighten it. At daybreak I cut the fan belt to get rid of that particularly misery, which was alright to do as the Aéro Minor had magneto ignition. As a result of that the dynamo didn't cause any trouble either. But that wasn't all however, as at approximately 6 o'clock in the morning the Bowden cable from the accelerator pedal to the carburettor broke, and that was not so nice. Using a piece of wire, I fixed the throttle at the fully open position and carried on. The engine therefore now ran constantly at maximum revs, and gear changing could no longer be done smoothly. In the corners I had to switch the ignition off in order to stay on the road. In desperation I stopped at the pit, where Henk and I managed to carry out a repair with a piece of twisted galvanized cable used for sealing the petrol tank cap. We found it on the floor by sheer luck, and it worked reasonably well for the remaining eight hours.

Our poor Aéro Minor neighbours, who had prepared everything so nicely, and who now had fought their way back up to fourth position again in the Index of Performance classification, met more misfortune at 9 o'clock. Their 'Smoky' was forced to retire with a broken front wheel bearing. We climbed to tenth position in the Index, first in the 750cc class, and twenty-first in the distance classification. Even so we were just as sorry for our Aéro Minor friends as they were themselves. They had so sportingly assisted us, but now had nothing to do than pack up after all their hard work had come to nothing. It was pure rotten luck. But we had not much time to worry about it, because our Aéro Minor was in the lead in its class and we intended to keep it there. The field had diminished considerably by now. Not only had all the Ferraris gone, but all the Gordinis too were parked at the side of the circuit. We began to devour the final hours as more and more people were lining the track to witness the finish of the great battle. Leading the race overall in the distance classification was Louis Rosiér in his camouflaged Talbot, which apart from one quarter of an hour spell he had driven himself throughout. The little Monopole of De Montrémy was leading the Index. In the smallest class though (750cc) we were in the lead ahead of the Monopole, but not in our opinion by a safe enough margin. Henk however admirably carried on keeping 'Smoky' in front, while our pit kept a careful check on our lead over the Monopole. Those last hours were considered to be a fleabite. But in fact, although we hardly realized it, we still faced a complete 500 Km Grand Prix. Five times as long as an average sports-car race at Zandvoort. At 12-noon Henk completed his last lap. I took over for the final four-hour stint, and Jan Apetz gave me the simple message: "You are in the lead, hang on there". That could prove to be a tall order, because those last hours at Le Mans can still hold many an unpleasant surprise.

The Delahaye drivers Pozzi and Flahout found that out when at 1 a.m. their car was taken out of the race, because at the pit stop there was no seal on the radiator cap. Le Mans can be as hard as nails. The public didn't like this decision, and started to boo loudly, whilst the drivers protested furiously. They thought it was the fault of the marshall who they claimed had not sealed the cap properly, but saying it and proving it are two different things. The bandaged Delahaye entrant Veuillet got so angry about this that his wound started to bleed again.

In order to consolidate our good position I increased speed, making laps of 7 minutes 4 seconds at 71.2 m.p.h., and so gradually began to gain on the Monopole in the Index of Performance classification, whilst at the same time increasing our lead over it in the 750cc class.

The sides of the circuit were now chock full of people, and there were many who had climbed trees, whilst others were on the roofs of houses, all anxious to get a clear view of the finish. Every vestige of tiredness had left me now. When I received the pit signal at about 3 o'clock that I had an advantage of approximately forty miles on the Monopole in distance (more than half an hour) I was confident that victory was ours. On every lap it was 'thumbs up' when passing the pits; Geert, Henk, Guy, and Jan began to prepare for the celebrations.

Then, at twelve minutes to four - as Jan Apetz told me later - our happiness changed suddenly to despair. The Dyna Panhards Nos. 56 and 57 passed the pits exactly on time. Then came the Renault, and the Dyna No. 55, after which 'Smoky' was due. But....no 'Smoky'. The pit crew stretched their necks in the direction from where 'Smoky' should appear, whilst all the time cold shivers were now running down their spines. One minute overdue, no 'Smoky', two minutes, no 'Smoky'. De Montrémy drove his Monopole under the Dunlop bridge for the last time. Jan told me later that these were the three longest minutes in his life. Geert, now looking very pale, stepped down from the pit counter. "Finished" he said, and out of pure despair he left the pit with tears in his eyes. Charles Faroux walked past, the chequered flag in his hand. The boys felt like hitting their heads against the wall. Twenty-four hours of hard work, sweat, and sleeplessness only to end like this and go stark raving mad! All this time I was by myself out on the circuit at the top of the hill just around the bend after the pits. Going uphill in that curve for the last lap but one I felt something strange with the steering, and at once saw the cause rolling away in front of me. The near-side front wheel had started to race all by itself. It rolled up the hill, right in front of Tony Rolt's Healey and disappeared over the top. "Damn" I said to myself, with a sickening feeling coming up from my stomach. "That's the second time this year". I got ready to leave 'Smoky' at 70 m.p.h. because I fully expected that it would turn over. But to my surprise it still steered alright. It could, with care, be brought to a stop running on the brake drum at that corner. I could have cried, for I was convinced that the brake drum and hub would be broken, and that defeat had come in the last quarter of an hour of those twenty-four long hours. But when I jumped from the stationary car my hopes returned. I could see all five of the wheel nuts holding five bits of the centre of the rim all still attached to the undamaged brake drum. The wheel rim had simply broken off. Like lightening I got the spare wheel and jack out of the car, but couldn't get the jack underneath as the car was down on its belly.

However, at such times there can be a mighty strength from somewhere within you, and I simply lifted 'Smoky' with my two hands and kicked the jack underneath. As I jacked the car up the public were shouting and cheering with a wild enthusiasm. I had never changed a wheel so quickly. I put the five broken pieces in my pocket as souvenirs, threw the jack in the car again and within four minutes 'Smoky' was back in the race again, still going strong. I had realized that I would have to retrieve the broken wheel because according to the rules I had to have it in the car. Luckily I found it at the side of the road about half a mile further on, picked it up and shot away, now joyfully thinking of the looks I would see on the faces of the pit crew. And what faces those fine chappies showed. Grinning broadly, and with my thumb up to the sky I flashed by for the last lap. I just had sufficient time to see them jump up and down, mad with joy. They yelled out: "Smoky, Smoky, Smoky, good old dear little Smoky", and almost kicked each other into hospital from sheer overwhelming joy. I had passed at four minutes to four to begin my last lap, with 'Smoky'

Four very happy Dutchmen after 24 hectic hours at Le Mans. L.to R. Geert Hoogeveen, Jan Apetz, Henk Hoogeveen and Maurice Gatsonides.

again running like an express train to the finish after twenty-four hours. The shouting, dancing and embraces which followed in the pit simply cannot be described in writing. Overcome with sheer happiness we didn't know what to do next. We watched the great homage paid to winner Louis Rosiér, who had driven his Talbot for twenty-three and three quarter hours at an average of 89 m.p.h. And yet I'm sure he could not have been any happier than we five Dutchmen who, through co-operation, steady nerves, and some pure luck, had managed to bring 'Smoky' home first in its class, eight in the Index of Performance, and twentieth in the Distance classification, averaging 103.36 k.m.h. (64.215 m.p.h.). It was a new record in the 750cc class.

We were anxious now to return home to Holland, where we arrived at the border with a large laurel wreath around 'Smoky's' proud little nose. We were toasted from all quarters, and Piet Nortier said that the old saying: "Long ago ships were made of wood and men were made of iron, but nowadays it is the other way round", didn't count for us, and stated that he was very touched for what we had achieved for Holland. My most cherished souvenir hangs on the wall in my office. It consists of a piece of mahogany on which one of the five pieces of broken wheel is displayed, and underneath it a small silver plate with the inscription: 24 Heures du Mans, 24/25-6-1950. Aéro Minor 1er Prix Categorie 750-c.c. 2,490,67 Km.

We all have this same souvenir: Geert, Henk, Jan, Guy, and I, for without any one of the five it could not have been done. And I think we shall at times all look at that small piece of broken wheel, reminding us always that a race is never won or lost until the chequered flag is down.

The 1950 Le Mans winning Talbot, driven by Louis Rosiér.

Shell lubricants kept the Aéro Minor going for 24 hours.

Chapter 19

French Alpine Rally 1950

> About a bend on a wall: sick passengers: tropical heat: and a threatening emergency slaughter.

The idea that I would take part in this Rally was born at the finish of the Monte Carlo Rally earlier in the year, when Klaas Barendrecht, Bobby Spencer and I had managed to bring the Humber Super Snipe in to such a favourable second place. Just as soon as that result was known, Norman Garrad, the Rootes competition manager, asked me if I would like to take part in the French Alpine Rally driving a 2-litre Sunbeam Talbot as a member of the factory team. I was most surprised, and delighted, as my Humber Super Snipe Monte Carlo Rally entry had not been a factory team affair at all, and as normally the British manufacturers preferred to use British drivers in their official factory teams, I felt this new offer from Rootes was quite an honour. I gladly accepted the suggestion, on the condition that I must have the car three months in advance of the event for my own thorough preparation. Garrad, however, told me that I needn't worry, as the factory would see to all that. And that was quite true, for when the Sunbeam Talbot (S.T.) was delivered there was very little left to be done to it. It was a beauty. A spare petrol pump was fitted, and there was a pair of hand-operated windscreen wipers in case of failure of the electrical ones. A very practical drawer in which to keep the maps was provided, and taking into account the well-being of the crew were a lovely set of large vacuum flasks. The S.T. held the road as if it were a train on rails, and although it had already competed in two previous Alpines and one Monte Carlo Rally, it looked brand new. After every event it had been completely stripped down and very carefully built up again. For both of us it was an added attraction that I could take my wife, Ciska, with me for the first time in a long international event. Ciska was quite experienced in rallies herself. She had competed in a pre-war Monte, had won the Coupe des Dames with the late Mrs. Germaine Trouïs in the first Tulip Rally, in 1949, and had finished in second place in the Rally Féminin de Paris. But for several reasons we had not yet been able to do a rally together. We tried out the Sunbeam in a local trial called the 'Ye Olde Boneshaker Trial', which was so named because the participants were all dressed in medieval clothes. The proceeds from this event were to go to a charity. We also took part in the local 'Delft Blue' treasure hunt, organized by the R.A.C. West. We won the first prize, a beautiful lamp shade on a Delft Blue vase. The car handled very well indeed by day and night. Altogether we were going to have a tough motoring fortnight's holiday, for immediately after the Alpine Rally I was due to compete with my 1.5-litre Gatso 'Flatty' in the '12 Heures de Paris', an international sports-car race on the Montléhry circuit. As its name suggests this is a twelve-hour race, and my co-driver was to be my good friend George Trouïs.

On our way to the start of the Alpine Rally we took 'Flatty' to Paris in readiness for the race, and where it could be parked in Trouïs' garage while we were away, during which time George could practice with it himself. From Paris we went to Valence where we intended to reconnoitre the Mont Ventoux, a mountain climb which had to be done during a night section of the rally. That mountain had to be taken at an exact average of 58 k.m.h., but unfortunately on the day we arrived there they were holding the annual Mount Ventoux Mountain Climb, a local event for all types of vehicles. The road therefore was crowded with cyclists, motor-cyclists, sports- and racing-cars. Nevertheless we found it could be done, although at St. Estève the sharp left hairpin in which the road had been built up into a banking on the curve (something like a miniature Brooklands) was somewhat frightening for beginners. That really was a peculiar affair, because when approaching the very sharp bend at high speed it seemed as if you were going to smash yourself up. However the curve was particularly well laid out, and if your speed was high enough the centrifugal force gave you plenty of adhesion which kept you tightly on the road, which was angled at 70 degrees. Behind this section was an alternative normal bend for those people who were less fond of thrilling sensations, but taken the specially-built 'wall of death' inclined curve, one could gain many seconds. We reconnoitered the whole night route, looking for open petrol stations which would be able to serve us on the Rally, and pre-arranging at several of these our refuelling during the night. Continuing along the known itinerary we went via Gap and Guillestre to the Col de Vars in order to memorize this mountain pass, where a 7 Km-long mountain test was to be held on the last day. Over some more low, but rather difficult mountain passes in the Alpes Maritimes we went to Monte Carlo, and here we stayed for the night. Driving around there a little, I suddenly saw a familiar figure enjoying a coffee on the terrace Quai Albert. I braked, reversed and saw it was indeed my friend Gerard 'Bud' Bakker Schut. On that terrace, situated close to the spot where in 1938 he had triumphed in the classifying test on the Monte Carlo Rally, we sat for some time digging up memories of the good old pre-war times. It was not without sadness that 'Bud', one of the greatest, and especially one of the most sympathetic rally drivers in the international motorsport world, watched us go on our way to a motoring event so dearly loved by him. He had driven in the pre-war Swiss Alpine Rallies with a works Ford V8 Roadster. The next day we continued to Marseilles where we spent the time before the start enjoying bouillabaisse (the famous fish soup), fitting new tyres, and discussing technicalities and the route with the other S.T. crews. It was decided between us that it would be a case of "each driver for himself, and the Lord for us all", because we knew at beforehand that this Rally would be so tough that everyone would have his hands full. This was because this time in addition to the French Alps, the route would also take us through the high Alps of Italy, Austria and Switzerland. Now that really promised something! There were no less than 148 competitors, a record entry, and the scrutineering this year was particularly strict. The small cars had to be examined by the scrutineers two days before the 'off' and locked up in the closed park, with the large cars being attended to the day before the start. Each competitor was allowed into his car five minutes before the start, and quickly drove it the compulsory 10 metres forward. Once outside the closed park you could work on your car ad lib should it be necessary. Our Sunbeam Talbot's engine fired up immediately, and we were able to drive of into the night stage without any problem. We quickly gained many minutes on the schedule, so giving me some time for a short stop to clean the windscreen and headlights before climbing the Mount Ventoux. From then on it was continuous high-speed driving. The banked curve on the wall was taken in fine style, but from then on things were not so favourable. A heavy thunderstorm began, its flashes of lightning momentarily blinding me as I concentrated on the road ahead. Patches of fog worsened the situation. It was a rotten sensation suddenly encountering this quite dense fog when rounding a bend at great speed. It was a rather dangerous business on that pitch dark road without protecting walls. A small car on its side in a ditch - the Dyna Panhard of Mr. and Mrs. Gerlach - warned us to go carefully. We came to the top with exactly 100 seconds in hand and stopped a short distance from the control point, and many well-meaning souls shouted to us that the post was a little further on, before we restarted to arrive there on time. A small setback awaited us at Malaucène, where no super-grade petrol was available, and therefore as the high-compression S.T. engine disliked the normal low-grade French petrol we had to use our reserve stock. There we met S.T. driver George Murray Frame, who was having electrical trouble with what appeared to be a non-functioning generator on his car. I was able to assist him by swapping our fully-charged battery for his, which then quickly became re-charged on our car. We did this change-over twice in fact on the next section until we could get assistance from the Rootes service crew. Changing the voltage regulator actually cured the problem, and George was able to continue with no marks lost for lateness. The next day, though, Murray Frame lost his chance of an Alpine Cup (for unpenalised drivers) when he was one fifth of a second too slow on the speed test on the closed autobahn section near Munich.

Later on, just before Sèrres, the Mercedes of Verkamman Van Keulen ran out of petrol, which resulted in him cursing the mountains. He had carried two full jerrycans to the start, but before leaving had then throw them out to save weight. Swearing in ever stronger terms, he began running the 5 miles towards Sèrres to find a petrol station. On the way he managed to borrow a bicycle and a petrol can. We saw hum puffing and blowing on his way back. Having solved that problem he was in so much of a hurry to make up the lost time that he rammed a wall, damaging a mudguard and bumper. That cost him more time and he collected his first, and many, penalties.

In the second half of this first stage which finished at Monte Carlo, we had to tackle the Col de la Cayolle. Since this twisting pass had to be taken in the dark it was not an easy task. On both the climb and descent we were right in amongst the cars of the 750cc class. Some of their drivers seemed to have the idea that they would profit by keeping the big cars behind, which was ridiculous because on the French Alpine there was no general classification. It was noticeable that the experienced competitors however would give way at the first signal. On this pass the Bristol saloon of O'Hara Moore, the strongest competitor to our Sunbeams, dropped into a ravine. We learned from a

Frenchman who had been driving behind him that the Bristol had overturned several times - just like in the movies - but thanks to the steel roof the crew came off quite lightly, with only a broken collarbone and some grazed skin.

At 7 o'clock in the morning we arrived at Monte Carlo with about twenty minutes to spare, which was sufficient to have the car lubricated and get the oil changed. We were almost suffocating from dust and heat, and it was unusually hot in Monte Carlo. The first stage had taken its toll amongst the passengers. The continuous dicing through the curves had demanded so much from their nervous systems and stomachs that many of them were physically sick. My wife Ciska was quite dizzy, and unable to swallow a bite of food. After a sleep, through which to my regret we missed the no doubt delicious luncheon at the Metropole Hotel, we learned at the official reception by the Monegask Automobile Club, held in the hall of the famous Monte Carlo swimming club, just how bad it had been for some co-drivers. Many of them, including Pat Appleyard-Lyons (daughter of Sir William Lyons) were totally done for, and in the end the organizers decided to allow crews with a sick co-driver to take on somebody from the crews of cars which, for whatever reason, had already dropped out. This was an unique decision in motor sport, because according to the rules the changing of crew members during an event was never allowed. I can assure you that it's no easy task to act as co-driver. The driver is usually too occupied to worry, but his passenger, who is watching deep ravines flashing past, and thinking at every hairpin this is probably the last one he'll still be alive to see, suffers from a series of sensations of which nobody need be jealous. Furthermore, having also to read the map, he has often his head down, and at speed on winding roads that can be very bad for the stomach.

However, at Monte Carlo all that was left of the crews re-assembled, and with not too much enthusiasm left very early the next morning for the Italian Alps, which were waiting to mix a new cocktail of frayed nerves and upset stomachs. At Monte Carlo we had handed over all our frontier documents, which were collected by an official who arranged clearance at the customs. All we had to do was to collect them again once we were back in France. Via the Castillon and the Brouïs passes the procession climbed to the Col de Tende at the top of which, in the middle of a two mile long tunnel, is the French-Italian border. On the French side we zigzagged through very sharp little hairpins to the top. Upon entering the tunnel we were treated to a shower of water dripping from the tunnel roof. However it felt nice and refreshing, which was something we needed because we were facing an enormously tough section which, via Turin, Bergamo and Bolzano, would see us landing in Cortina d'Ampezzo. In daylight, the S.T. crews of Murray Frame and ourselves both drove as fast as possible to the time control at Turin, in order to get sufficient time in hand for the second change of batteries, his once again being almost flat against my fully-charged one. The hoped for Rootes service crew had apparently driven directly to the finish of this section at Cortina, and did not turn up in Turin. On the 200 Km Autostrada to Bergamo an average of 95 k.m.h. (60 m.p.h.) was compulsory for our 2-litre class, and that was not so easy as it might seem. It was a single-carriageway road on which you had to watch for oncoming traffic. Occasionally the road climbed, and we had to stay behind huge Italian trucks because their drivers did not allow us to overtake. Quite often we would come across one of the freight trains damaged at the side of the road following a crash. It was on this Autostrada that the 'Kilomètre Lancé' test, of which the exact location was kept secret, was being held. The start was indicated by an Italian flag, but there was no clear warning sign when this was coming up. By sheer luck I happened to spot a small notice with '2 Kilomètres' written on it and further on another with '1 Kilomètre'. Intuitively I pushed the accelerator down hard, and the hunch proved right. Due to that piece of luck I made the fastest time in my class with 137 k.m.h. (85 m.p.h.). As the test section was on a slight climb, this suggested the level maximum speed of the Sunbeam Talbot was apparently somewhere around 140 k.m.h. (87 m.p.h.). On the same test Ian Appleyard's Jaguar XK 120 did 109.5 m.p.h., whilst the small Panhards made no less than 72 m.p.h., a fantastic achievement for this little French miracle-car which has made all previous thoughts about top speed in the 750cc class very old fashioned indeed.

At Bergamo we left the Autostrada with fifteen minutes in hand and were refreshed by an Italian Rootes dealer, who offered a complete service station on wheels, from which petrol, oil, and ice-cooled drinks could be obtained. A couple of completely dehydrated French officials, who were handling the Printogines clock, looked at us with a sad longing in their eyes, and so we took the chance to provide them with some of our refreshment. The heat was unbearable, and this plus the tension of the Rally resulted in us being bathed in perspiration. After Bergamo we came to the time control at Bozzana. This was a madhouse! The time control was situated in a narrow street which had become blocked by waiting cars. To add to the 'joy' an old fashioned tram, its bell ringing loudly, rode through the swearing throng of drivers and their cars. Everyone was manoeuvering their car trying to get a favourable position for the start of the following tough section.

The next section to Cortina was only 100.5 miles; but everyone prepared themselves for the Grand Prix race it was undoubtedly going to be. There was practically no straight bit of road at all throughout the whole section. Soon after we started out we found that we could have easily left our top gear at home. There was no chance to use it, it was a case of second and third gear all the time. It was a terrible trip through the Italian dust, which hung in great clouds on the mountain roads. With its engine screaming at maximum revs our Sunbeam Talbot diced along the gravel roads, with lumps of stone, thrown up by other cars, whizzing by on both sides. At the end of this stage there was hardly an unbroken headlight glass left, and I was pleased that I had taken the precaution to protect our lamp glasses with aluminium covers which fitted them exactly. Our nastiest moment came just before Nova Levante. We were driving at 75 m.p.h. in third gear along a short straight stretch of gravel road, when suddenly a fat cow crossed the road. Now ever since my first Dumonceau Cup Rally, which I did on a motor-bike, I have been frightened to death of cows. It was a mutual fear, however, which I realized when the panic-stricken milk-producer danced a 'boogie' in the middle of the road. I stood on the brake pedal and swung the car over to one side, intending to slip past. But with mathematical correctness the cow jumped the same way, and then back again the other way just as we did that too. Complicating the situation was a small rock in the road which had to be avoided. Things didn't look good for us. Not until the last moment did the cow decide to move in such a direction as to avoid an 'emergency slaughter', at which Ciska and I sighed with relief.

Everywhere at the sides of the road were cars showing evidence of an overdose of speed, and to make matters worse the last 60 miles was across the Costalunga, Pordoi, and Falzarego passes. Over this same road the Coppa Dolomiti, a famous Italian race, was going to be staged the next day, running in the opposite direction. This meant that at any moment we were faced with practising sports- and racing-cars hurtling towards us, which really livened things up. Many times just as we felt safe again another Ferrari or Maserati would come thundering down and almost take the paint from our mudguard. It was a shocking affair, a complete madhouse. Such had been the problems on this section that I was happy as a child to arrive at the Cortina time control with only one valuable minute in hand. In later years the Alpine still included this 303 Km circuit, but run counterclockwise in the same direction as the Coppa Dolomiti.

At Cortina d'Ampezzo, where there was a rest day, we faced another problem. Due to dust and perspiration we were absolutely filthy, but had to argue a long time before we could get a bath. Then we realized we had no clean clothes, as we had given our suitcase to an official that morning and it was now somewhere in a Rootes service car. Arriving for dinner in our birthday suits would have no doubt caused a scandal, but fortunately Humber Motor Company's director Mr. Loyd Dixon came to our rescue. Bit Ciska, in the clothes of the much taller Mrs. Dixon, looked like a baby girl in a christening frock. However, Mimi Descollas came to her aid with some quite professional needle and thread work, a most interesting example of international co-operation.

That second section had produced a clearer picture of the possible outcome of this Rally. In our class there were now only two cars with clean sheets, our Sunbeam Talbot and George Hartwell's. That seemed hopeful, and we decided to have a good rest on our day off at Cortina. We were awakened in the morning by the thunder of engines, which to our disappointment was not a dream but the start of the Coppa Dolomiti. Almost every type of car was taking part, from tiny hotted-up Fiat Topolinos to mighty Ferraris. We saw record holder Bracco, who this time improved his own record by four minutes in his Ferrari. Unfortunately for him, however, Marzotto, driving a Maserati, covered the 200 miles through the Dolomites in 14 seconds less. These chaps had averaged 54 m.p.h. over those winding, tortuous mountain passes.

The rest of the Sunday we spent scouting the Tre Groce mountain climb, which had only just been included as a replacement for the Mont Ventoux climb. That speed test in France had been cancelled because as a result of car trouble the timekeepers had not been able to get to the top in time to check all competitors. A similar test was now being held here. We also used our day off to hide two cans of petrol in the bushes just after the Tre Groce pass, because I wanted to do the timed test with an empty car and just sufficient fuel, whilst knowing that later there would be no time for refuelling at a pump. Talking about petrol I may mention that on that last section we consumed almost our last drop. Normally the S.T. could be expected to do about 210 miles on its 10-gallon tank, but continuous driving in the lower gears resulted in the tank being empty after 95 miles, and our jerrycans having to be used.

Gatso and Ciska tackle the Tre Groce mountain climb in their works Sunbeam Talbot. Alpine Rally 1950.

After having done the test according to plan, we hurried further along towards the control at San Stefano di Cadore, where we met our friends Marc and Nicole Angelvin, who were this time acting as timekeepers. They wished us all the best. Alas, it didn't help. Immediately after leaving their control we heard a suspicious noise from under the rear of the car. The worst proved to be true. A tooth had broken off the crownwheel. At Rigolato we had to retire from the Alpine, which had seemed so hopeful for us as we were still unpenalized. Ciska and I didn't say much to each other, but we were very disappointed and angry that a mechanical failure had finished our Rally.

However, we did not get much time to worry about our troubles whilst we waited for the 'broom car', because two accidents occurred quite close to where we were. The Greek driver Gérarkis had left the road in his Citroën and come to rest in a very precarious position on the edge of a ravine, only held there by a wooden pole. His white-as-a-sheet co-driver had jumped out a little before, and luckily the Citroën had kept its balance whilst waiting to be towed back to the road.

Absolutely unrecognisable after rolling some 200 feet down a ravine, the completely wrecked Allard of the two British boys Potter and Gill.

The Britons Leonard Potter and Arthur Gill in their Allard two-seater were not so fortunate. Driving blind following the dust-cloud of Swiss driver Hervé's Jaguar XK 120, with no sight of the road ahead Leonard Potter had driven straight on at a curve. The Allard fell about 200 feet down into a ravine. We immediately went to the spot. Down below us I could see the car, so smashed up that it was almost impossible to tell that is was an Allard two-seater. Only observing its Rally plate told me that it was this British crew. Leonard Potter was at the wheel during the first of the many roll-overs performed by the car, and had got the steering wheel in his chest, but seemed to be in the better condition of the two men when I had climbed down. Seemingly unconscious, he was sitting on a stone, but had no serious visible injuries, although he could not move his right arm when he came round. Gill's case looked far more serious. This young fellow had been catapulted out of the car at the top, and had rolled about 250 yards down, well past the car. He was obviously suffering from very serious shock, and he was bleeding from deep wounds on the top of his head and in his face. Very carefully we carried the two boys to the road again, and then using ladders for stretchers we got them to the nearest police station. A doctor soon arrived. Gill, who had been moved onto a proper stretcher, was delirious. Then, to everyone's fright he suddenly sat upright, spilling blood, uttered a few words and collapsed. All the Italians there immediately began making the sign of a cross and started saying prayers, believing that he was passing away. It was a horrible moment. However, it was a great relief for us when we heard in the hospital later that apart from shock, a deep wound in his skull and a slight concussion, the poor fellow had only a bleeding nose, and when he had seen all that blood he'd fainted. In fact it was Potter who was the worse. The hospital examination revealed that he had broken several ribs, one of which had pierced his right lung which as a consequence had collapsed like a punctured inner tube. Additionally was some internal bruising and a broken arm, but this 'hard as nails' rally driver hadn't complained about that. Altogether he was in rather a bad condition. After being assured that our British fiends didn't lack anything, and having informed their relatives by telephone, it was time to take care of the fate of our Sunbeam. We had it towed to the railway station at Tolmezzo, where with some difficulty, but eventually thanks to the untiring efforts of a helpful Italian who spoke French, we managed to get the car on the train to Paris. Two days later we also left Tolmezzo, dirty and tired in our muddy clothes (our luggage was somewhere with the Rootes service car), my shorts full of holes from the battery acid spilled all over the ravine by Potter's car. We were going to Cannes in Gérarkis' Citroën Traction Avant '11', and from there we took a train to Paris.

We were deeply disappointed of course, but had a pleasant outlook now with thoughts of the coming twelve-hours race at Montléhry in my Gatso 1500 'Flatty'. At Paris however we received another blow. This time quite devastating. To our great regret we learned that George Trouïs' wife, Germaine, had suddenly passed away. For Ciska, who had won the Ladies Cup with her in the first Tulip Rally only the year before, this was especially upsetting. Under these tragic circumstances there was no question of George participating in the race, but he had taken the trouble to try and find another co-driver for me. But I also didn't now feel at all like competing in it either. However, we went to have a look at the race - noticing, incidentally, that the organization could not compare with that in other countries - and it was an understandably rather miserable couple that returned to Holland. It could have been so nice.

An action shot of Gatsonides crew's Sunbeam Talbot was chosen to illustrate a Ferodo advertisement.

DYNA PANHARD
610 cc. 2 cylinder luchtgekoeld 4 d. sedan.

Een kleine automobiel met grote prestaties.

PANHARD overwinningen 1950

Rallye de Monte Carlo	1		Zuid West rit	1
Winterrallye Zweden	1		Circuit van Draiguignan	1
Sandviken Rallye	1 en 2		Atlas (Marokko) rit	1
Rallye van Lissabon	1 en 2		Coupe des Alpes	
Rallye Aix in Provence	1		6 coupes voor Panhard.	

Importrice: N.V. DELFTSCHE MOTORENHANDEL
THERESIASTRAAT 145 — TELEFOON 77 20 43 — DEN HAAG

Advertisement depicting the Dyna Panhard in the Alps, and listing the car's competition achievements in 1950. These small French cars were powered by a 610cc two-cylinder aircooled engine.

Chapter 20

Liège-Rome-Liège 1950

About an 'atomic crew': a victorious race: a monotonous superiority: a blown cylinder head gasket: and a dispirited cycle ride.

If I ever started a tough motoring event full of self-confidence it was my first post-war Liège-Rome-Liège. This confident feeling was largely because my co-driver on this great trial was going to be the four-times winner, Ginette Trasenstèr. This friendly Belgian, who with his fellow countryman Breyre, in an old Bugatti had on four pre-war occasions won this marathon of European motor sport. And now he had just one wish: to win the event one more time, post-war. Being older now, he expected this to be his last rally.

I felt it was a great honour that he suggested to me that together we form the crew. Now it so happened that for this extremely tough event I had a very suitable car indeed, the closed 4-litre Gatso Coupé with which I had competed in the Zandvoort sports-car races that same year. This Gatso was reckoned to be one of the fastest sports-cars I had ever driven, although in fact I did not know its top speed because I had never had an opportunity to let it go flat out. I am certain that the lead-grey car could exceed 120 m.p.h., and of course I already knew well enough that its acceleration was fantastic. At Zandvoort it had proved to be faster than the 3.4-litre Jaguar XK 120, and that is quite something. When it became known that the crew was to be Gatsonides-Trasenstèr (my sporting co-driver insisted that my name should come first, although I had proposed to leave that honour with him), a prominent Belgian motor sport journalist, Jacques Ickx (father of Jacky Ickx, in later years an excellent racing driver) wrote in his newspaper column: "Gatsonides-Trasenstèr, l'équipe atomique".

213

In 'Parc Fermé' at Liège before the start in 1950.

Ever since the end of the war I had wanted to compete once more in a Liège-Rome-Liège, but apparently it had not been easy for the organizers to start their well-known event again. In 1949 there were some rumours about a Liège-San Sebastian-Liège Rally, but the financial backing, some of which was to have come from two local Casino managers, failed to materialize. A year later, however, I spoke to Maurice Garot of the Motor Union de Liège, the top man of the organization. He assured me that this time the rally would be held. Out of some 300 enquiries already received, he hoped for about 240 entries. Well, he didn't get that many, but when the final list was published it still had many impressive names on it. There were cracks such as Trévoux, Lesurque, Chinetti, Bècquart, Secrèt, a number of Italians with fast 2-litre Alfa Romeos, and very reliable Fiat 1400s. It certainly looked as though we were getting a hard nut to crack. Remarkably there were no British entries, perhaps due to currency restrictions. However, Klaas Barendrecht and Henk Richten had entered a new six-cylinder Morris (the first one to be assembled in Holland). The crew Bakkum-Baars entered a Buick, whilst the 'medicine men' crew Groenhart-Kokkes were driving a Dyna Panhard. These two doctors were so busy with their medical practice that they feared being unable to get their car ready in time, but eventually were able to leave there pill-making three days before the event and went to Liège in order to have some time there to prepare their car. The Germans, who in the past had always had a strong representation in this event, had wanted to compete gain, but there was still understandably considerable antagonism towards them, and their applications were not accepted. Having worked hard on the Gatso, which in some respects was still not completely finished, we arrived at Liège. Here, the first thing I heard was that unfortunately, for various reasons, some of the aforementioned crack drivers had been forced to cancel their entries. Because of that our chances obviously went up, and when Trasenstèr had tested the Gatso in the outskirts of Liège, he was so enthusiastic about the car that he was most optimistic about his wish coming true. After a quick scrutineering and then some hours in the closed park, full of confidence we drove at the head of the procession (we had been given the honour of starting No. 1) through Liège, escorted by mobile police. The roads were lined with thousands of spectators who warmly cheered their favourite Trasenstèr. The procession didn't quite pass without trouble, because in front of Barendrecht a Standard Vanguard suddenly lost a wheel. Its rather nervous crew had apparently simply forgotten to tighten the wheel-nuts.

In the dark all cars drove via Spa to Francorchamps, where the start would take place on the circuit in front of the crowded grandstand. Our 11.30 p.m. starting time gave us the opportunity to have a meal in the small hotel at the sharp La Source hairpin, which was already crowded with drivers becoming rather bored with hanging around all day, a situation which occurs often at the start of other rallies. Three cars started together, at intervals of three minutes. The starts resulted in an immediate display of maximum acceleration, as each driver sought to impress his opponents and amuse the crowds. For us this was easy. The Gatso seemed to be doing 60 m.p.h. before the others left the line. We kept that lead all the time. This was not an enviable position, gaining time when already running at No. 1, because the waiting traffic police were still asleep when we arrived before schedule, acting as an alarm clock. Trasenstèr had the wheel from the beginning, and judging by the way he started off it wouldn't be his fault if for some reason we went too slow. A pleasant aspect of the Liège-Rome-Liège is that there is no fixed maximum average speed as in other rallies. This enables you to take time in hand to stretch your legs at the controls, having placed your car in the closed park. Those short resting periods are priceless. On the 3,000 miles route there were 47 time control posts, in the early stages approximately every 25 miles. Our minimum compulsory average was 50 k.m.h. (32 m.p.h.), 60 (38) on some stretches in France, and 72 (45) on the Italian Autostradas. Maintaining these speeds could be tough in the mountains on some of the narrow passes.

The first disadvantage of our leading position was experienced at the Belgian-Luxembourg frontier, where the Customs officer acted as though he had never heard of the Liège-Rome-Liège, which resulted in many minutes delay before he opened the barrier, which is never closed during the day. This didn't make much difference though, because we had already gained about three quarters of an hour, and so could afford to lose a little time.

At daybreak we went into the Alsace mountains. We began to do a bit of mountaineering across the Ballon d'Alsace, so often used for specials tests in later rallies. It is only a mild climb, but still driving in darkness it gave us some trouble because there was thick fog on the hairpins. We carried on cheerfully, continuously watching our petrol stock, which had to be replenished regularly at the controls. This was because to keep the car as light as possible we never filled the 20 gallon tank to the full. The Gatso consumed about 1 gallon every 15 miles at such high speeds. Upon our arrival at Annécy during daytime I realized we had some trouble in store. Trasenstèr, who had told me that during a rally he hardly ate or drank anything, simply living on his nerves, was now beginning to go slightly green in the face. At the control, where my friend Marcel Bècquart was in charge, he took only a cup of soup. Always preferring not to forget the culinary side of things no matter what the circumstances are, I ate his portion also just to keep things balanced. Fortunately the unwell feeling in his stomach didn't stop Trasenstèr from doing his crew duties to perfection. He had made a detailed route card, showing roadsigns and exact maps of towns through which we had to pass. He used these all the time.

After Annécy I drove over some passes which were known to me from previous Alpine rallies. Notwithstanding continuously falling rain, everything went like clockwork. We continued to always arrive first at each control, a situation which had a certain charm. Trasenstèr took the wheel again at Grenoble, in order to deal with the Col de Lautarèt, the Izoard, and the Vars. Despite now feeling very sick, he took the Gatso to the summit and down again, displaying such an inspiring mastery which at last gave me the key to the puzzle why all those previous times he had shown the tail of his ancient Bugatti to the whole field. Approaching the Col de la Cayolle I took over again, as only a month before I had practised thoroughly on that pass for the Alpine Rally. It was a great pity that between Barcelonette and Pugèt-Theniers, the stretch of the '1000 tunnels', came in the dark. We could not see the beautifully coloured scenery.

In the dark, turning and skidding through all those narrow passages I thoroughly enjoyed myself at the wheel, but my poor co-driver became sicker and sicker. He suddenly had to open the window....! We swapped places again after that, because when driving you are too busy to be sick, and he safely guided the Gatso to Nice. Indeed, he can't have felt too bad at all at the wheel, as at one stage he happily fought hard against a Jaguar SS 100, whose driver obviously wanted to get to Nice before us. On the straights he drove at 95 m.p.h., but when he was obviously intent on continuing like that through villages I stopped the race. Why? Because I remembered four serious accidents on that stretch in a previous Alpine Rally. Even so, it was with a sad look in his eyes that Trasenstèr let the Jaguar overtake.

At the Promenade des Anglais at Nice, at half past eleven at night, we found the control post at the big Shell service station on that famous Boulevard, where the service was indeed perfect. We were not even allowed to touch the car, which was immediately treated to a wash, then lubricated and topped up with oil. Meanwhile we had soup, sandwiches and coffee, and there was even champagne if you wanted it. I had some trouble when I had been outside the station and wanted to come in again. Wearing dirty old clothes as usual, I looked like a tramp, and also I wasn't displaying my competitors badge clearly. They thought I had some nefarious intention and promptly pushed me out again. I got in of course when I proved who I was. From Nice I drove across the Cols de Braus, de Brouïs and de Tende, (not particularly high, but quite nasty) to Cuneo in Italy. On that section Klaas Barendrecht and Henk Richten unfortunately had to give up due to trouble with their car's electrical system. The never-say-die Klaas struggled on for a while, driving on his sidelights and following other competitors, but in the end this was proving too risky.

The Italian Customs had given splendid service by meeting the cars twelve miles inside French territory to check our papers together with their French colleagues. When we arrived at the top of the Tende pass, where you have to go through a two-mile tunnel drilled through the mountain where it straddles the frontier, the barrier on the French side was down. There was a light burning in the Customs office, but however much we hooted nobody came out. I decided to push the barrier up, and although Trasenstèr objected I jumped out of the car and lifted the barrier. We shot through the tunnel, bud had apparently triggered some sort of alarm, for when we arrived on Italian territory five frontier guards with machine guns awaited us. They probably thought we were smugglers, but a glance at our rally plates was sufficient for them to let us pass by. After we were spoiled with delicious coffee espresso at the Cuneo control and accepted a bouquet of Edelweiss, Trasenstèr took the wheel again to drive to Genoa. After Savona came a game of 'tag' with a train over a distance of thirty miles. The railway crossed our road sixteen times. Furthermore the stations are situated in such unfortunate positions that when a train stops it blocks the level crossing. If you are unlucky much time can be lost because of that. Shortly after Genoa this 'joke' is repeated eleven times, but all the waiting had a least the advantage that I could eat cold chicken offered to us at Briançon by my friends Marc and Nicole Angelvin who were managing the time control. They had also given us some cigarettes for Ginette, bottles of Perrier, two mountain caps, and a cordial embrace, which tired as we were, raised our spirits no end. My eating chicken was watched by Ginette as if it were poison, and his stomach almost overturned in his belly. Reaching Genoa at sunrise we had trouble finding the control because nobody, not even the police, knew its whereabouts. We hired a taxi driver to act as guide, who immediately demonstrated with Italian passion that he could beat any racing driver. On our way to La Spezia we came across a beautiful stretch along the Italian Riviera called the Flower Road. Then it was on to Pisa where, no matter how much we looked, we couldn't find the Leaning Tower. The welcome was excellent, mobile police on fast Moto Guzzi motor-bikes, with their whistles blowing piloted us through the town to the Autostrada leading to Florence. On the Autostrada we drove continuously near to maximum speed, with the speedometer steady on 165 k.m.h. (103 m.p.h.). At last Ginette could catch some sleep. But not for long. I had to wake him up because I heard a disturbing noise. I first thought it was caused by the macadam joints between the concrete slabs which made up the road surface, bit it became worse. Switching off the engine and coasting it still continued. I stopped the car and Trasenstèr got out, but he couldn't see anything wrong. I suspected that one of the wheel bearings was damaged. Very worried by now we left the Autostrada and drove into a little town. In a garage there we raised the car and checked the bearings, finding them all to be in order. We had to run the car to find out what the cause might be. The noise worsened, and eventually the car began to zig-zag and could hardly be kept on the road. Jacking the car up again we now discovered that between the tread and sidewall of one of the tyres there was a hole big enough to put your hand in. It was one of the special competition tyres ordered by Trasenstèr who had no faith in my usual Dutch Vredestein tyres. I had therefore followed his advice and fitted Belgian Englebert tyres. However the trouble was over when one of our spare wheels was fitted.

At Florence we were again met by police who took us to the control, situated in a very expensive hotel. We hardly dared to enter in our dirty clothes. However, the staff accepted but charged us - poor rally drivers - ridiculous prices for a bottle of soda water. Via Viterbo we drove to Rome where we had completed the first, but not the toughest half of the Rally. The control was again in the seven-stories high garage, but this time on the ground floor. The cars had a shampoo wash, whilst I, against my principles, had a shave just to please friend Trasenstèr, who himself shaved twice a day. On the return journey from Rome we had some rotten luck in a village called Spoleto. We asked a fellow there for directions. Perhaps he couldn't accept that he had to use a bicycle whilst we had a car, but whatever, the blighter sent us over a narrow goat path which resulted in us entering Foligno from the wrong side. We were eight minutes late and penalised eighty marks. Sheer bad luck! "We've lost it", I said to Trasenstèr, who could have cried. This was an exaggeration from me, because nobody ever returned at Liège without penalties. So we carried on along the East coast via Ferrara to Padua. It was getting dark for the third time and Ginette who was driving, began a pleasant race with a hotted-up Alfa Romeo 2-litre. Then the Gatso began to swing about again. The italian driver, a non-competitor, overtook and signalled us to stop. Another of those special tyres was suffering from the same loose tread problem. The smell of burning rubber was awful, and Trasenstèr added a burned finger to his miseries when he touched the hot wheel rim. There was no immediate reason to worry, because we had started out with eight tyres in total.

From Padua we went via Cortina over a road which proved difficult to find. In those days the maps were not always clear, and navigating was not easy in Italy, the more for us as we were exhausted now due to lack of sleep. On top of that everything was filthy in the car. It was a miserable situation. However, without any more penalties we arrived at Cortina d'Ampezzo, from where we faced the toughest section. A whole series of formidable passes, of which the Stelvio and Gavia were the toughest to be conquered. We prepared ourselves for the first. Just outside Cortina, as we climbed the Falzarego pass, we were suddenly flagged down near a hotel by an excited girl waving her arms at us. She told us that according to a phone call to the hotel we had to return to the control at Cortina, from where we had just come. Something like this is never nice. Trasenstèr and I looked at each other. A thousand possibilities went through our minds. Had we forgotten something? Had we missed a stamp? Had we forgotten our road book? Had we not paid for our coffee? Or was somebody playing a dirty trick on us? We quickly ascertained that our documents were alright. "Carry on, nothing to do with us", said Ginette. I doubted that we should, but my team mate was so determined that I gave in. The mystery was never solved. From Cortina we drove to Bolzano, and then to Gomagio at the foot of the notorious Stelvio pass. Climbing from 800 to 2,757 metres, this is Europe's second highest pass, with 56 hairpin bends to challenge the rally driver. In the meantime we had heard that everyone now had more penalties than us. We were in the lead again. Looking at each other we thought: "Everything is ours". I tore up the Stelvio knowing that, if anywhere, it was here where we could beat the entire field. It was a hard, furious ascent. When we reached the top we had completed the 20 kilometre test in twenty-two minutes. That was two minutes within the time limit, and five minutes better than the existing record, set up before the war by Trasenstèr himself with his Bugatti. It was there at the top of the Stelvio that we became convinced we had the Rally in our hands, and that if nothing unforseen happened Trasenstèr's fifth victory would become a reality. 'If nothing unforseen happened'. At an altitude of over 2,000 metres (6,000 feet) the tuned Mercury engine had not been quite right. It was red hot, and during the descent we had to top it up with three gallons of water, equal to half of the total capacity. This caused us to have frightening suspicions. The replenishing had to be done very carefully, and took ten minutes, which resulted in us being two minutes late at Bormio. Things looked bad. When we started the climb of the narrow Gavia pass, a mule path made during World War One for military purposes, it became clear just how bad. The engine coughed badly, and quickly boiled its water. Again I said: "We've had it", but I really needn't have bothered to say it, as it was all too obvious. A blown cylinder head gasket had destroyed our certain hopes of victory at a moment when it was practically ours. Ginette was beaten. I had no thoughts of carrying on and completely ruining an expensive engine. I borrowed a bicycle and went back to Bormio on two wheels to get help. What a difference that was from considering yourself the certain winner of the Liège-Rome-Liège. The cause of the problem came to light two hours later, when we had removed one of the cylinder heads. As recalled in an earlier chapter the engine had boiled in the race at Zandvoort when running without a fan. Next day I had started the engine and because it turned over and ran alright I had not taken the trouble to strip it down. A fortnight before the Liège-Rome-Liège I wanted to make sure, and found that one cylinder head was slightly damaged. That was quickly put right by refacing the head slightly, which raised its compression ratio and so similar treatment had to be given to the other cylinder heads of the V8 engine. The problem then was that I had trouble finding a pair of the correct Mercury gaskets. I had to use the normal Ford V8 ones which had narrower water holes, so these had to be widened to ensure the proper water circulation. Widening the water passage holes damaged the reinforcing rings around them. This was alright for normal use, but for this very high-compression engine which had been used in a definitely abnormal way it had proved fatal. The hot steam had worked its way between the gasket's layers and that was it. By using a spare gasket and one we bought on the way we could drive home via main roads in Switzerland. Twice on the way the gasket failed again because the head was now warped. It was poor consolation when we read in Jacques Ickx's newspaper report: "The dropping out of the Gatsonides-Trasenstèr crew was very sad, but brought tension back into the rally, because nobody will deny that it was the rally of Gatsonides-Trasenstèr. As long as they were in they had a monotonous superiority". It was bad luck for Trasenstèr not seeing his heart's desire fulfilled. It was just as hard for me who, after a season of rather silly bad luck in which victory after victory had slipped through my fingers at the very last moment, was beaten in a motorsport event which more than any other I would have liked to win. Not so much for my personal honour, but for the satisfaction of my Gatso. The car had proved its superiority, but definite acknowledgement only comes when the care takes the place of honour on the results list. In this sport unexpected things can always happen. Having started it was said without a chance three times on the Monte Carlo Rally I got high places as many times. And now when sure, even too sure, of victory, the atomic crew stumbled with the trophy in sight. It only goes to show that in motorsport there are no crews without chance. The 1950 Liège-Rome-Liège Rally was eventually won by the couple Dubois-De Cortanze, who drove marvellously throughout in their supercharged Peugeot Special.

The Culprits

Whoever is looking for the writer William Leonard, should seek out lonely canals or gently flowing streams. Ten-to-one you will find him there, totally engrossed in his efforts to disentangle his fishing line from the water's plant life. Many other hours of his busy life he spends on horseback, and he claims to know much about horses, although who is there to tell us whether there is any truth in that? During the little time he spends away from fishing and his one-horsepower travel he tries his hand at newspaper reporting. He is very proud of being a reporter for all kinds of papers in which he writes about all kinds of sports. Even motorsport, of which he knows nothing at all, but pretends he does. On the road he is the captain of a Fiat road-louse, which has a speedometer which exaggerates by about 15 m.p.h. That is his way of getting high-speed thrills. He is 6 feet, 4 inches tall, and has the most ugly nose you can imagine, from which you can conclude that he is not married. He is 30 years old and his favourite drink looks like weak tea.

Our artist Jan Apetz received his first drawing lessons in the kindergarten. From fear of contravening any ruling of the Government's Department of Human Form and Beauty, we publish no photograph of him, only the caricature he produced of himself. It is most flattering. Too much so in fact. No long ago he reached the age of 32 years. He has a wife, a four-year old daughter, a dog called Minx and a cat called Ascari, from which you can judge that the dog is unlikely to ever catch the cat. He wants so much money for his drawings that he is always very busy. He seems to find plenty of time to draw cars because he has a burning love for them, especially when he can borrow one at no cost and preferably with a tank full of petrol. Indeed, this love is so burning that he has already twice short-circuited William's road-louse (Fiat Topolino), by putting the key in the wrong hole. "Beautiful sparks", he said with a happy smile. In the police files you can find his name with a note attached: "A nice chap, but rather unstable".

Our photographer Maurice Gatsonides is the same as the 'I' in this book. He can take such nice photographs that he once won the Concours de Photographie in a pre-war Monte Carlo Rally. Following that his Contax-camera was promptly stolen by cunning Greeks who thought that it must be a very good camera if Gatso could take good pictures with it. Maurice is tall and thin, but that didn't stop him getting married and producing two kids. He is already 40 years old, but doesn't consider that as being too old to imitate an accordion on the push-buttons of hotel lifts in Lisbon or Monte Carlo. The hotel owners just love him for that. He never smokes, but he likes garlic, not only when he is in France. When he was very young, which was a long time ago, he was always keen to go poaching on a winter's night. Preferably by car, but sometimes on a motor-cycle. On these escapades his greatest joy was to be chased by the mobile police, because he gave them a lovely race along the seaside boulevard, shaking them off his tail by fast cornering four times round a block. He always won the race, and that resulted in a wide grin on his face. Such were his youthful sins. If you haven't realized it yet after reading this book, we must grudgingly admit that he knows how to drive a car. Almost as well as us (William and Jan). This we openly acknowledge, because of course we are very fair.

'Gatso' on the 'Monte'

Nine attempts, then succes at last. 1953 event easier than anticipated

By Maurice Gatsonides

The reader has already learned of the many adventures I have had on the way to Monte Carlo between taking my first tentative steps in 1936, and that memorable near-miss in 1950 in the Humber Super Snipe. My six attempts at this famous Rally had resulted in me twice winning the magnificent Barclays Challenge Cup which was always awarded to the highest-placed British car. That Barclays Bank Cup, the biggest of all the fantastic array of prizes at Monte Carlo, has fas-

Gatso dreaming of the Barclays Bank Cup.

cinated me ever since I first won it, but my efforts in 1951 with a Sunbeam Talbot, and in 1952 driving a Humber Super Snipe once again, failed to add to that total.

Always considered to be the most important Rally from the publicity point of view. the Monte was taken seriously by many car manufacturers, and that is why with the experience of eight Montes behind me I was approached by several manufacturers for the 1953 event. Once again the Barclays Bank Cup was the reason I decided on driving a British make. My choice was a Ford Zephyr Six, because Ford of Britain not only asked me to take part in 1953 in four rallies with their car, but also wanted my advice in preparing the team of three Zephyrs. This last fact appealed to me enormously, as it gave me an opportunity to use the experience I had acquired in earlier rallies. I was glad to discover that the Ford experimental department were most receptive to my advice. With no factory-entered British Fords having competed before they didn't have any previous experience of this kind, and my requests therefore were quite out of the ordinary. Both management and technicians of that department did an excellent job, and never before have I started a rally in such a beautifully-prepared car.

It was equally important that my co-driver, Peter Worledge, who had done the Rally with me in 1952, knew exactly what I wanted. As

My ten-year-old son Tommy operated the stop-watches, fastened on the front seat with a luggage-strap. Safety-belts were not yet invented.

Peter lived in London he could often be at the factory during the preparation of the cars. In the final months of 1952 I travelled to England several times to survey the work myself. On the occasion of my last trip, I took a Zephyr back with me to Holland. Around Christmas I went to the South of France in this car with my family. I used this Zephyr extensively for my daily reconnoitering of the Col de Braus, for on this 74.35 kilometres (46.6 miles) circuit the 1953 Rally would be decided. In the four weeks that I stayed there my ten-year-old son Tommy kept me company on all the practice runs. He operated the stopwatches, being himself strapped securely in the front seat with a belt (in case I had to brake suddenly and hard). A lot of time was spent practising passing the timing points at the finish of each of the six sections exactly on the second. This was vital if total regularity was to be attained, and the extensive practice enabled me to pass those six finishing lines in the final test on the Rally itself with discrepancies of only one second each at the first two checks, whilst the remaining four were passed exactly on time. Those 1, 1, 0, 0, 0, 0, results were just sufficient for me to win the Rally outright, which also secured for me the Barclays Bank Cup for the third time, and that meant it became mine to keep.

For the first test after arrival at Monte Carlo, the acceleration and braking test, I did not practice very much. As this test served only to select 100 cars for the decisive second regularity test, it was only necessary to be amongst the 100 best times. The acceleration of the Zephyr was such as to give me the safe feeling of knowing that I could do this test well above the average.

In the 1952 Rally I had run with a crew of three in the Humber Super Snipe, with Peter Worledge and Count Van Zuylen Van Nyevelt joining in with me. During the Rally our team spirit had been excellent, and we all agreed that we would form the same crew to try again. The Zephyr, though, was better suited to a crew of only two, and my friend Van Zuylen who realized this, voluntarily stood down. With him I entered for the 1953 Le Mans 24 Hour race, where we were to drive a Jowett Jupiter.

For the Rally our Zephyr engine was unchanged, as tuning was not allowed by the regulations. Only the interior was altered, with the front bench seat being replaced by two comfortable bucket seats. The backrest on the passenger's seat could be folded back so that we could sleep in turn - which we did to the tune of 10 hours per day, and we were not in the least tired on arrival at Monte Carlo.

However, the long road section of the Rally was rather easy this year. The enormous quantities of snow which had rendered the roads of the Massif Central and the Alps impenetrable two weeks before, had either thawed away of formed a hard frozen cover over the roads. Only at night did we experience trouble with fog, which covered the windscreen, headlights and foglights with an icy layer. Driving through the fog however was less of a problem for me than it was to the other drivers, as our Zephyr was fitted with my own-designed anti-glare shield over the foglights. One particular incident on the Le Puy-Valence section is worth mentioning. I had studied this stretch with its three alternative routes for three years, but this time against my own instincts I followed the advice of somebody who was alleged to have inspected the different routes only the day before. The seven minutes which we had in hand at Yssingeaux with one third of the distance covered, we lost later on the high and winding roads past Tence, St. Agrève and Lamastre. We were even three minutes behind on our 50 k.m.h. schedule. The Monastère average speed indicator fitted in our car indicated this fact to us in one look, simply by comparing two dials. Having discovered that we were loosing on our scheduled aver-

'He woke up with a jerk, pulled the wheel right over ....
the hay-cart swayed like mad....'

age, I really had to step on it despite the roads on this section being covered with rutted frozen snow. When descending from the Massif Central to the Rhône Valley we went like smoke. Consequently, I was not particularly surprised when rounding a blind corner to suddenly observe a tractor with a cart-load of hay plumb in the middle of the road. This happened at seven o'clock in the morning, and I suspect that the driver was still asleep. He woke up with a jerk, desperately pulled the wheel right over so that the haycart swayed like mad. The man standing behind him on the tractor must have broken the high-jump record by several feet. He saved his skin by landing on the hay while we scraped past with the Zephyr.

Luckily this was the only narrow escape, and we made the Valence control with three minutes in hand. Others, however, who had taken the longer route via Bourg Argental, had over 15 minutes to spare. Apart from that Le Puy-Valence stretch though our Rally had not been a difficult one, and it were the days of festivities afterwards which were really the most hectic. Extremely busy days in Monte Carlo were followed by a flight from Nice to London in a specially chartered Bristol Freighter aircraft in which our Zephyr also travelled. The British Ford works had arranged this trip to London where we were feted again. Those days after the Rally were more exhausting than the Rally itself, but I am very glad indeed to have had them, and I enjoyed them immensely.

TYRESOLES
News Letter

VOL. 5 No. 8   WEMBLEY, MARCH, 1953   For Private Circulation only

We are proud of our product

XXIIIrd RALLYE MONTE-CARLO 1953
Won on TYRESOLES

The winning "Ford Zephyr" together with Mr. Maurice Gatsonides and his co-driver, Mr. Peter Worledge, were flown back from Monte Carlo to London Airport by Bristol Air Freighter. Mr. Gatsonides poses with one of the many trophies which his achievement brought.

Congratulations to Mr. Maurice Gatsonides and Mr. Peter Worledge

Postscript to the Monte Victory

Sadly, in Holland there was no time to celebrate the Dutch Monte Carlo Rally victory, as torrential rain and abnormal high tide had brought flooding which turned the coastal regions of that country into a disaster area. Dutch authorities were naturally pre-occupied with the clearing up, and vital relief operations necessary to assist the inhabitants of the affected areas.

The Dutch people were noted for the warm hospitality with which they always welcomed motoring and motorsport visitors to their country, and as news of the disaster broke relief funds were quickly set up in many neighbouring countries. In Britain the magazine Autosport organized one such fund, and amongst the first monies to arrive were donations from Gatso's friends. The names P.M. Appleton, the Farrel Family, John Gott, and F. Harrison were at the top of the Autosport list, each of whom had befriended Gatso as fellow competitors on many events. Similar spontaneous actions were started in France by the Ecurie Méditerranée at Marseilles, and the Ecurie Monégasue at Monaco. Gatso was an honorary member of both these prestigious clubs, a situation which, incidentally, was sometimes a cause of embarrassment to him, on those ocasions when he had to choose which he was going to represent when both clubs wanted to enter a three-car team for the Club Team Award in an event.

Renewed international contacts: Some years after world war II the anomosity towards the German drivers receded, and they were once again accepted in international motorsport. Pictured here in 1994 are a group of veteran German drivers at the prize-giving following a rally for historic cars over 30 years old. On the front row at the left of the pucture is the only foreign guest, Dutchman Maurice Gatsonides, who was invited to compete in the event. Seated alongside Gatso is Baron Huschke von Hanstein, whose name has figured several times in this book. Both Gatso and von Hanstein were born in 1911, and there paths have crossed many times since they first competed against each other during the 1930s in European rallies.

From left to right:
seated: Maurice Gatsinodes, Fritz Baron Huschke von Hanstein, Walter Schock, Hans Herrman.
standing: AvD director Adalbert H. Lhota, Paul Ernst Strähle, AvD President Wolfgang Ernst Fürst zu Ysenburg und Büdingen, Rolf Moll, Eugen Böhringer, Herbert Linge, Bernd Hahne.

International motorsport competititons

Maurice Gatsonides competed in approximately 150 Dutch national, and over 200 international events, beginning in 1931 on two wheels, continuing for a short period on three, and for many years on four wheels. A record which has not yet finished by march 1995.

Below is an abbreviated record listing many of the principal events amongst those over 200 onternational competitions made up of approximately 150 rallies, 60 races plus some 20 hill climbs. Total distance covered including test and reconnoitring runs: 2.000.000 kilometeres.

23 Monte Carlo Rallies of which 3 not finished. Continued with historic Mont Carlo Challenges.

Year	Co-driver	Make of car	Starting place
1936	W. van Huut, R. Sillevis	Hillman Minx	Amsterdam
1937	H. Sanders	Hillman Minx	Umea
1938	H.J. Blijdenstein	Hillman Minx	Athens
1939	K. Barendregt	Am. Ford V8	Athens
1940 - 1948 *no rally during and after World War 2*			
1949	K. Barendregt	Hillman Minx	Monte Carlo
1950	K. Barendregt, B. Spencer	Humber Super Snipe	M.C.
1951	A. van Luijk	Sunbeam Talbot 2	M.C.
1952	H. van Z. van Nijevelt, P. Worledge	Humber Super Snipe	M.C.
1053	P. Worlodgo	Ford Zephyr	M C
1954	M. Becquart	Ford Zephyr	Lisbon
1955	M. Becquart	Aston Martin DB2/4	Lisbon
1956	M. Becquart	Standard Vanguard	Lisbon
1957 *no rally due to Suez-crisis*			
1958	M. Becquart	Triumph TR3A	Athens
1959	M. Becquart	Triumph TR3A	The Hague
1960	I. Langestraat	Austin Mini	Warsaw - non finish (technical)

Year	Co-driver	Make of car	Starting place
1961	L. van Noordwijk	Facellia	M.C.
1962	A. Jetten, J. Bronzwaer	Vauxhall Cresta	M.C.
1963	J. Rupert	Renault Gordini	M.C. - non finish (bad weather)
1964	A. Ilcken	Hillman Imp	M.C.
1965	A. Ilcken	Sunbeam Tiger V8	M.C. - non finish (illness)
1968	Veteran Cat. W. Lier	Triumph TR6	M.C.
1969	Veteran Cat. W. Lier	Porsche 911	M.C.
1970	Veteran Cat. W. Lier	Porsche 911	M.C.
1993	M.C. Challenge: M. Verbeek	Citroën ID 19 - 1957	Noordwijk
1994	M.C. Challenge: P. Günther	Citroën ID 19 - 1957	Noordwijk
1995	M.C. Challenge: M. Verbeek	Ford Zephyr - 1953	Noordwijk

Rallies
11 x Alpine
9 x Liège - Rome Liège
7 x Tulip
6 x Great Britain - RAC
14 x Economy Run (Caltex, Chevron, Mobil
4x Scheveningen - Luxemburg - Scheveningen
Iberian, Lisbon, del Fiori, Deutschland, Wiesbaden, Limousin, Midnightsun, Geneva, Deutsche Alpenfahrt, E.A. (Coronation) Safari, Harzfahrt, Sestrières, Travemünde, Tour de France,
Benfralux, Austrian Alpine. Dumonceau Cup, Neige et Glace, Kohle und Stahl, de L'Europe, GP de Paris, Monte Carlo Challenge.

Races
4 x 24 hours of Le Mans, 1000 Km-Rennen Nürburgring, International Sportscar Races at Monthéry, Reims, Paul Ricard, Rouen, Goodwood, Silverstone, Dundrod TT, Auvergne, Grenzland Ring, Francorchamps, Monza, Hockenheim, Zandvoort.

Hill Climbs
Freiburg-Schauinsland. Ballon d'Alsace. Puy de Dôme, Prescot, Mont Ventoux, Chamrousse, Mont Cénis.

Gatso celebrated his 84th birthday by competing in his replica Monte 1953 winning Ford Zephyr in the M.C. Challenge 1995

```
                                              M.G.
                                              RILEY
1931  N. BLACK                       GARDNER BENTLEY
1932  MRS. L.S. STANILAND                    TRIUMPH
1933  LORD DE CLIFFORD                       TRIUMPH
                                              TRIUMPH

1934  D.M. HEALEY
1935  J.C. RIDLEY                            HILLMAN
1936  D.M. HEALEY                             TALBOT
                                            SS JAGUAR

1937  N. GATSONIDES - C.L. SANDERS
1938  N. GARRAD - S.C.H. DAVIS               BRISTOL
1939  J. HARROP                              HUMBER
                                              JAGUAR

1949  T. DOBRY - Z. TREYBAL
1950  N. GATSONIDES - K.S. BARENDREGT
1951  C. VARD - A. YOUNG                     ALLARD

1952  S.H. ALLARD - G. WARBURTON
1953        REMPORTÉ DEFINITIVEMENT       FORD ZEPHYR
      N. GATSONIDES - P. WORLEDGE
```